T. P. Ying

1983. 12.

J. P. T.

1983. 19.

Ada® for Programmers

Eric W. Olsen
Stephen B. Whitehill

THE TAN CHIANG BOOK CO.
Taipei, Taiwan

Reston Publishing Company, Inc.
A Prentice-Hall Company
Reston, Virginia

First printing . . . . Nov. 1983

Published and Reprinted by

THE TAN CHIANG BOOK COMPANY

Taipei, Taiwan

The Republic of China

臺 灣 版

臺內著字第　　　號

原著者：Eric W. Olsen
　　　　Stephen B. Whitehill

發行者：邱　如　升

發行所：淡江書局有限公司

地　址：重慶南路一段一三七號

電　話：三三一二五五四

郵撥帳號：6680 號

行政院新聞局出版登記證
局版台業字第〇八一四號

印刷所：百麗印刷廠有限公司
　　　　台北市長順街107巷4號

電　話：三〇六六七二一

中華民國72年10月第一版

Library of Congress Cataloging in Publication Data

Olsen, Eric W
　　Ada for programmers.

Includes index.
　1. Ada (Computer program language) I. Whitehill,
Stephen B.　II. Title.
QA76.73.A35O38　1983　　001.64'24　　82-20462
ISBN 0-8359-0149-1

Contents

Preface

Ada® is a complex language and the Reference Manual for the Ada® Programming Language (LRM) is a tremendously detailed document, but the LRM is clearly not intended for use by anyone not already familiar with Ada. The initial impetus for this book was our desire to make some sense out of Ada and the LRM in conjunction with our work at Irvine Computer Sciences Corporation, which is currently engaged in the production of Ada language translators and associated support tools. We were also encouraged in our pursuit by the activities of the Programming Environments Project at the University of California at Irvine, which is involved in research into new programming environments based upon Ada.

The production of this book was a task that involved many people other than ourselves and those who contributed to the evolution of the manuscript should be recognized: Dan Eilers and Scott Ogata of Irvine Computer Sciences Corporation; Bill Crosby of Local Network Systems; Norm Jacobson, Dave Schulenberg, and Steve Willson of UC Irvine; and Jack Graham and Ricke Clark of Rockwell International were all kind enough to provide valuable comments on the content and layout of early drafts of the manuscript. Professor Thomas Standish, principal investigator of the UC Irvine Programming Environments Project, was instrumental in providing background and motivation prior to our decision to embark on this project.

Eric W. Olsen
Stephen B. Whitehill

Ada® is a registered trademark of the U.S. Government, Ada Joint Program Office.

chapter 1

Introduction

In the early 1970s, the United States Department of Defense (DoD) observed that the cost of software development and maintenance was rising dramatically relative to the cost of hardware and, further, that the situation was likely to get worse, not better. Scores of different languages were being used by all branches of the service for software development. Even languages with the same name were likely to differ among development sites. In response to this situation, in 1975 DoD formed the Higher-Order Language Working Group, whose purpose was to establish a single high-level language appropriate to the programming tasks encountered by the Army, the Navy, and the Air Force.

The programming language Ada was designed in accordance with requirements established by DoD for embedded computer systems development (such as those used in radar installations or aircraft navigation systems). Ada is also intended for use in more conventional environments as an applications programming language or as a large-scale program development tool. The language includes many of the features of the language Pascal, upon which it is loosely based, as well as many other more specialized facilities. In particular, modular programming and real time programming are supported.

As indicated, one of the primary goals in the design of Ada was to define a languge that would improve program reliability and simplify program maintenance. As a result, the language emphasizes readability rather than writeability. To many programmers familiar with more ''concise'' languages, this aspect of Ada will prove somewhat of a shock; however, when it comes down to reading and maintaining someone else's program, Ada should be appreciated.

It has been predicted that Ada will become the most important programming language of the 1980s and 1990s; some have even suggested that it will be the last new major programming language developed prior to the advent of automatic programming. Ada therefore deserves some serious study. This book should provide a sound basis for programmers wishing to become familiar with Ada and its intricacies.

1.1   PRESENTATION

The ordering of chapters has been carefully considered to provide the reader with the most logical development of language concepts. This book is not intended as a tutorial on computer science in general or computer programming in particular; rather, it is intended to provide the reader who is generally familiar with at least one other programming language with an understanding of Ada. Nor is this book intended to replace the Ada Language Reference Manual. A reference manual is a useful tool once a language is understood; however, you do not learn French by reading a French-English dictionary. A tutorial presentation, as provided by this book, is more appropriate to the learning process. We do not pretend to cover all the subtleties of Ada, but we do provide the information necessary for most programmers to write significant Ada programs.

This book has been written with two principal stylistic goals in mind:

1. Avoid forward references: never refer to a concept or language feature before it is defined.

2. Avoid expert problem domains: provide examples that do not require special knowledge or expertise.

Nothing is more annoying to the reader of an introductory manual than forward references. We believe that an author who refers the reader to material later in the book has failed his readers. The Ada Language Reference Manual is replete with forward references: there are references to the last chapter as early as Chapter 3. (To be fair, the reference manual was not written as an aid to learning the language, but rather as a definition of the language.) The reader will find no forward references in this book. In service of this goal, from time to time we postpone discussion of certain subtleties of the language. If two features of the language interact in some way, interaction is described only after both features have been explained.

Another aspect of programming language tutorials that can be annoying is the use of expert problem domains in programming examples. Scientific or mathematic examples are easy to produce and are excellent teaching aids— if you are a scientist or a mathematician. If not, you spend more time trying to understand the problem than you spend understanding the solution. We have avoided such examples in this book. We have also tried to avoid systems programming examples. It is true that Ada's main purpose is as a systems programming language, but we believe that systems programmers can learn the Ada language just as well with the examples provided. It is simply not the case that an introductory text must be confusing to beginners to be useful to more advanced programmers. The examples we use most often are simple data processing problems such as maintaining employee records. These examples can be understood by nearly anyone, so the reader is able to concentrate on how Ada is used to solve these problems.

Chapters 2–7 present the fundamental Ada semantics, including declarations, standard types, expressions, basic statement forms, and subprograms. An understanding of this material will enable the reader to write simple, but complete, Ada programs.

Chapter 8 discusses packages, which are the means of encapsulating collections of related subprograms and their associated data. This facility is one of Ada's most important improvements over other programming languages.

Chapters 9–12 detail the Ada type definition facility. This material is very important to an understanding of Ada.

In the remaining chapters (on overloading, derived types, generics, program structure, exceptions, and tasking) new material is presented which is generally unique to Ada. As a result, this material builds on the knowledge of Ada acquired from previous chapters.

The several appendices provide additional information on various topics, including implementation dependent features, notes for Pascal programmers, Ada input-output, general reference information, and some examples of real Ada programs.

1.2   SYNTACTIC NOTATION

In addition to numerous examples, the formal syntax for each Ada construct is given to provide the reader with specific syntactic guidance. In many cases, the syntax presented differs from that defined in DoD's Ada Reference Manual. This is the result of a vigorous attempt to avoid forward references when at all possible. Complete syntax definitions may be found in Appendix III.

Throughout this book, a simple variant of the Backus-Naur Form is used for syntactic definition. Using this BNF variant, non-terminals are represented using lower-case words, with optional dashes. For example:

```
upper-case-letter =
      A | B | C | D | E | F | G | H | I | J | K | L | M
      | N | O | P | Q | R | S | T | U | V | W | X | Y | Z
```

This example illustrates what we call a *production*, which is a portion of a syntactic description. The name of this production is upper-case-letter. Usually, we try to give meaningful names to productions so that we have some intuitive feel for what a production is meant to represent. The production upper-case-letter is used to define the set of English upper case letters, A through Z. The equal-sign = separates the name of the production from the syntactic definition. We use several conventions in such definitions. For example, the vertical bar | separates *alternatives*. If a production has more than one alternative, then each of the alternatives may be used to satisfy part of what we call the *parse* of a program. In the case of upper-case-letter, this means that any one of the upper case alphabetics matches the input stream.

Productions are used in combination with other productions to match larger and larger parts of a program. For example, we might define another production identifier which is used to match strings of characters that represent programmer-defined names:

```
identifier =
    upper-case-letter {upper-case-letter}
```

This production introduces another convention we use in syntactic definitions. The use of matching curly braces { } is meant to indicate that the enclosed definition may be repeated zero or more times. Thus, the identifier production matches any string of one or more upper case letters. Literally, the production says to match one upper case letter and then continue scanning while upper case letters are matched. For example, the identifier production given above matches each of these strings of letters:

```
A          or
ADA        or
MAX        or
LIST       or
VERYLONGIDENTIFIER
```

Fortunately, as in many other programming languages, identifiers in Ada may consist of more reasonable constructions, including lower case letters, digits, and underscores. The syntactic definition of identifiers in Ada corresponds to these five productions:

```
identifier =
    letter { [underscore] letter-or-digit }
letter-or-digit =
    letter | digit
letter =
    upper-case-letter | lower-case-letter
```

```
digit =
     1 | 2 | 3 | 4 | 5 | 6 | 7 | 8 | 9 | 0
underscore =
     _
```

This new version of identifier uses another common convention used in syntactic definition. The square brackets, [ ] surround part of a syntactic definition that is optional (that is, which may appear once or not at all). Thus, Ada identifiers consist of a sequence of characters that starts with a letter and is followed by any number of letters or digits. Each letter-or-digit may be preceded by an underscore character; this means that only isolated underscores are permitted. The following examples illustrate legal Ada identifiers:

```
i                       or
Ada                     or
VAR1                    or
a1223                   or
max_value               or
Very_long_identifier
```

Most languages use certain symbols called *keywords* to distinguish different statements or definitions. Keyword symbols are eproduced in boldface, as in this example:

```
goto-statement = goto label_name ;
label-name = identifier
```

The keyword **goto** is used to distinguish the goto statement. Literal text for certain special sequences of characters may also be used in a production. For example, the semicolon ; is used in the production goto-statement. Special characters must be matched exactly, meaning that a semicolon must terminate a goto statement. Multiple character sequences must also be matched exactly, as in this example which includes the colon-equals : = sequence:

```
assignment-statement =
     variable-name := expression ;
variable-name = identifier
expression =
     identifier
   | . . .
```

The production assignment-statement is matched by the following examples:

```
a  : = b;                or
i  : = max_value;        or
currval  : = lastval;
```

In order to avoid references to material that has not been presented, another convention is used. The ellipsis ... denotes that additional alternatives occur for this production but are omitted from the definition because they describe features not yet introduced. In all cases, a production is reproduced at each point in the text where a new feature is discussed that results in a change to that production.

The general term *token* is used to refer to any identifier, keyword, number, or special symbol in a program.

chapter 2

Conceptual overview

The example and accompanying discussion below are presented in order to provide the reader with a conceptual basis and some intuition about Ada programs. The details of the environment in which an Ada program runs are not specified; it is assumed that the reader is familiar with a suitable program development environment.

2.1 A SIMPLE EXAMPLE

The following example is a complete, though simple, Ada program. It is discussed throughout the remainder of this chapter.

```
with ada_io; use ada_io;        -- context specification
procedure double is             -- program specification
   x,y: integer;                -- declarative part
begin                           -- start of body
   get(x);          -- read a number
   y := x * 2;      -- multiply it by 2
   put(y);          -- print the result
   new_line;        -- advance to the next line
end double;                      -- end of body
```

The program consists of a procedure called double which reads a number, multiplies it by 2, and prints the result. There may be some local conventions that must be observed for this program to run with a particular Ada compiler, but we won't deal with these here.

An Ada *program* is composed of a sequence of basic units called tokens. The following classes of tokens are used in the example program above:

1. Reserved keywords whose meanings are known to an Ada compiler, including **with**, **use**, **procedure**, **is**, **begin**, and **end**

2. Punctuation symbols called *delimiters*, including

```
,        (
:        )
;        *
:=
```

3. Predefined names whose meanings are known to an Ada compiler, including integer

4. Names whose meanings are determined by examining a program library, including ada_io, get, put, and new_line

5. User-defined names, including double, x, and y

6. Constants, including 2

The above list includes all of the tokens in the example program, although Ada defines many more such tokens.

Programs may also contain *comments*, which consist of two dashes -- followed by arbitrary text and terminated by the end of the line. Comments may appear anywhere in a program. They are meant to clarify the meaning of the program for the human reader and are ignored by an Ada compiler.

With respect to the Ada language, spaces, tabs, and end-of-lines (collectively called *white space*) serve no purpose other than to separate tokens. In the example above, white space is required between the tokens procedure and double because, without separation, these two words would appear to be a single token proceduredouble. (For those programmers familiar with BASIC, this behavior is new.) White space is also used to separate pieces of a program in order to enhance readability. For example, we use a particular indenting style developed for Ada in the examples throughout this text; however, such usage is largely dependent on local conventions.

All Ada programs have four components: a *context specification* (line 1), a *program specification* (line 2), a *declarative part* (line 3), and a *body* (the remaining lines). The context specification instructs the Ada compiler to look in a *library* for specified portion of the program. A library is a collection of previously compiled routines that can be made accessible by using context specifications. In the example above, the context specification tells the Ada compiler to look for ada_io which contains the procedures get, put, and new_line.

The collection of routines called ada_io is not part of the standard Ada library. It is a simplified version of the standard library unit text_io which defines an extensive set of input-output facilities. The use of text_io requires knowledge of concepts that are not discussed until the latter part of the text. We assume that most Ada implementations include simplified input-output routines like those in ada_io; the programmer should refer to the reference manual for the local implementation of Ada. All examples in this text requiring input-output facilities use the simplified input-output library unit ada_io.

The program specification gives the name of the program. The declarative part includes any *object declarations* (x and y in this example) as well as many other kinds of declarations that will be described later. The body of a program consists of a *sequence of statements* that specify the action of the program. These statements may refer to any of the objects declared in the declarative part.

The declarative part in the example above contains definitions for two variables, x and y, both of which are integers. In Ada, variables are named by *identifiers*. An identifier consists of a sequence of letters, digits, and isolated underscores and must begin with a letter. The case of letters used in identifiers is not significant; upper case letters are equivalent to lower case letters. Ada does not permit two consecutive underscores in an identifier, nor may an underscore be the final character of an identifier. All characters in identifiers are significant. There is no language restriction on the length of identifiers except that they may not cross source line boundaries.

A *type* defines a set of possible values for a variable. Ada is a strongly typed language, meaning that all data objects must be declared prior to their use and each declaration must specify a particular type for the data object. The identifier integer represents a predefined Ada type that corresponds to an implementation-dependent subset of the integers (non-fractional numbers).

The body of the program above contains four distinct statements. The first one,

```
get (x) ;
```

is a call to the input procedure get from ada_io which reads an integer from a standard input device and sets the variable x to that integer. The second statement,

```
y : = x * 2;
```

is an assignment statement. An assignment statement evaluates the expression on the right side of the : = (in this case, x is multiplied by 2) and assigns that value to the variable on the left side (y in our example). Types are used to insure that the programmer does not accidentally use variables in unintended ways. For example, an Ada compiler checks that the expression x * 2 is correct by determining that the operands x and 2 are both appropriate types (in this case, integers). Then, the compiler insures that the expression and variable in an assignment statement are also of the same type. The third statement,

```
put (y) ;
```

is a call to the output procedure put from ada_io which outputs the value of the expression y to a standard output device. Ada input-output is character oriented (as opposed to line-oriented, as in FORTRAN) and the output routines do not output any white space either before or after the data being output. The final statement,

```
new_line;
```

is a call to the output procedure new_line from ada_io which terminates the current output line and causes subsequent output to occur on the next line.

Expressions are composed of constants, variables, operators, and parentheses. Most operators, like + and * (addition and multiplication, respectively) are familiar from other programming languages and conventional arithmetic usage. Parentheses constrain the order in which operations are performed.

The preceding discussion should give the reader a feel for the essentials of Ada adequate for an understanding of the examples and related material to follow. The remaining chapters expand upon the basic concepts briefly described here.

2.2   SOME CONCEPTS AND RELATED TERMINOLOGY

It is important to understand the distinction between *compile time* and *runtime*. The term compile time refers to the period during which a compiler (in this case, an Ada compiler) is processing or *compiling* the text of a program. The term runtime refers to the period during which a program that has already been processed by a compiler is executing or *running* and carrying out the actions specified by the program text. The text given to a compiler is called a *compilation unit*.

For example, the following program causes a compile time error:

```
procedure compile_time is
   x: integer;
begin
   x := 3.7; -- illegal
end compile_time;
```

The assignment is illegal because a real number cannot be assigned to an integer variable. The Ada compiler reports this error when the program text is processed. In the chapters to follow, we point out some errors that are detected by Ada compilers; however, we do not itemize all such errors.

Many errors cannot be detected at compile time. For example:

```
procedure run_time is
   x: integer;
begin
   get(x);
   put(1/x);
end run_time;
```

Execution of this program results in a runtime error on the division if the value of the object x is 0. As with compile time errors, we occasionally point out situations that may result in runtime errors, but we do not enumerate all such errors.

Quite frequently, the computer intended to run an Ada program is not the same computer used to compile the program. This situation occurs most often in embedded systems environments since an embedded computer may not support the tools, including an Ada compiler, necessary for program development. To distinguish between the two (possibly different) computers, we use the terms *target machine* (the machine that runs a program) and *host machine* (the machine that compiles a program).

This text contains hundreds of examples, most of which are compilable and many of which are executable. Don't hesitate to try these examples with the local Ada compiler. Doing so will provide several illuminating pieces of information including:

- How to run the compiler.
- The general appearance of output from the compiler, such as error messages, program statistics, and so forth.
- How to execute programs generated by the compiler.

One final note before we begin in earnest. Beyond this book (or others like it), there are three sources of answers to questions about Ada that are not explicitly answered in subsequent chapters. The first is the Ada Language Reference Manual, which should only be used once the programmer is familiar with Ada. The second is a friendly colleague, who is less cryptic but also possibly less reliable than the Reference Manual. The third and most important is the Ada compiler itself, which should be the oracle of the first resort when additional questions arise. The best way to understand a language feature is to write a simple program and try it.

chapter 3
Predefined types and operations

The type in an Ada object declaration can represent many different kinds of values. Indeed, much of the rest of this book deals with the definition of those things that can be used as types. This chapter, however, deals only with Ada's predefined types. For each predefined type, we describe the predefined operations that may be performed on objects of that type, and the representation for literal constants of that type.

3.1   THE TYPE INTEGER

We have already encountered the type "integer", whose possible values are a subset of the integers (nonfractional numbers). The subset represented by integer may be different for each implementation of Ada, depending upon the capabilities of the target machine.

The textual representation for integer literals in Ada is similar to those in most programming languages: a sequence of one or more digits. Ada's integer literals may also contain isolated underscore characters; that is, any digit (except the first) may be preceded by an underscore. These underscores do not change the value of an integer literal, but are used to improve its readability. These are some examples of integer literals:

```
37                     -- the number thirty-seven
1_328_845_426          -- using the '_' like a comma
                       -- for a very large number
723_14_1598            -- using the '_' to emphasize that
                       -- this is a social security number
```

By default, integer literals are assumed to be decimal numbers. Ada provides an additional mechanism for specifying the base of an integer literal. Such literals, called *based numbers*, are preceded by the desired base and surrounded by the number sign # as in the following examples:

```
8#377#              -- 377 octal (255 decimal)
16#FF#              -- FF hexadecimal (255 decimal)
16#ff#              -- lower case OK
2#1111_1111#        -- 11111111 binary (255 decimal)
```

The base is always specified in decimal. Based numbers are often useful in machine-level programs when it is necessary to specify hardware-defined bit patterns. It is possible to specify based literals for any base between 2 and 16, but bases other than 2, 8, and 16 will almost certainly never be needed.

The following arithmetic operations are defined for any integers x and y and yield results of type integer:

Expression	Meaning
x + y	addition
x − y	subtraction
x ∗ y	multiplication
x / y	division (result is truncated)
− x	negation

Integer-valued expressions may replace any of the simple references to x and y, so that more complex expressions can be constructed. For example:

```
x + y * z
-(x / y)
```

Technically, negative integers are expressions rather than literals, but this distinction is not important until we discuss expressions in more detail.

Two predefined procedures used for integer input-output were mentioned earlier in conjunction with ada_io. The procedure put takes an integer expression and prints its value:

```
put(i);
put(2*i+3);
```

The procedure get takes an integer variable. An integer is read from input and the variable is set to its value:

```
get(i);
get(2*i+3);  -- Illegal! Must be a variable.
```

3.2   THE TYPE FLOAT

The predefined type float is used to represent approximate values of real numbers. Like integer, this type is dependent on the floating point capability of the machine on which programs are executed. Numeric literals of type float are distinguished by the presence of a decimal point. They may also include an exponent. This usage is consistent with most programming languages. These are examples of float literals:

```
12.0
0.456
3.14159_26
1.34E-12
1.0e+6
```

The following arithmetic operators are defined for float variables x and y and yield results of type float:

Expression	Meaning
x + y	addition
x − y	subtraction
x * y	multiplication
x / y	division
− x	negation

Note that integer and float values cannot be mixed in an expression.

The predefined procedures put and get in ada_io may take expressions and variables of type float.

3.3   THE TYPE BOOLEAN

A boolean value is a logical truth value. Boolean values are denoted by one of two predefined literal identifiers true and false, which are the only two values associated with the type boolean.

The following operators are defined for boolean values x and y and yield results of type boolean:

Expression	Meaning
x **and** y	logical conjunction
x **or** y	logical disjunction
x **xor** y	exclusive or
not x	logical negation

These operators have their conventional meanings. The language defines several ways to compare the values of two data objects and determine their relationship to each other. Relational operations are defined for most Ada types and yield boolean results.

Expression	Meaning
x = y	equality
x /= y	inequality
x < y	less than
x <= y	less than or equal to
x > y	greater than
x >= y	greater than or equal to

The operands of a relational operator must be the same type. For x and y of type integer or float, the relational operators have the conventional meaning (except that the two types cannot be mixed in a single relational expression). For x and y of type boolean, the relational operators are defined because the type boolean is specified such that false is less than true.

3.4   THE TYPE CHARACTER

The predefined type character is used to represent values that are defined by the American Standard Code for Information Interchange (ASCII). Character literals consist of a single printable character enclosed in single quotes. Mechanisms for accessing nonprintable character values are described in Appendix V. The following examples are literals of type character:

```
'a'      -- lower case letter a
'%'      -- punctuation symbol percent sign
''''     -- a single quote
' '      -- a space
```

The only operations defined for the predefined type character are the relational operations. The operations = and /= have their usual meaning when applied to characters. The operations <, >, <=, and >= are defined in terms of the underlying numeric representation of character values (see Appendix IV).

Such operations are useful for determining, for example, if a character is in the range of ASCII values which define letters.

The predefined procedures get and put in ada_io may also take character variables and literals.

3.5   THE TYPE STRING

All of the predefined types discussed thus far are *scalar types*; that is, they have atomic values that cannot be divided into smaller parts. Ada has a predefined type string which is a *composite type*. Composite types have values that consist of one or more component values. For example, the type string is used to represent values that consist of a sequence of character values. (Composite types are discussed in greater detail in subsequent chapters.)

A string literal is a sequence of zero or more characters enclosed in double quotes:

```
"this is a string"
"abcd"
" "              -- the null string (zero characters)
"123" "56"       -- using double-quote in a string
```

This last string shows the mechanism used to include the double-quote character in a string—it is written twice. This string is 6 characters long; the fourth character is a double quote.

Ada provides a mechanism for declaring variables of type string, but we'll postpone discussion of string variables until we know a little more about Ada.

The predefined procedure put in ada_io may take a string that is simply output character by character:

```
put ("hello");
```

Recall that put does not implicitly cause a new_line.

chapter 4

Expressions

The concept of an expression appears in all major programming languages and Ada's expressions do not differ from other languages' in any fundamental ways. An expression is a sequence of operands (such as variables, literals or sub-expressions) separated by operators (such as + or −). All expressions in Ada have a type, and the compiler checks for incorrect combinations of types in expressions. This chapter details the aspects of expressions that are unique to Ada.

4.1 NUMERIC TYPE CONVERSIONS

In many programming languages, it is legal to mix integer and real operands in an expression. In FORTRAN or Pascal, for example, if an integer is added to a real, it is first converted to a real. Ada allows no such implicit type conversions. It does, however, provide a mechanism for explicitly converting from one numeric type to another. For example:

```
with ada_io;  use ada_io;
procedure type_conversion_demo is
   i: integer;
   x: float := 3.7;
begin
   i := integer(x);          -- set i to 4 (rounds 3.7 up)
   x := x + float(2 * i);    -- add 8.0 to x
   put(x);                   -- prints 11.7
end type_conversion_demo;
```

A type conversion consists of a type name followed by a parenthesized expression to be converted. Conversion of floating point values to integer values involves rounding.

The type conversion facility described here is only for use with numeric types. It is illegal, for example, to convert a character to an integer in this manner.

4.2   THE MEMBERSHIP OPERATION

Ada provides a convenient mechanism for testing if a value is within a given range. The expression

```
i in 1..n
```

is equivalent to this more complicated expression:

```
i >= 1 and i <= n
```

Only values from scalar types can be used to define the bounds of the range of a membership operation.

A variant of the membership operation is used for testing whether a value is not within a given range:

```
i not in 1..n
```

This expression is equivalent to

```
not(i in 1..n)
```

but is more readable.

4.3   SHORT-CIRCUIT OPERATIONS

The operators and and or evaluate both operands before computing the result. Sometimes, what is needed is to evaluate the left operand first, and then evaluate the right operand only if necessary. The operators and then and or else provide such a capability. For example:

```
2 < 1 and then 3 < 4
```

In the expression above, the right operand is not evaluated because the expression is known to be false after the left operand has been evaluated. This is not crucial in the above expression, but consider a construct such as

```
x /= 0 and then 20/x < 9
```

If an ordinary and is used, a run-time error occurs if x is 0 because the expression 20/x is evaluated and leads to division by 0.

4.4   THE MOD AND REM OPERATORS

Most languages provide an operator for computing the remainder of a division operation. There are subtle differences between different languages when either operand is negative. Ada attempts to solve this problem by providing two separate remainder functions, mod and rem. The best way to explain the differences between these operations is with Table 4-1.

Table 4-1. Difference Between Mod and Rem

A	B	A/B	A rem B	A mod B
10	5	2	0	0
11	5	2	1	1
12	5	2	2	2
13	5	2	3	3
14	5	2	4	4
10	−5	−2	0	0
11	−5	−2	1	−4
12	−5	−2	2	−3
13	−5	−2	3	−2
14	−5	−2	4	−1
−10	5	−2	0	0
−11	5	−2	−1	4
−12	5	−2	−2	3
−13	5	−2	−3	2
−14	5	−2	−4	1
−10	−5	2	0	0
−11	−5	2	−1	−1
−12	−5	2	−2	−2
−13	−5	2	−3	−3
−14	−5	2	−4	−4

Note that mod and rem may be used only with integer values.

4.5   EXPONENTIATION

The exponentiation operator ** is used to form expressions that compute integer exponentials of integer or float values. The language does not permit noninteger exponents. Some examples:

```
2 ** 8
n ** 2
n ** (m - 1)
e ** 7
5.1 ** (4 ** n)
```

All binary operators other than exponentiation (like * and /) group left to right, meaning that the expression

```
a / b / c
```

is equivalent to

```
(a / b) / c
```

But a similar expression using exponentiation is not legal Ada:

```
2 ** 3 ** 2
```

because there is no default grouping for exponentiation. The grouping must be explicitly indicated with parentheses:

```
(2 ** 3) ** 2        -- 8 ** 2 = 64
2 ** (3 ** 2)        -- 2 ** 9 = 512
```

The standard mathematical convention groups exponentiation right to left, which is exactly the opposite of all other operators. The distinction has caused confusion in other programming languages. To avoid this confusion, Ada's exponentiation operator does not have a default grouping.

4.6   ABSOLUTE VALUE

The predefined operator abs is used to compute the absolute value of a numeric quantity, both integer and floating point. For example:

```
abs (-3)             -- value is 3
abs (3)              -- value is also 3
abs (-2.7)           -- value is 2.7
                     -- assume a = -1, b = 3
abs (a)              -- value is 1
abs (a - b)          -- value is 4
abs (b * a)          -- value is 3
abs a                -- parentheses optional, but recommended
```

The operator abs may be used as part of an expression. For example:

```
3 + abs (a - b)      -- value is 7
1.3 + abs (x)        -- assume x = -4.3, value is 5.6
```

4.7   STRING CONCATENATION

The concatenation operator & is used to construct a single string from two smaller strings: *

```
"abcde" & "fghijk" & "lmn"
```

The expression above is equivalent to:

```
"abcdefghijklmn"
```

String concatenation is often useful for building long string literals because Ada does not allow a string literal to cross a source line boundary. (That is, the text inside a string literal must be written on a single source text line.)

The concatenation operator can be used with values of type character as well as values of type string. The result of a concatenation operation is always of type string.

```
"ab" & 'c'            -- result is "abc"
'a' & "bc"            -- result is "abc"
'a' & 'b' & 'c'       -- result is "abc"
```

String concatenation is explained more fully when string-typed variables are discussed.

4.8   STATIC EXPRESSIONS

The notion of *static expression* is used in several Ada language constructs. In general, a static expression is an expression whose value can be computed at compile time. The following examples should give the programmer an intuitive feel for static expressions. Any literal by itself is a static expression:

```
3           -- static expression of type integer
'a'         -- static expression of type character
```

A constant initialized to a static expression is a static expression. For example:

```
length: constant integer := 5;
```

An expression that uses only the predefined operations and static operands is also a static expression:

```
3 * length
abs(length - 1) + 4
```

An expression containing a value that can change at runtime is not static.

When a static expression is required by the language, a compile time error is generated if a static expression is not supplied.

4.9   OPERATOR PRECEDENCE

A precedence relationship between two operators determines the order in which the operations are done. For example, in this expression:

```
3 + 4 * 5
```

the multiplication 4 * 5 is done before the addition because Ada's expressions generally follow normal algebraic conventions. Multiplication is said to have a *higher* precedence than addition. Using this convention, the value of the expression given above is 23. If the precedence of multiplication were lower than addition, the result would be 35. Parentheses can be used to alter the order of expression evaluation, as in this example:

```
(3 + 4) * 5
```

If the relative precedence of two operators is not known, it is advisable to use extra parentheses in expressions.

The expression

```
x * -2      -- Illegal
```

is not allowed by Ada's expression syntax; however, a slight modification of this expression is permitted:

```
x * (-2)
```

We suspect that this unconventional rule can be traced to the need to avoid two consecutive minus signs, as in this example:

```
x--2        -- probably not what you want
```

The two minus signs -- are treated as the comment delimiter and the rest of the source line is ignored.

The only major departure from conventional arithmetic precedence is the precedence of unary operators. In this expression:

```
-2 * x
```

the multiplication 2 * x is evaluated *before* the unary minus, because the expression -2 is not an integer literal. According to the language definition, all numeric literals are positive and the unary minus has a lower precedence than multiplying operators.

In the previous example, the value of the expression is the same regardless of the precedence of unary minus. However, because of the strange precedence of unary operators, the following expression does not give the apparent result indicated by Table 4-1:

```
-11 mod 5
```

The value of this expression appears to be 4; however, the actual value is −1, because the unary minus is evaluated after 11 mod 5 rather than before. It is probably a good idea to always use parentheses whenever unary operators are used.

Table 4-2 lists the various classes of operators and their relative precedence (from lower to higher precedence):

Table 4-2. Precedence of Operators

LOW		
	logical operators	and then or else and or xor
	relational operators	not in in = /= < <= > >=
	adding operators	+ − &
	unary operators	− +
	multiplying operators	* / mod rem
	exponentiating operators	** not abs
HIGH	highest precedence	

Note that although the logical operators all have the same precedence, they may not be intermixed at the same level of an expression. For example, the following two examples are legal Ada:

```
a and b and c
a or b or c
```

but the following example is illegal:

```
a or b and c    -- illegal
```

because the and and or operators have no relative precedence with respect to each other. We must indicate the grouping explicitly using parentheses.

```
(a or b) and c
a or (b and c)
```

4.10   FORMAL SYNTAX

The syntax for Ada expressions is fairly imposing; however, it is included for reference purposes (on page 24):

```
name =
    simple-name                           -- like x or line_count
    | ...
simple-name = identifier

primary =
    name
    | numeric-literal                     -- like 37 or 3.14
    | string-literal                      -- like " Enterprise"
    | ( expression )
    | type-conversion
    | ...

type-conversion =
    type-name (expression)

type-name = name                          -- like integer

expression =
    relation {and relation}
    | relation {or relation}
    | relation {xor relation}
    | relation {and then relation}
    | relation {or else relation}

relation =
    simple-expression [relational-op simple-expression]
    | simple-expression [not] in range

range =
    simple-expression .. simple-expression
    | ...

simple-expression =
    [unary-op] term {adding-op term}

term =
    factor {multiplying-op factor}

factor =
    primary [** primary] | abs primary | not primary

relational-op =
    < | > | <= | >= | = | /=

adding-op =
    + | - | &

unary-op =
    + | -

multiplying-op =
    * | / | rem | mod
```

chapter 5
Object declarations

In this chapter, we present an overview of object declarations, which are used to define data objects and the storage associated with them. The concepts presented here are used throughout the remaining chapters, although many of the details concerning the definition of object types are deferred to later chapters.

5.1 OVERVIEW OF OBJECT DECLARATIONS

There are two classes of objects in Ada programs: *variables* and *constants*. The value of a variable may change during the execution of a program, but the value of a constant must remain the same throughout the program's execution. All variables and constants (collectively referred to as *objects* in Ada) must be declared prior to their use. An object declaration associates a name and a type with an object. Thus, the object declaration

```
x: integer;
```

says that x is the name of a variable object whose possible values are those of the standard Ada type integer. The object declaration

```
length: constant float := 7.0,
```

says that length is the name of a constant object of type float whose value is the floating point literal 7.0. The following statements illustrate some of the uses of the two objects declared above.

```
x := 3;              -- set the value of x to 3
x := x + 1;          -- increment the value of x
put (x);             -- print the current value of x
length := 5.0;       -- ILLEGAL!! the value of a
                     -- constant cannot be changed!!
```

Constant object declarations must include an initialization clause which defines the value of the object. Variable object declarations may include an optional initialization clause, which specifies an initial value for the object:

```
n:  integer := 37;               -- variables may be given
                                 -- initial values as
                                 -- shown here
p:  integer := n + 2;            -- initialization values
                                 -- can also be arbitrary
                                 -- expressions
c:  constant integer := n * 3;   -- constants may be given
                                 -- nonstatic initial values
```

The first declaration defines an object named n of type integer which is to have the initial value 37. The second declaration defines object called p, also of type integer, which is initialized to the expression n + 2 (in this case, 39). The third declaration declares a constant and illustrates that the initial value for a constant object need not be specified using a static expression. At runtime, initialization of variables occurs in the order that initialization clauses are encountered in the program text.

Normally, variables are not automatically initialized. All variables must be initialized (either in the declaration or in the program text) before they may be correctly used. If a program uses an uninitialized variable, its result is unpredictable. The type of an initialization expression must be the same as the type of the object. In the last example, the literal value 37 is indeed of type integer.

An object declaration may declare more than one object of the same type. For example, the object declaration

```
i,j,max: integer;       -- declaration of more than one
                        -- object
```

defines three objects, with names i, j, and max, which are all of type integer.

5.2   FORMAL SYNTAX

The specification for the syntax of an object declaration is as follows:

```
declaration =
    object-declaration
  | ...
object-declaration =
    identifier-list : [constant] type-indication [:= expression]
  | ...
identifier-list = identifier {, identifier}
type-indication =
    type-name
  | ...
```

The reader has already been introduced to the use of the predefined type names (such as integer and character) as type-indications. Other sorts of type-indications will be introduced as we progress with our discussion.

chapter 6

Basic ada statements

Ada defines a number of statements that permit the programmer to manipulate data and control the sequencing of actions in a program, many of which are similar to statements in other programming languages. In this chapter Ada's basic statements are discussed in detail. In particular, discussion centers on the assignment statement (used for establishing a value for variables), and the control statements (used for organizing a program's flow of control).

Ada permits a sequence of statements (that is, one or more statements) to appear anywhere a single statement may appear. The language designers felt that this rule would simplify program modification, since statement insertion can occur anywhere without the addition of **begin** and **end** delimiters, as used in many other languages. Ada uses the **begin** and **end** keywords to designate statement sequences which may have declarations associated with them (such as the body of a program).

Note that Ada uses the semicolon as a statement *terminator* and every statement must therefore end with a semicolon. This usage differs from many languages (such as Pascal and Algol) which employ the semicolon as a statement *separator*.

6.1   ASSIGNMENT STATEMENT

The assignment statement is used to establish a *value* for a variable. Values are represented by *expressions* which compute a particular value to be assigned. Variables are represented by the Ada names used in object declarations. Assignment is written using the colon-equals token : = to separate the variable from the value to be assigned. The variable is often called the *left hand side* of an assignment and the expression is normally called the *right hand side* of the assignment. The following program illustrates several simple assignment statements:

```
procedure assignment_demo is
   i, j: integer;
   b: boolean;
begin
   i := 1;
   j := i * 5;
   b := true;
   b := i <= 31 or not b;
end assignment_demo;
```

Ada is a strongly typed language. The type of the expression on the right hand side of an assignment must be the same as the type of the variable on the left hand side. The following program contains three erroneous assignment statements:

```
procedure bad_assignment_demo is -- illegal
   i, j: integer;
   b: boolean;
begin
   i := '?';        -- illegal
   j := 3.7;        -- illegal
   b := 23;         -- illegal
end bad_assignment_demo;
```

Ada compilers give error messages whenever type conflicts are encountered in assignment statements.

6.1.1   Formal Syntax

```
sequence-of-statements =
     statement {statement}
statement =
     assignment-statement
   | ...
assignment-statement =
     name := expression ;
```

6.2   IF STATEMENT

As in most higher level languages, the if statement is used to select a sequence of statements for execution based on the value of a boolean condition. The following program illustrates a simple use of the if statement.

```
procedure if_demo is
  line_count, page_count: integer;
begin
  if line_count > 66 then
    line_count := 1;
    page_count := page_count + 1;
  end if;
end if_demo;
```

When the boolean condition is true, the then clause is executed. This is illustrated in the example above. When the value of the integer object line_count is greater than 66, line_count is reset to 1 and another counter, page_count, is incremented. Note that since Ada permits a sequence of statements anywhere a statement may appear, both assignment statements are part of the then clause of the if statement. However, in order to avoid the ambiguity that might result from allowing a sequence of statements anywhere, Ada requires that the tokens **end if** terminate an if statement.

Ada also permits an alternative action if the boolean condition is false. This is written, as shown in the example below, using the reserved word **else** to separate the false alternative from the true alternative.

```
procedure else_demo is
  i: integer;
  max: constant integer := 511;
begin
  if i < max then
    i := i + 1;
  else
    i := 0;
  end if;
end else_demo;
```

The statement after the **else** keyword is called the ''else clause'' and may also be a sequence of statements terminated by the **end if** token sequence.

Ada formalizes a very common programming construct. In addition to the else alternative just described, Ada defines optional elsif alternatives which may appear between the initial then clause and the (optional) else clause. Consider the following program:

```
with ada_io; use ada_io;
procedure elsif_demo is
  ch: character;
begin
  get(ch);
  if ch in 'a'..'z' or ch in 'A'..'Z' or ch = '_' then
    put("this character is an identifier character");
  elsif ch in '0'..'9' then
    put("this character is a decimal digit");
  else
    put("this character is a special character");
  end if;
  new_line;
end elsif_demo;
```

This example determines if a character is an identifier character (that is, a letter or an underscore), a decimal digit, or something else. Only one "elsif clause" is shown here, although any number (including zero) of such clauses may appear. Each elsif clause may include a sequence of statements terminated by another elsif clause, an else clause, or the tokens **end if**.

6.2.1   Formal Syntax

```
if-statement =
    if boolean-condition then
      sequence-of-statements
    {elsif boolean-condition then
      sequence-of-statements}
    else
      sequence-of-statements
    end if ;
boolean-condition = expression
statement =
    assignment-statement
  | if-statement
  | ...
```

A boolean-condition is simply an expression that has a boolean result such as a boolean variable or constant, or a relational expression.

6.3   LOOP STATEMENTS

Loop statements are used to cause the execution of a statement or sequence of statements zero or more times, generally depending on a condition specified by the programmer. Ada provides three forms of the loop statement: the basic loop, the while loop, and the for loop. Each of these forms defines a different mechanism for initialization, execution, and termination of the loop.

6.3.1   Basic Loop

The simplest of the loop statements, called the basic loop, specifies that the sequence of statements enclosed by the basic loop is to be executed repeatedly. For example, consider the basic loop statement below.

```
with ada_io; use ada_io;
procedure basic_loop_demo is
   a: integer;
begin
   loop -- forever
      get(a);
      put(a);
   end loop;
end basic_loop_demo;
```

Notice that no condition for loop termination is specified; the basic loop specifies perpetual execution of the statements to read and print an integer value. This kind of statement is often useful in systems programming applications when some activity is expected to continue as long as the computer is in operation. For example, operating system schedulers, radar tracking systems, or database request handlers might use such "infinite" loops.

6.3.2   While Loop

The while loop is an enhancement of the basic loop through the addition of an *iteration clause* that specifies a boolean condition upon which continued execution of the while loop is predicated. The following example illustrates a while loop.

```
with ada_io; use ada_io;
procedure while_demo is
   n:  integer
begin
   n := 0:
   while n < 32 loop       -- while n is less than 32
     if n mod 2 = 0 then   -- is n an even number?
       put (n) ;
       new_line;
     end if;
     n := n + 1;           -- increment n
   end loop;               -- go back up to test
end while_demo;
```

This program prints all the even numbers between 0 and 31. The while condition is tested *before* each execution of the body of the loop and, if the condition is false, the body will not be executed. Thus, if the condition is initially false, the body of the loop will never be executed. If the condition becomes false as a result of execution of the loop body, execution of the loop will terminate prior to the next execution of the loop body.

6.3.3   For Loop

The for loop is an enhancement of the basic loop using a different iteration clause. The for loop iteration clause implicitly declares a new variable, called the *control variable*, and a range of values that the control variable is to acquire during execution of the for loop.

The range specified must be a *discrete range*. A range is discrete if the associated type is discrete. A type is discrete if it is a scalar type and the values represented by the type can be enumerated; that is, if the values can be counted using the whole numbers. Thus far, the discrete types that have been discussed are integer, character, and boolean. The type float is not discrete because the values represented by float cannot be enumerated.

During the first execution of a for loop body, the control variable has the value of the lower bound of the specified discrete range. During each subsequent execution of the loop body, the control variable is assigned the value of the successor of the previous value. The for loop terminates following execution of the loop body when the control variable has the value of the upper bound of the specified range.

```
with ada_io; use ada_io;
procedure for_demo is
begin
  for n in 0..31 loop    -- declares n and defines its range
    if n mod 2 = 0 then  -- is n an even number?
      put(n);
      new_line;
    end if;
  end loop;
end for_demo;
```

This example also prints the even numbers between 0 and 31; however, use of the for iteration clause simplifies the resulting program somewhat. In this example, the control variable n acquires values in the range 0 to 31, beginning with 0 during the first execution of the loop and terminating with 31 during the final execution of the loop.

The example above uses a for loop which assigns values to the control variable in order of increasing arithmetic value; that is, a sequence like 0, 1, 2, 3, 4, . . . , 31. By using the keyword **reverse**, the programmer may also specify that control variable values should be assigned in descending rather than ascending order. The following iteration clause could be used in the example above:

```
for n in reverse 0..31
```

Using this iteration clause, the control variable will acquire a new sequence of values: 31, 30, 29, 28, 27, . . . , 0.

The iteration clause

```
for n in 31..0
```

is not the same as the previous example. The range 31..0 is called a *null range* because the first value is greater than the last value. Null ranges are often ranges whose bounds are not constant:

```
with ada_io; use ada_io;
procedure null_range_demo is
  m: integer;
begin
  get(m);
  for i in 0..m loop    -- if m is less than zero
    put(i);             -- nothing is printed
  end loop;
  new_line;
end null_range_demo;
```

When a null range is used in a for iteration clause, the body of the loop is executed zero times.

The for iteration clause acts as a declaration of the control variable (i in the last example). If another object with the same name as the control variable has been declared at the point where the for loop is written, then that other object is hidden from the statements within the body of the for loop. For example:

```
with ada_io; use ada_io;
procedure scope_demo is
   m,n: integer;
begin
   n := -1;
   m := n;
   for n in 1..20 loop     -- implicitly declares a new n
      m := n;               -- n is the control variable
   end loop;               -- not the object declared earlier
   put(n);                 -- n is explicitly declared object
end scope_demo;            -- this program prints -1
```

All statements in the body of the for loop refer to the loop control variable when they use the variable n—the n declared earlier is not visible within the loop. After termination of the for loop, the value of m will be 20, the final value of the loop control variable. The value of the object n declared outside the for loop will be −1, unchanged from its value on entry to the for loop code.

The control variable acts as a constant within the for loop. The control variable may not be changed by statements in the body of the loop, nor may the control variable be passed to procedures in a manner that permits alteration of the control variable (as in get(i) if i is a loop control variable). Ada compilers report errors at compile time if control variables are misused in this manner.

The type of the control variable is determined by the type of the bounds in the range specification that follows the **in** keyword of the for iteration clause. Any discrete type is suitable. For example:

```
for ch in 'a'..'z' loop ...
```

The type of the control variable ch is character because the bounds 'a' and 'z' are literals of type character.

For loop ranges need not use constants as upper and lower bounds. Any simple expression involving constants or variables of a discrete type is acceptable. The upper and lower bounds of a for loop range are computed only once, during initialization of the for loop, insuring that alteration of any variables that appear in a for loop range by the body of the for loop cannot alter the action of the for loop. Consider the following example:

```
with ada_io; use ada_io;
procedure loop_demo is
   n: integer := 2;
begin
   for i in n*2 .. n*4 loop
     n := n + 2;
   end loop;
   put(n);   -- prints 12
end loop_demo;
```

The bounds of the for loop are computed before the loop is executed (the initial value is 4 and the terminating value is 8). Thus, these values are not affected when the value of n is changed inside the loop. The loop is executed five times (for the values 4, 5, 6, 7 and 8).

6.3.4   Exit and Exit When

The exit statement is used to terminate an enclosing loop, causing execution to resume at the statement immediately following the body of the loop exited. The exit statement may be used to terminate a basic loop, while loop, or for loop and must appear within the body of the loop to be terminated. Exit statements may not be used to terminate non-loop statements, such as if statements. Consider the following program.

```
with ada_io; use ada_io;
procedure exit_demo is
   n: integer;
begin
   loop   -- forever
     get (n);
     if n = -1 then
        exit;
     end if;
     put (n*2);
   end loop;
   put ("Goodbye...");
end exit_demo;
```

This program reads a value, prints twice the value, and then repeats. The program runs until the value −1 is read by the call to get. Execution of the exit statement immediately transfers control to the statement following the loop statement; no further statements in the body of the loop are executed.

The exit statement also permits an optional conditional expression which is evaluated to determine whether or not the loop should be terminated. The exit statement in the example above:

```
if n = -1 then
   exit;
end if;
```

should be written:

```
exit when n = -1;
```

This causes loop termination when the expression n = -1 is true. The conditional expression may be of arbitrary complexity, provided only that the result is of type boolean.

6.3.5   Formal Syntax

loop-statement = [iteration-clause] basic-loop;

basic-loop =
   loop
      sequence-of-statements
   end loop

iteration-clause =
   for identifier **in** [**reverse**] discrete-range
   | **while** boolean-condition

discrete-range =
   range
   | ...

exit-statement =
   exit [**when** boolean-condition] ;

statement =
   assignment-statement
   | if-statement
   | loop-statement
   | exit-statement
   | ...

6.4   CASE STATEMENT

The case statement is used to select for execution one of a number of alternative statement sequences based on the value of an expression called the *case selector*. The type of the selector must be discrete. Each statement sequence is preceded by a list of *choices* specifying those values of the selector that cause execution of that statement sequence:

```
with ada_io; use ada_io;
procedure case_demo is
  n, x: integer;
begin
  get(n);
  case n is
    when 0 | 1 =>
      . x := 1;
    when 2 =>
      x := 2;
    when 3 =>
      x := 6;
    when 4 =>
      x := 24;
    when 5 =>
      x := 120;
    when 6 =>
      x := 720;
    when others =>
      put("number too big");
      x := 0;
  end case;
  put(x);
end case_demo;
```

Each choice value must be a static expression of the same type as the selector. Every element of the value set of the selector type must be represented once and only once in the set of choices; however, there is no requirement that the choice values be listed in any particular order. Consider this (erroneous) example:

```
with ada_io; use ada_io;
procedure bad_case_demo is -- illegal
  n, x: integer;
begin
  case n is
    when 2 =>
      x := 3;
    when 0 | 1 =>
      get(x);
      x := x * 2;
  end case;
end bad_case_demo;
```

This example is erroneous because every value of the selector type (integer in the example) must be given in some when clause.

The choice **others** may be used to specify all values of a selector type that have not been listed in prior choices. It may only appear as the final choice in the list of choices. As in the examples above, the vertical bar | may separate choice values to indicate that more than one choice value is associated with a single sequence of statements. In addition, value ranges (such as 1..5) may be used to associate a range of choice values with a single sequence of statements. These features are illustrated in this example:

```
with ada_io; use ada_io;
procedure case_range_demo is
   ch: character;
begin
   get(ch);
   case ch is
     when 'a'..'z' | 'A'..'Z' | '_' =>
       put("this character in an identifier character");
     when '0'..'9' =>
       put("this character is a decimal digit");
     when others =>
       put("this character is a special character");
   end case;
   new_line;
end case_range_demo;
```

When a case statement is executed, the value of the selector is used to determine and transfer control to the proper statement sequence. Once that statement sequence has executed, control transfers to the next statement following the case statement.

6.4.1   Formal Syntax

```
case-statement =
    case expression is
        {when choice {| choice} =>
            sequence-of-statements}
    end case ;

choice =
    static-simple-expression
    | discrete-range
    | others

statement =
    assignment-statement
    | if-statement
    | loop-statement
    | exit-statement
    | case-statement
    | ...
```

6.5   NULL STATEMENT

The null statement specifies an empty action or no-operation and is defined primarily for increased program readability. It is frequently used with other statement forms to indicate that no action is to be performed under certain circumstances. For example:

```
with ada_io; use ada_io;
procedure null_statement_demo is
    n: integer;
begin
    get(n);
    case n is
        when 1 =>
            put("one");
        when 2 =>
            put("two");
        when others =>      -- must specify all cases
            null;
    end case;
end null_statement_demo;
```

In situations where a statement is required, but no action is necessary, the null statement is useful.

6.5.1   Formal Syntax

null-statement = **null** ;

statement =
    assignment-statement
  | if-statement
  | case-statement
  | loop-statement
  | exit-statement
  | null-statement
  | . . .

chapter 7
Subprograms

As in most languages, Ada allows the programmer to define *subprograms* consisting of object declarations, optional nested subprogram declarations, and a sequence of statements. There are two kinds of Ada subprograms: *procedures* and *functions*. Functions return a value as a result of execution; procedures do not.

Procedure and function declarations associate a procedure or function name with an optional list of formal parameters, some optional related declarations and a required sequence of statements. A function declaration also specifies the type of the returned value. For example, consider the following program.

```
with ada_io; use ada_io;
procedure spaces_demo is
   n: integer : = 4;

procedure spaces(count: integer) is
begin
   for i in 1 .. count loop
     put(' ');
   end loop;
end spaces;

begin
   spaces(6);
   spaces(n*2);
end spaces_demo;
```

The program spaces_demo contains a procedure declaration. The declaration of procedure spaces includes a single *formal parameter* called count.

The text between the keywords **procedure** and **is** is called the procedure specification; the text between the keyword **begin** and **end** spaces is called the body of the procedure. The identifier after the keyword **end** is optional, but, if present it must be the same as the identifier given in the corresponding subprogram specification.

A *subprogram call* names a subprogram to be executed and specifies *actual parameter* values that correspond to the formal parameters. For example, the program spaces_demo includes two calls to procedure spaces, each of which gives an actual parameter corresponding to the formal parameter count. The first call to spaces associates the actual parameter 6 with the formal parameter count and then executes the statements in the body of procedure spaces, printing 6 spaces. The second call evaluates the expression n*2 (the actual parameter) and associates the result with the formal parameter count. Then the body of spaces is executed, which prints 8 spaces.

Subprograms can be used to avoid repetition of program fragments, but they are useful even if they are called only once. They allow the programmer to logically associate related statements into a single named entity, thus clarifying their intended meaning. A good rule of thumb is to restrict the length of a subprogram to no more than a single source page. Small subprograms allow readers of a program to visualize the operations of a program more easily.

A program is a subprogram whose declarations contain zero or more subprograms in its declarative part (like spaces_demo above). In all of the examples given in this book, programs are parameter-less procedures. Every Ada implementation is required to support programs of this form. Some implementations may support parameters or return values for programs. Programmers should consult local Ada documentation to determine whether or not other forms of program specifications are allowed.

7.1   FORMAL PARAMETERS

The procedure specification not only supplies the name of the procedure, it may also declare any number of formal parameters. Formal parameters represent objects that are *local* to the procedure being declared (that is, not accessible outside the region of text bounded by the procedure specification and the end of the procedure body).

For each formal parameter, the programmer supplies a *parameter access mode* either explicitly or implicitly. The keywords **in**, **out**, and **in out** are used to designate the access mode of a parameter; the meaning of these keywords is explained below. If no explicit access mode is specified for a formal parameter, **in** is assumed. Thus, the parameter count to the procedure spaces is implicitly an in parameter.

in   An in parameter acts as a constant, local to the procedure, whose value is given by the corresponding actual parameter. As with constants, the programmer may not alter the value of an in parameter.

out   An out parameter is a variable which may only be assigned a value by the procedure. When the procedure returns, the value of the out parameter is assigned to the corresponding actual parameter (which must be a variable). The predefined procedure get has an out parameter.

in out   An in out parameter acts as a local variable, which is initialized to the value of the actual parameter. It may be assigned a value by the procedure, which is assigned to the actual parameter variable when the procedure returns.

If the programmer attempts to compromise the access mode of a parameter (by attempting to assign to an in parameter, for example), Ada compilers report an error at compile time.

7.2   PROCEDURE CALL STATEMENTS AND ACTUAL PARAMETERS

In order to execute the body of a procedure, the programmer writes a procedure call, consisting of the name of the procedure to be executed and a list of actual parameters corresponding to the formal parameter list. Actual parameters either specify values for the formal parameters of the procedure or indicate variables to be used to return information. When an actual parameter is used solely to pass information to a procedure (that is, an in parameter), the actual parameter consists of an expression specifying the value to be associated with the corresponding formal parameter. When an actual parameter may be used to return information from the called procedure (an out or in out parameter), the actual parameter must be a variable. In either case, the types of the actual and formal parameters must be the same. Some examples are:

```
with ada_io; use ada_io;
procedure parameter_demo is
   x: integer;

   procedure add_and_put(a,b: integer) is -- in parameters
   begin
      put(a+b);              -- simple in parameter
      new_line;              -- no parameters
   end add_and_put;
```

```
begin
  get (x) ;                    -- uses an out parameter
  add_and_ put (2, x) ;        -- simple actual parameters
  add_and_ put (x, x*4) ;      -- more complex expressions
end parameter_demo;
```

Ada defines two notations for actual parameters: *positional* and *named*. Positional parameters are written in the actual parameter list in the same order as the corresponding formal parameters are written in the subprogram specification. This form of parameter passing is familiar to most programmers. Named parameters permit the programmer to specify actual parameters in any order by giving the name of the formal parameter to which an actual parameter is to be bound. Positional and named parameters may be mixed in the same procedure call statement, with the restriction that all positional parameters must precede any named parameter associations.

Some examples of procedure calls with named parameter associations are:

```
spaces (count => 37) ;
add_and_ put (a => 2, b => x) ;
add_and_ put (b => x, a => 2) ;
add_and_ put (2, b => x) ;
add_and_ put (x, a => 2) ;          -- illegal
```

The first two procedure calls illustrate the normal use of named parameter notation. The third procedure call shows that named parameters may be passed in any order. The fourth call demonstrates that the two notations may be mixed, provided that all positional parameters precede any named parameters. The last call is erroneous because the formal parameter a may not be named once its position has already been used. In deciding which notation to use, the readability of the program should be the primary consideration. Programmers should use common sense and choose a consistent style of notation.

7.3   DEFAULT ACTUAL PARAMETERS

When appropriate, default values may be specified for an in parameter and the corresponding actual parameter may be omitted from procedure calls. For example:

```
procedure spaces(count: integer := 1) is
begin
  for i in 1 .. count loop
    put(' ');
  end loop;
end spaces;
```

In this new declaration of spaces, the parameter count is given a default value of 1. Thus, the parameter to spaces may be omitted and only one space will be output. Such a procedure call would simply read:

```
spaces;
```

The default value must be a member of the same type as the parameter. If a default parameter is not last, named notation must be used to specify any remaining actual parameters in a subprogram call. Multiple commas are not allowed.

```
with ada_io; use ada_io;
procedure default_demo is

procedure dummy => demo (a: integer;
                         c: character := ' ';
                         b: float) is

begin
  null;
end dummy => demo;

begin
  dummy => demo (1,'-',2.0);              -- no defaults
  dummy => demo (a => 1, b => 2.0);       -- c defaults to
  dummy => demo (1,,2.0);                 -- illegal
end default_demo;
```

The final call to dummy => demo is not legal Ada.

The expression specifying the default value for a parameter is evaluated each time the subprogram is called without a corresponding actual parameter. Consider the following program:

```
with ada_io; use ada_io;
procedure default_demo is
   n: integer;   -- initially undefined

   procedure p(a: integer := n*2) is
   begin
     put(a);
   end p;

begin
   p(5);         -- prints 5, "n*2" never evaluated
   n := 5;
   p;            -- prints 10
   n := 3;
   p;            -- prints 6
end default_demo;
```

This procedure illustrates that the default value for the parameter a is recomputed each time it is needed. Since it depends on the global variable n, the default value is changed when n is changed.

Notice that a compiler cannot determine the difference between an erroneous omission of a parameter for which a default value is specified and an intentional use of a default parameter value. Further, the use of global variables in default expressions can lead to obscure dependencies that may not be understood by later readers of a program. For these reasons, default parameter values should be used with care.

7.4   SUBPROGRAM OVERLOADING

Ada provides a facility called *overloading* which allows several different subprograms to share the same name, provided the parameters of each subprogram are sufficiently different in type or number. The standard procedure put is actually defined as several procedures which take different argument types. Complete specifications for versions of put for characters and integers are:

```
procedure put(item: character);
procedure put(item: integer; width: integer := 0);
```

A call to put with a character argument indicates that the first function above is intended, while an integer argument implies the second. Notice that, for integers, put takes an optional second parameter that specifies a minimum width for output. If the number uses fewer characters than the specified width, leading blanks are output so that exactly width characters are output. If the number requires more than width characters, the width is ignored—no truncation of the output is performed. Thus, the default width 0 means to output the number using as many characters as is required. The width parameter is useful for printing tables of numbers.

```
with ada_io; use ada_io;
procedure put_demo is
begin
  put('z');               -- the character version of put
  put(123);               -- the integer version
  put(123, 6);            -- 3 spaces are output first
  put(123, width => 6);   -- named notation
end put_demo;
```

The rules for deciding which version of an overloaded subprogram to use can get very complicated if the parameter specifications are similar, or if default parameters are used. There is no need for an Ada programmer to be an expert on the rules since Ada compilers complain if a subprogram reference cannot be resolved.

Overloading should only be used to define a collection of subprograms that perform the same sort of action for all of the associated types. It is possible to give two unrelated subprograms the same name if their parameters are different, but such usage is unwise because it implies to a subsequent reader of the program a relationship that does not actually exist.

7.5   FUNCTIONS AND RETURN STATEMENTS

Function subprograms return a value that can be used as part of an expression, exactly as variables are used in expressions. Like variables, functions must have a type, which defines the set of values that may be returned by the function and the operators that apply to the function values. Function declarations are like procedure declarations, except that function declarations begin with the keyword **function** and include the type of the function in the function specification following the keyword **return**. Function parameters must use the in parameter access mode. Consider the following function declaration.

```
function total(n: integer) return integer is
  t: integer := 0;
begin
  for i in 1..n loop
    t := t + i;
  end loop;
  return t;
end total;
```

This function computes the sum of the integers from 1 to n for a given integer n. The type of this function is integer and any expression that may include an integer value may also include a call to the function total:

```
x:  integer;
.  .  .
x  : = total (4)  + 7;
```

The return statement is used in a function to pass a value back to the calling environment. The value returned is computed by an expression that must be of the same type as the enclosing function. In the function total above, the statement

```
return t;
```

causes the value of t to be returned as the value of the function total. Every call to a function must return a value—which implies that a correctly written function must be terminated by a return statement.

In addition to specifying a value to be returned, the return statement causes immediate termination of a function. The following example (page 50) illustrates a return statement used to exit a loop statement.

```
with ada_io; use ada_io;
procedure function_demo is
  n: integer

  function yes_no return boolean is
    ch: character;
  begin
   loop    -- forever
     get (ch);
     skip_line;    -- ignore rest of input line
     case ch is
       when 'y' | 'Y' =>
         return true;                -- return immediately
       when 'n' | 'N' =>
         return false;               -- return immediately
       when others =>
         put ("type y or n: ");  -- loop continues
     end case;
    end loop;
    -- can't get here
  end yes_no;

begin    -- function_demo
  loop
    get (n);
    put (n*2);
    new_line;
    put ("continue? ");
    exit when not yes_no;           -- call to yes_no
  end loop;
end function_demo;
```

The call to yes_no near the end of the example illustrates the form of a call to a parameter-less function. Some other languages require an empty parameter list for such a call:

```
exit when not yes_no ();   -- Not legal Ada
```

Readers of Ada programs should beware that a call to a parameter-less function cannot be distinguished from a simple variable reference.

A return statement without a return value can also be used to exit a procedure. An implicit return statement is generated at the end of every procedure, so it is not necessary for the programmer to write an explicit return there.

7.6   RECURSION

Ada subprograms may use a programming technique called *recursion*; that is, they may call themselves with successively less complex arguments until a limiting case for which an answer is known is encountered. An answer to the limiting case is returned and more complex answers are built as each recursive call returns with an answer. For example, the function total could be written like this:

```
function total(n: integer) return integer is
begin
   if n= 0 then
      return(0)
   else
      return n + total(n - 1);
   end if;
end total;
```

Each call to total creates a separate *invocation* of the function. There is a separate copy of all parameters and local variables for each invocation of a function. For computing total of 4, the following calls occur:

```
total(n => 4)
   total(n => 3)
      total(n => 2)
         total(n => 1)
            total(n => 0)
            return 0
         return 1
      return 3
   return 6
return 10
```

The above sequence is equivalent to the expression

```
4 + 3 + 2 + 1 + 0
```

A recursive function is an effective way for the programmer to dynamically create and evaluate arbitrarily long expressions like the one above.

Many mathematical results are defined by recursive algorithms. The traversal of tree data structures is a problem for which recursion is the simplest, most elegant solution. While recursion is very often an elegant solution to a problem, an iterative solution is usually more efficient. The programmer should evaluate alternative solutions to a problem and choose the most appropriate.

7.7   VISIBILITY OF IDENTIFIERS

A subprogram may contain declarations of local entities, which are *visible* only within the subprogram. Like formal parameters, they are said to be *local* to that subprogram. For example, the parameter n is local to the function total. Ada does not permit references to this identifier outside of the body of total. We say that the *scope* of the identifier extends from its definition to the end of the enclosing subprogram.

If the function total appeared in a context where the identifier n already had meaning, the previous meaning of n would be *hidden* within the scope of the local parameter n.

Ada scoping rules are technically called *lexical scoping* or *static scoping*. The following example illustrates this concept:

```
with ada_io; use ada_io;
procedure scope_demo is
   i: integer := 1;

   procedure h is
   begin
      put(i);
   end h;

   procedure g is
      i: integer := 2;
   begin
      h;
   end g;

begin -- scope_demo
   g;
end scope_demo;
```

The procedure h prints the value 1. When h is called, the invocations of scope_demo and g are both active. A reference to i inside of h refers to the i defined in procedure scope_demo, even though there is a more recent invocation (that of g) which contains an object named i. This is because the i declared in procedure g is not visible inside of procedure h. Figure 7-1 illustrates lexical scoping for this example.

7.8   ORDER OF DECLARATIONS

The declarative part of a subprogram consists of object declarations and subprogram declarations. The object declarations must precede the subprogram declarations.

A subprogram specification may appear separately from the body of the corresponding subprogram. This is useful if two subprograms are mutually recursive, since otherwise it would be impossible to decide which subprogram to define first. Consider the example mutual_recursion_demo (on page 53).

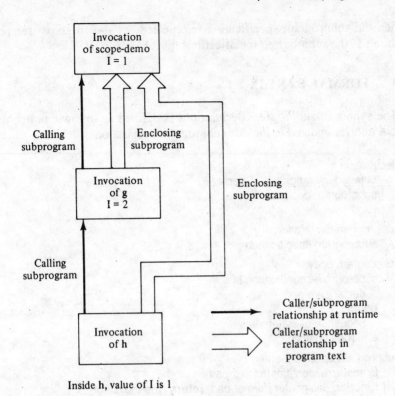

Inside h, value of I is 1

Figure 7-1. Lexical Scoping

```
procedure mutual_recursion_demo is

  procedure f1(n: integer);      -- body comes later

  procedure f2(a, b: integer) is
  begin
    ...
    f1(a);  -- needed declaration of f1 here
    ...
  end f2;

  procedure f1(n: integer) is    -- it's later now
  begin
    ...
    f2(n, n*4);
    ...
  end f1;
begin
  f1(37);
end mutual_recursion_demo;
```

When the subprogram specification is repeated, as shown above for procedure f1, the subprogram specifications must be identical.

7.9   FORMAL SYNTAX

The syntax of subprogram declarations is defined as follows; notice that declaration is updated to include subprogram declarations.

```
declaration =
    object-declaration     -- Chapter 5
    | subprogram-declaration
    | ...
subprogram-declaration =
    subprogram-specification ;
subprogram-body =
    subprogram-specification is
        declarative-part
    begin
        sequence-of-statements
    end [designator];
subprogram-specification =
    procedure identifier [formal-part]
    | function designator [formal-part] return type-indication
formal-part =
    ( parameter-declaration {; parameter-declaration} )
parameter-declaration =
    identifier-list : mode type-name [:= expression]
mode = [ in ] | out | in out
designator =
    identifier
    | ...
declarative-part =
    { declaration }
    { body }
body =
    subprogram-body
    | ...
```

The syntax of procedure and function calls is defined as follows. Note that procedure calls are a form of statement, while function calls are a form of expression.

```
statement =
    assignment-statement            -- Chapter 6
  | if-statement                    -- Chapter 6
  | case-statement                  -- Chapter 6
  | loop-statement                  -- Chapter 6
  | exit-statement                  -- Chapter 6
  | null-statement                  -- Chapter 6
  | procedure-call-statement
  | return-statement
  | . . .

procedure-call-statement =
    procedure-name [actual-parameter-part] ;

procedure-name = name

return-statement =
    return [expression] ;

primary =
    name                            -- Chapter 4
  | numeric-literal                 -- Chapter 4
  | string-literal                  -- Chapter 4
  | ( expression )                  -- Chapter 4
  | type-conversion                 -- Chapter 4
  | function call
  | . . .

prefix =
    name                            -- Chapter 4
  | function-call

function-call =
    function-name [actual-parameter-part]

function-name = name

actual-parameter-part =
    ( parameter-association {, parameter-association} )

parameter-association =
    [formal-parameter =>] actual-parameter

formal-parameter = simple-name

actual-parameter = expression
```

chapter 8

Packages

— a Module

—contains a few programs.

In the management of any large or complicated activity, organization is essential. In Ada, *packages* provide a mechanism for the organization of large or complicated programs.

As an analogy, let's consider the organization of a company. The president of a company is not concerned with all of the day-to-day aspects of the company. Instead, departments are created within the company and general guidelines are set forth for running them. The department managers take all the information about their departments and distill it down, reporting only general trends and developments to the president. Any manager who attempts to understand all the details of the organization will get bogged down in these details and lose track of the big picture. An effective manager not only decides what information is required, but also what information can be done without.

The same thing is true in programming. Large programs consist of large numbers of data objects and large numbers of subprograms which can interact in an even larger number of ways. Like the manager of a large organization, the programmer must find a way to organize a program so that it can be understood. In Ada, packages provide a mechanism for collecting logically related subprograms and their associated data. This is similar to the use of subprograms to collect logically related statements and associated data.

A package consists of two parts: a *specification* and a *body*. The specification gives the name of the package and describes its external characteristics, while the body defines the implementation details of the package. The user does not need to see the body of a package in order to use that package. The programmer, like the manager, must decide which details can be ignored in order to get a clearer view of the "big picture". The information

56

inside a package body is never relevant outside the package. Sometimes, knowledge about how a package is implemented can even be dangerous. A programmer might use such knowledge to use the package for some purpose for which it was never intended. Then if the body of the package were modified to use a new algorithm or data structure, the package might no longer work for that programmer.

8.1   A SIMPLE PACKAGE

The following program defines a mechanism for generating unique numbers. These numbers could be used, for example, as employee numbers in a payroll system. This program can (and will) be expressed better using a package.

```
procedure id_number_demo is
   next_id_number: integer := 0;

   function id_make return integer is
   begin
     next_id_number := next_id_number + 1;
     return next_id_number;
   end id_make;

   procedure demo is
      x, y: integer;
   begin
      x := id_make;
      y := id_make;
   end demo;
end id_number_demo;
```

The procedure id_make returns a different value each time it is called. The next available value is kept in the object next_id_number. There are a number of organizational problems with this scheme. One problem is that there is no reason for the object next_id_number to be available to the rest of the program. This object can be used or modified anywhere in the program, defeating the purpose of the procedure id_make. Also, the fact that ID numbers start at zero should be irrelevant to the rest of the program. We should use a package to hide these details.

The package specification for a package that generates unique numbers might look like this:

```
package id is
   function make return integer;
end id;
```

The ID numbers are generated by incrementing an integer object which is hidden from the user of the package. This example illustrates how the function make in package id is called.

```
procedure demo is
   x, y: integer;
begin
   x := id. make;
   y := id. make;
end demo;
```

Notice the notation used for referencing items that are in the specification of a package. The item is preceded by the package name and a dot . character.

The specification for a package describes its external behavior; we also call this the *interface* to the package. The body of a package defines the implementation details of the package. The body of package id is defined as follows:

```
package body id is -- repeats name of package specification
   next: integer := 0;

   function make return integer is
   begin
      next := next + 1;
      return next;
   end make;
end id;
```

The body consists of local object declarations, followed by subprogram declarations. For every subprogram specification that appears in the package interface, there must be a corresponding subprogram body. The programmer may also declare any number of subprograms that are local to the package. (There are no local subprograms in package id.) In package id, the object next is declared as a local integer which is initially 0; and the body for procedure make, which was defined in the package specification, is declared as well. The procedure make increments the current value of next and then returns the new value.

The complete program id_number_demo containing package id is written as follows:

```
procedure id_number_demo is
   package id is
      function make return integer;
   end id;
```

```
package body id is
   next: integer := 0;

   function make return integer is
   begin
      next := next + 1;
      return next;
   end make;
end id;

procedure demo is
   x, y: integer;
begin
   x := id.make;
   y := id.make;
end;
end id_number_demo;
```

There are several organizational advantages to this scheme, even though it is functionally equivalent to the example given at the start of this section. First, the object next is local to the body of package id. This placement prevents unauthorized access to it. It may only be accessed through the procedure make. Also, the initialization of next is not visible, which is good because the initial value is an implementation detail of the package. Furthermore, if the algorithm for allocating ID numbers changes, the external behavior, as defined by the package specification, does not change.

Perhaps the most important reason for using a package in this example is that it logically associates related entities. The only association between the original disjoint entities next_id_number and id_make is an implicit one which is indicated, but not enforced, by the similarity in the names of the two items. The package id makes this association explicit, and prevents incorrect usage of the associated entities.

In later chapters, we introduce additional package features and refine the definition of package id further.

8.2   THE USE CLAUSE

The notation for referencing items declared in a package interface is an excellent feature for improving program readability. The package name is always written with the referenced item, which clarifies package references for the human reader. We know that id.make is the function make from the package id. However, in some contexts, this notation is too cumbersome. In such a context, a *use clause* can be employed.

A use clause causes the items in a package interface to become directly visible. For example:

```
use id;
```

This use clause allows the programmer to reference the items in package id without using dot notation. The procedure demo above could be rewritten with a use clause as follows:

```
procedure demo is
  use id;
  x, y: integer;
begin
  x := make;  -- no "id." required
  y := make;
end;
```

Name conflicts may arise in some situations involving the use clause. For example, if an identifier is visible in the current context, and the same identifier appears in a package being used, then the identifier in the package is not made directly visible; the dot notation is still required. Consider the following example.

```
with ada_io; use ada_io;
procedure conflict_demo is
  package p is
    a: integer := 1;
    b: integer := 2;
  end p;

  a: integer := 3;

  use p;
begin
  put (a);        -- prints 3 (local a, not p.a)
  put (p.a);      -- prints 1 (p.a)
  put (b);        -- prints 2 (p.b)
  put (p.b);      -- prints 2 (p.b) "p." not required but ok
end use_demo;
```

Note that the package specification in this example contains only object declarations. This feature is useful for associating related data objects. Such data is often called *common data*. A package interface that does not contain any subprogram specifications does not require a corresponding package body.

If two or more packages are used, and an identifier, say x, appears in more than one package interface, *none* of the instances of the identifier x are made visible. This rule prevents the programmer from being confused by inadvertent name conflicts, since such identifiers must be named using dot notation. The following program should clarify this point:

```
with ada_io; use ada_io;
procedure package_conflict_demo is
   package p is
      a,b: integer := 1;
   end p;

   package q is
      b,c: integer := 2;
   end q;

   use p,q;
begin
   put(a);          -- prints 1  (p.a)
   put(b);          -- illegal (p.b or q.b needed)
   put(p.b)         -- prints 1
   put(q.b)         -- prints 2
   put(c);          -- prints 2  (q.c)
end package_conflict_demo;
```

The conflict resolution problem described above does not generally apply to subprograms. Subprograms are usually made directly visible by a use clause since the arguments in a call can be used to determine which subprogram is intended; however, if two overloaded subprograms are so similar that a call may be ambiguous, the resolution method described above does apply.

A use clause may appear anywhere an object declaration may appear, and the identifiers made visible by a use clause are visible until the end of the enclosing scope. We would advise that the use clause be used sparingly since the explicit use of the package name in references to the items in a package interface generally results in more readable programs.

8.3   SEPARATE COMPILATION

Ada provides a facility for separately compiling packages or subprograms (compilation units). The package id could be presented to the compiler as a separate compilation unit:

```
package id is
  function make return integer;
end id;

package body id is
  next: integer := 0;

  function make return integer is
  begin
    next := next + 1;
    return next;
  end make;
end id;
```

Once such a package has been compiled, programs (or other packages) may use it. A context specification is used to make separately compiled compilation units available. For example, a compilation unit requiring the services of package id would contain the following context specification:

```
with id;
```

The following compilation unit uses the separately compiled package id. The first line is the context specification.

```
with id;
procedure context_demo is
  x, y: integer;
begin
  x := id. make;
  y := id. make;
end context_demo;
```

If a context specification is used, it must appear first in the compilation unit. A context specification may contain an optional use clause if dot notation is not desired:

```
with id; use id;
```

8.4   THE PACKAGE "ADA_IO"

Most of the programs we have seen so far have used this context specification:

```
with ada_io; use ada_io;
```

As we mentioned in Chapter 2, we have assumed the existence of a package ada_io which implements several simple input-output functions. We expect that most implementations of Ada will support a similar package.

The following is a specification for package ada_io.

```
package ada_io is
  procedure put(item:  integer; width:  integer := 0);
  procedure put(item:  float; width:  integer := 0);
  procedure put(item:  character);
  procedure put(item:  string);
  procedure new_line(spacing:  integer := 1);
  procedure get(item:  out integer);
  procedure get(item:  out float);
  procedure get(item:  out character);
  function end_of_line return boolean;
  procedure skip_line(spacing:  integer := 1);
end ada_io;
```

Since package ada_io has already been separately compiled, any program may use its services by naming the package in a context specification.

Notice that the body of package ada_io is not given. The implementation of this package is of no concern to the programmer who uses it. This illustrates one of the advantages of using packages. The body of ada_io might be fairly complex, but this complexity is completely hidden from the user.

The standard Ada input-output package text_io includes several complex input-output facilities, none of which are required in order to learn Ada. For the interested reader, the complete specification of text_io appears in Appendix X. Note, however, that text_io uses several features of Ada that have not yet been discussed.

8.5   THE PACKAGE "STANDARD"

The predefined subprograms and types in Ada are effectively defined in a package named standard. This package is implicitly used by every Ada compilation unit. This fact is most useful for resolving name conflicts with user-defined names. For example:

```
procedure standard_demo is
  integer:  boolean;              -- a bad idea
  false:  standard.integer        -- another bad idea
begin
  integer := standard.false;
  false := -4;
end standard_demo;
```

In this example, the object integer hides the predefined type integer and the object false hides the predeclared boolean value false. The predeclared items are specified by using the dot notation with the package name standard. It is really a poor idea to declare a boolean object named integer, but Ada allows it and this example illustrates the point.

8.6   THE ADVANTAGES OF PACKAGES

Any nontrivial program should be built using packages. Even if it is not immediately clear how a problem can be broken up, it is worth the effort to find a way. Such an effort is certain to clarify and simplify the problem. If several programmers are involved, it may be the only way to allow them all to work on the problem at once. The motto of a good programmer should be ''divide and conquer''.

The use of packages provides an additional advantage. Libraries of reusable *software components* can be created. Much of the code being written today has been written countless times before. If common useful programming activities are written as packages, the same package may be reused in many different applications.

8.7   FORMAL SYNTAX

The name production is updated to include package dot notation and declaration is updated to reflect packages. Package-body is added to the production body.

```
name =
     simple-name                    -- Chapter 4
   | selected-component
   | . . .
selected-component =
     prefix . selector
selector =
     simple-name
   | . . .
declaration =
     object-declaration             -- Chapter 5
   | subprogram-declaration         -- Chapter 7
   | package-declaration
   | use clause
   | . . .
package-declaration =
     package-specification ;
package-specification =
     package identifier is
         {declaration}
     end [simple-name]
use-clause =
     use package-name { , package-name } ;
package-name = name
body =
     subprogram-body                -- Chapter 7
   | package-body
   | . . .
package-body =
     package body simple-name is
         declarative-part
     [ begin
         sequence-of-statements ]
     end [simple-name] ;
```

chapter 9

User-defined types

A type defines a set of possible values for a variable or expression. This concept is central to an understanding of Ada. For example, earlier we saw that in the declaration

```
x: integer;
```

the type-indication integer defines a set of possible values for the variable x.

With the exception of a very few predefined types (see Chapter 3, Predefined Types and Operations), all types in Ada are programmer-defined types that must be explicitly declared prior to their use. Using type definitions, the programmer specifies the properties of a set of values and associates a name or identifier with the type thus defined. Subsequently, the type name is used to refer to the set of values. Consider these declarations:

```
type day_of_week is (sun, mon, tue, wed, thu, fri, sat);
payday: day_of_week;
```

A new type, day_of_week, is defined, whose possible values are enumerated in the type definition. The variable payday is of type day_of_week and thus may assume any of the possible values of that type. The statement

```
payday := thu;
```

causes the variable payday to have the value thu, which is a member of the set of values defined in the declaration of day_of_week. In this example, the expression thu has the same type as the variable payday. On the other hand, the assignment

```
payday := 4;      -- illegal
```

is an error because the integer literal 4 is not a member of the set of values defined by day_of_week. This sort of error is called a *type clash*.

9.1   ENUMERATION TYPES

The type day_of_week defined above is called an *enumeration type*. Enumeration type declarations define a new type and a set of values (literals) of that type. Enumeration types are discrete types; their values may be used as the limits in a discrete range. An enumeration literal is a static expression.

In addition to day_of_week we have already seen another enumeration type. The standard type boolean is defined by

```
type boolean is (false, true);
```

Some additional examples of enumeration types are:

```
type color is (red, yellow, blue, green);
type status is (off, on);
type gender is (female, male);
type marital_status is
    (single, married, divorced, widowed);
type direction is (north, west, south, east);
```

Enumeration types define an ordering on enumeration literals and the relational operators may therefore be used to compare literals or variables of the same enumeration type. If we use the whole numbers to number each successive enumeration literal in the order it appears in the enumeration type definition, then the same relations hold between enumeration literals as hold between the corresponding whole numbers. For example, using the type color defined above, the following relational expressions are true:

```
red < green       yellow > red       blue <= green
```

In addition, any discrete type name may be used to specify a discrete range as in the following examples:

```
for ch in character loop ...
for i in integer loop ...
for day in day_of_week loop ...
```

In the first loop, the loop control variable ch takes on all possible values of the type character. The second loop uses integer as the range of values for the loop control variable i. The actual limits of this loop may vary across implementations of Ada, but the corresponding range certainly contains a very large number of values and, in any case, is probably not useful. The third loop could be rewritten as

```
for day in sun..sat loop ...
```

but the use of the type name day_of_week makes it unnecessary for the programmer to know the names of the first and last elements of the enumeration. This can be very important if the declaration of the enumeration type is changed.

9.1.1   Formal Syntax

In this section, we give the syntax of type declarations in general and of enumeration type declarations in particular. Note that the syntax of declaration is updated here.

```
declaration =
    object-declaration       -- Chapter 5
    | subprogram-declaration -- Chapter 7
    | package-declaration    -- Chapter 8
    | use-clause             -- Chapter 8
    | type-declaration
    | ...

type-declaration =
    type identifier is type-definition ;
    | ...

type-definition =
    enumeration-type-definition
    | ...

enumeration-type-definition =
    ( enumeration-literal {, enumeration-literal} )

enumeration-literal =
    identifier | ...
```

9.2   CONSTRAINTS AND SUBTYPES

Up to now, the type-indication used in object declarations has simply been a type identifier. However, a type-indication may be followed by a *constraint*. Consider the following example.

```
x:  integer;
y:  integer range 1..10;
```

The declaration of y includes a *range constraint* which indicates that y may only be used to hold values in the range 1 to 10. Constraints do not define a new type, they define a *subtype* by placing a restriction on a *base type*. Thus, a variable or expression of a constrained type may be used anywhere that a variable or expression of the corresponding base type may be used. We say that a subtype is *compatible* with its base type and other subtypes of the same base type. In the example above, the two objects x and y are compatible: the type of x is integer and the type of y is a constrained subtype of integer.

The use of constraints may have an effect on program execution. Consider this assignment statement:

```
x := y;
```

This statement is always valid because the range of permissible values for y is a subrange of those for x. However, the converse assignment may not be valid.

```
y := x;
```

This statement may result in an error at runtime if the value of x is not in the range 1 .. 10. The error is caused by a *constraint check*. An Ada compiler automatically ensures that constraint checks are done to verify that constraints are not violated. If the programmer defines types carefully, such checks can be extremely valuable during the debugging phase of a program's lifetime since constraints can be used to insure that variables and expressions always have expected values.

The following examples present some additional uses of range constraints:

```
a: integer range 0..99;
b: integer range -5..-1;
weekday: day_of_week range mon..fri;
```

Notice that a range constraint may be applied to an enumeration type. The expressions in a range constraint must be compatible with the base type, and the lower bound may not be greater than the upper bound.

A subtype declaration permits the programmer to name a constrained version of a type:

```
subtype year is integer range 1900..2100;
```

Subtype declarations do not introduce new types, merely constrained versions of existing types. An object declaration using year can be written

```
current_year: year := 1983;
```

The subtype year is compatible with integer and other subtypes of integer. The operations available for integer (such as + and *) are also available for subtypes of integer, so that on New Year's Eve the current year can be incremented:

```
current_year := current_year + 1;
```

This assignment will cause a constraint error in the year 2101.

To understand how constraints interact, consider this example.

```
with ada_io; use ada_io;
procedure constraint_demo is
   small_numbers: integer range 1..10;
   big_numbers: integer range 1000..2000;
begin
   get(small_numbers);    -- constraint error if input value
                          -- out of range
   get(big_numbers);      -- same here
   small_numbers := big_numbers; -- always a constraint error
end;
```

The final assignment statement will always cause a constraint error because the range constraints on small_numbers and big_numbers do not overlap—they have no values in common.

9.2.1   Formal Syntax

Notice that the productions declaration and type-indication are updated.

```
declaration =
    object-declaration        -- Chapter 5
  | subprogram-declaration    -- Chapter 7
  | package-declaration       -- Chapter 8
  | use-clause                -- Chapter 8
  | type-declaration
  | subtype-declaration
  | ...

subtype-declaration =
    subtype identifier is type-indication ;

type-indication =
    type-name                 -- Chapter 5
  | type-name range-constraint
  | ...

range-constraint =
    range simple-expression .. simple-expression

discrete-range =
    range                     -- Chapter 6
  | type-name [range-constraint]
```

9.3   ATTRIBUTES OF DISCRETE TYPES

Ada defines several *attributes* of discrete types. Attributes of a type are obtained by following the type name by a quote mark ', and an identifier specifying the attribute:

```
day_of_week'first
```

The type of above expression is day_of_week, and its value is sun, which is the first enumeration literal in the definition of day_of_week. The attribute last is defined as well. The attributes first and last may be applied to any discrete type:

```
day_of_week'last        -- value is sat
integer'first           -- smallest possible integer
integer'last            -- largest possible integer
```

There are five other attributes that apply to discrete types: pos, val, succ, pred, and image. Unlike first and last, these attributes are functions.

For a given type t, the expression t'pos is a function that takes a value of type t and returns an integer that corresponds to the position of the value within the type:

```
day_of_week'pos (sun)   -- value is 0
day_of_week'pos (mon)   -- value is 1
boolean'pos (false)     -- value is 0
integer'pos (3)         -- value is 3
integer'pos (-5)        -- value is -5
```

For an enumeration type, the position of t'first is always 0.

The attribute val is the inverse of pos. The expression t'val is a function that takes an integer expression and returns the corresponding value in type t:

```
day_of_week'val (4)     -- value is thu
boolean'val (1)         -- value is true
direction'val (0)       -- value is north
day_of_week'val (7)     -- constraint error
```

As indicated in the last example, this attribute performs a constraint check to verify that the supplied value is a legitimate position in the type.

The attributes pred and succ are used to get the successor and predecessor of a value. They are used primarily with enumeration types. With integer types, they are equivalent to adding or subtracting 1. The function t'succ is applied to an expression of type t and returns the succeeding value. The expression

```
t'succ (x)
```

is equivalent to

```
t'val (t'pos (x) +1)
```

The attribute pred is defined similarly. Both succ and pred perform constraint checks on their result values. For example:

```
day_of_week'succ(sat)
day_of_week'succ(day_of_week'last)
```

These expressions are equivalent and each generates a constraint error. This is unfortunate, because the day after Saturday is Sunday. The following example illustrates a method for computing the next day that overcomes this difficulty.

```
function tomorrow(day: day_of_week) return day_of_week is
  week_length: constant integer :=
        day_of_week'last - day_of_week'first + 1;  -- 7
  i: integer;
begin
  i := day_of_week'pos(day);      -- convert day to integer
  i := (i + 1) mod week_length; -- always in range 0..6
  return day_of_week'val(i);      -- convert integer to day
end tomorrow;
```

The attribute image is a function that returns the string representation of its argument.

```
boolean'image(false)      -- the string "FALSE"
integer'image(7+9)        -- the string " 16"
character'image('a')      -- the string "'a'"
```

Note that enumeration images are upper case, a numeric image contains a leading blank for the sign if it is positive, and a character image includes the single quotes.

This attribute is most useful for printing values of enumeration types, as demonstrated by this example.

```
with ada_io; use ada_io;
procedure image_demo is
  type day_of_week is (sun,mon,tue,wed,thu,fri,sat);
begin
  for day in day_of_week loop
    put(day'image);
    put('.');
  end loop;
  new_line;
end image_demo;
```

The procedure image_demo cycles through the values of the type day_of_week and prints the image of each value. For an enumeration type,

SUN. MON. TUE. WED. THU. FRI. SAT.

This attribute is most useful during program debugging, since the programmer is able to produce symbolic output that can be directly related to a program.

An attribute whose value is static is a static expression. For example:

```
day_of_week'first              -- value is sun
day_of_week'pred(day_of_week'last)   -- value is fri
```

are static expressions. But an attribute that returns a dynamic value is not a static expression:

```
day:  day_of_week;
. . .
day_of_week'pred(day)    -- value only available at runtime
```

9.3.1   Formal Syntax

```
name =
    simple-name              -- Chapter 4
  | selected-component       -- Chapter 8
  | attribute
  | ...

attribute =
    name ' attribute-designator

attribute-designator =
    simple-name
  | simple-name ( expression )
```

chapter 10

Array types

An *array* is used to group objects of the same type into a single *data structure*, which may be a simple one-dimensional vector or a more complex multi-dimensional matrix. This sort of structure is found in most programming languages. Arrays are composite types defined by specifying a type used to select components of the array (called the index type) and the type of the underlying components. Arrays are manipulated by indexing single components, or by selecting some number of contiguous elements (called a slice), or as a whole by specifying entire array objects or array valued expressions (called aggregates).

10.1 SIMPLE ARRAYS

An example of a very simple array object declaration is:

```
count: array(1..5) of integer;
```

This declaration defines an array variable count with 5 elements, each of which is an integer. The elements of an array are accessed by *indexing* the array. For example, the third component of the array count is accessed by writing count(3). Indexed variables may appear anywhere that simple variables may. For example:

```
count(3) := 0;        -- set the value of the third
                      -- element of count to 0
x := count(3);        -- set x to the value of the
                      -- third element of count
count(i) := 0;        -- set the value of element i
                      -- of count to 0 (i must have a
                      -- value in the range 1..5)
```

74

```
count (n) := count (n) + 1;
                          -- increment the value of element n
                          -- of count (n must be in the
                          -- range 1..5)
put (count (n) );         -- print the value of element n
```

The index type defines the set of values that may be used to index an array. If the type of an index value is not compatible with the index type, a compile-time error occurs.

```
count ('a') := 7;         -- compile-time error
```

In the example above, the index value is a character but the index type given in the definition of count is a subtype of integer. Thus, an Ada compiler flags this statement to indicate that an index type clash has occurred.

Further, if an index value is not in the range of values specified by the index type, a constraint error occurs at runtime. For example:

```
with ada_io; use ada_io;
procedure index_error_demo is
   n: integer;
   count: array (1..5) of integer;
begin
   get (n) ;
   count (n) := 37;        -- runtime error when n not in 1..5
end index_error_demo;
```

When the value input by the call to get is not in the range given in the definition of count (that is, 1 to 5), a constraint error occurs. Runtime index checking is another useful debugging aid.

The best way to understand arrays is to look at an example for which they are useful. Consider the following programming problem.

- Read a sequence of numbers (one per line) terminated by −1. Each number must be in the range 1 . . 5.

- Produce a frequency count for each of the 5 possible input values.

The basic outline for this program is

```
-- initialize counters
loop
   get (n) ;               -- read a number
   skip_line;              -- one per line
   exit when n = -1;       -- terminated by -1
   -- add 1 to nth counter
end loop;
-- print results
```

The easiest way to implement this program is to use an array to store the frequency counts:

```
count: array(1..5) of integer;
```

We use a for loop to initialize the counters:

```
for i in 1..5 loop
  count(i) := 0;
end loop;
```

As we read data into the variable n, we increment the appropriate frequency counter by writing

```
count(n) := count(n) + 1;
```

Finally, we use a second for loop to print the results. The entire program is given below.

```
with ada_io; use ada_io;
procedure frequency_count_demo is
  endval: constant integer := -1;
  max: constant integer := 5;
  count: array(1..max) of integer;
  n: integer range 1..max;
begin
  for i in 1..max loop      -- initialize counters
    count(i) := 0;
  end loop;

  loop
    get(n);                  -- read a number
    skip_line;               -- one per line
    exit when n = endval;    -- terminated by -1
    count(n) := count(n) + 1; -- add 1 to nth counter
  end loop;

  for i in 1..max loop       -- print results
    put(i, width => 6);
    put(count(i), width => 6);
    new_line;
  end loop;
end frequency_count_demo;
```

Notice that we have introduced two constants, max and endval. Use of these constants does not change the meaning of the program, but does illustrate a good programming practice. If the problem specification is changed (if the input range were to become 1 .. 1000, for example), the program can be modified correctly by simply changing the definition of the constant max.

Suppose the data to be examined were in a second array:

```
data: array(1..100) of integer range 1..5;
```

Each of the 100 input values must still be in the range 1..5. Use of this array changes the counting loop in our example program above:

```
for i in 1..100 loop
   n := data(i);
   count(n) := count(n) + 1;
end loop;
```

Notice that the two arrays are used in different ways. The elements of data are accessed in order, but the elements of count are accessed at random.

The two statements inside the for loop could be written more concisely as follows:

```
count(data(i)) := count(data(i)) + 1;
```

This example illustrates an important point: the index in an array reference may be any kind of expression including a simple variable, a complex calculation, another array reference or even a function call. The only requirement is that the type of the index expression be compatible with the index type in the array declaration.

It is not necessary that a subtype of integer be used as the index type in an array declaration. Any discrete type may be used as an index type. For example:

```
type day_of_week is (sun, mon, tue, wed, thu, fri, sat);
hours_worked: array(day_of_week) of integer range 0..24;
```

The array hours_worked has seven elements. It could be used to keep track of weekly work hours. Instead of indexing the array with numeric values we use the enumeration values of the type day_of_week. For example:

```
with ada_io; use ada_io;
procedure day_array_demo is
   type day_of_week is (sun, mon, tue, wed, thu, fri, sat);
   hours_worked: array(day_of_week) of integer range 0..24;
begin
   for day in day_of_week loop        -- loop through days
      put(day_of_week'image(day));     -- prompt the user
      put("? ");
      get(hours_worked(day))           -- read integer into
      skip_line;                       -- array component
   end loop;
end day_array_demo;
```

Consider the following declarations:

```
type char_class is (letter, digit, special);
char_table: array(character) of char_class;
```

The array char_table can, when properly initialized, be used to determine the class of a character.

```
ch: character;
...
case char_table(ch) is
  when letter =>
    put("this character is an identifier character");
  when digit =>
    put("this character is a decimal digit");
  when special =>
    put("this character is a special character");
end case;
```

The case statement above has the same effect as the case statement presented on page 39. In the following section, we show an efficient method for initializing the array char_table.

10.2   ARRAY AGGREGATES

Initialization of arrays, such as count and char-table in the last section, can be written concisely using an *array aggregate*. The notation of array aggregates takes a number of forms. For example, the statement

```
count := (0, 0, 0, 0, 0);
```

specifies the value of each element of the array in ascending order of array indices. The value of each expression in an array aggregate must be compatible with the type of the array elements defined in the array declaration (in this case, each element must be of type integer). In addition, an aggregate must provide a value for every element of the structure for which it defines a value.

The elements of an array aggregate may simply be expressions as illustrated above or each element may consist of a position indication and a value:

```
count := (1=> 0, 2=> 0, 3=> 0, 4=> 0, 5=> 0);
```

Several position indications may be associated with a single value by separating them with the | token.

```
count := (1 | 2 | 3 | 4 | 5 => 0);
```

Position indications may also be specified by discrete ranges:

```
count : = (1..5 => 0);
```

Finally, the reserved word **others** is used to mean all positions that have not yet been explicitly mentioned. It must appear last in the list of choices:

```
count : = (others => 0);
```

This last example is the easiest way to set all the elements of an array object to a single value.

Additional examples of aggregates using more complex position indications:

```
hours_worked : = (mon..fri => 8, sat | sun => 0);
                           -- normal work week;
hours_worked : = (sat | sun => 0, others => 8);

char_table : = ('a'..'z' | 'A'..'Z' | '_' => letter,
                'O'..'9' => digit,
                others => special);
```

10.3   ARRAY ASSIGNMENTS

Entire array objects may be assigned to other array objects of the same array type using an assignment statement. Array type declarations are used to define several compatible array objects. For example:

```
procedure array_assign_demo is
   type v is array(1..5) of integer;
   a,b: v;
begin
   a : = (1,2,3,4,5);
   b : = a;
end array_assign_demo;
```

The first assignment is legal because the array aggregate satisfies all the requirements for an object of type v. The second assignment copies all five values of array a into array b. It is legal because a and b have exactly the same type.

Normally, Ada requires that the type in an object declaration must have been previously defined. The sole exception to this rule is the provision that array types can be defined as part of an object declaration, because it is sometimes easier than declaring it separately. However, textually identical array type specifications create distinct types. The following example contains several illegal assignments·

```
procedure array_assign is -- illegal
   a: array(1..5) of integer;
   b,c: array(1..5) of integer;  -- not compatible with a
begin
   a := (1,2,3,4,5);            -- this is ok
   b := a;                      -- this is illegal
   c := a;                      -- this is illegal
   b := c;                      -- this is illegal too
end array_assign;
```

The types of the objects a, b, and c are distinct, so the objects are not compatible for assignment. This sort of type is called an *anonymous type* because, since it has not been explicitly declared, it does not have a name. Such types should be avoided in all but the simplest of situations. Instead, array types should be declared explicitly.

10.4   ARRAY PARAMETERS

Array objects may be passed as subprogram parameters and returned as function results. The following program contains a function that adds two arrays, element by element, and returns a third array containing the sum.

```
with ada_io; use ada_io;
procedure array_param_demo is
   type v5 is array(1..5) of integer;

   a, b: v5;

   function add5(x,y: v5) return v5 is
      z: v5;
   begin
      for i in 1..5 loop
         z(i) := x(i) + y(i);
      end loop;
      return z;
   end add5;

begin
   a := (1,2,3,4,5);
   b := add5(a, (10,8,6,4,2));
   for i in 1..5 loop
      put(b(i));
      put(' ');
   end loop;
   new_line;
end array_param_demo;
```

This program prints the following:

```
11 10 9 8 7
```

10.5   MULTI-DIMENSIONAL ARRAYS

Ada's arrays can be *multi-dimensional*; that is, more than one index may be used to reference an array element. For example:

```
m:  array(1..10,1..10)  of integer;
```

This declaration defines an array object m with 100 elements that are logically organized into 10 groups, each with 10 integers. A multi-dimensional array is accessed by specifying multiple indexing expressions:

```
m(i,j)  := 0;
x := m(a+b, c);
```

A two-dimensional array like m is often referred to as a *matrix*.

Consider the following declarations:

```
type matrix is array(1..10,1..10) of integer;
p: matrix;

type vector is array(1..10) of integer;
q: array(1..10) of vector;
```

There is a subtle difference between the arrays p and q. Both contain 100 elements and are indexed quite similarly:

```
p(i,j)   -- two-dimensional array
q(i)(j)  -- array of one-dimensional arrays
```

The definition of q permits us to refer to individual rows of the matrix as a separate array:

```
q(6)  := (1..10 => 0);
```

The array p can only be indexed by a pair of values. The individual rows of p cannot be referenced as a unit.

Now consider a programming example using a two-dimensional array. The problem is to write a program that takes two primary colors as input, and determines what color results when you mix them. For example, mixing red and yellow results in orange. If we make the following declarations, the problem is easy to solve.

```
type color is
      (red, yellow, blue, green, purple, orange);

subtype primary is color range red..blue;

mix: array(primary, primary) of color :=
     -- red   --yellow  --blue
   ((red,     orange,   purple),   --red
    (orange,  yellow,   green),    --yellow
    (purple,  green,    blue))     --blue
```

The array mix is indexed by the two primary colors to be mixed and the value is the resulting color. For example, the value of mix (red,yellow) is orange.

Notice the structure of a multi-dimensional array aggregate. Since aggregates are one dimensional, a two (or more) dimensional array aggregate is an aggregate whose components are themselves aggregates.

Also, notice how comments are used to clarify the meaning of the array aggregate used to initialize mix. It is a matter of individual choice whether using positional notation improves the readability of this aggregate:

```
mix: array(primary, primary) of color :=
   (red    => (red=> red,    yellow=> orange, blue=> purple),
    yellow=> (red=> orange, yellow=> yellow, blue=> green ),
    blue   => (red=> purple, yellow=> green, blue=> blue ))
```

10.6   UNCONSTRAINED ARRAYS

The declaration of an *unconstrained array type* defines a class of possible array types; each member of the class has the same element type, the same number of indices, and the same index types. For example:

```
subtype positive is integer range 1..integer'last;

type matrix is
    array(positive range <>, positive range <>) of integer;
```

This declaration defines a class of two-dimensional array types whose elements are integers and whose index types are subranges of type positive. In order to declare an object of this type, the programmer must give an *index constraint* for the type

```
x: matrix(1..5, 1..5);
```

The discrete ranges are used to define a constrained instance of the type. All array objects must be constrained.

Two constrained array objects of the same unconstrained array type can be assigned if they are the same length. For example:

```
procedure array_assign is
   type vector is
      array(integer range <>) of integer;
   a:  vector(1..5);
   b:  vector(6..10);
begin
   b := a;
end array_assign;
```

The index constraints on the objects a and b are different, but since each defines the same number of elements the assignment is permitted.

A subtype declaration may be used to give a name to a constrained instance of an unconstrained array type:

```
subtype square10 is matrix(1..10,  1..10);
subtype skinny is matrix(3..5,  1..1000);
```

The simple array types described in section 10.1 are equivalent to constrained instances of unconstrained array types. For example, the following array type declaration:

```
type v1 is array(1..10) of integer;
```

is equivalent to the following sequence of declarations:

```
type vector is array(integer range <>) of integer;
subtype v1 is vector(1..10);
```

Both definitions of v1 create constrained array types. In the first case, the underlying constrained array type is said to be anonymous. In the second case, the unconstrained array type is declared explicitly and can be used to create other compatible constrained array subtypes:

```
subtype v2 is vector(11..20);
```

Array subtypes are not compatible when the underlying unconstrained array types are distinct. In particular, when an anonymous unconstrained type is involved, there can only be one subtype and that subtype is compatible only with itself. The subtype v2 is compatible with the second definition of v1, since the base type is the same and each has the same number of elements. However, v2 is not compatible with the first definition of v1 because, even though they have the same number of elements, they have different base types.

In the examples above, both index types were integer ranges, but in general, it is not necessary that all index types be of the same type. For example, the following unconstrained array declaration is perfectly legal:

```
type weird is
  array(character range <>, day_of_week range <>)
  of boolean;
```

Unconstrained array definitions must appear in type statements and all array object declarations must be constrained, either by using constrained array declarations as we saw earlier:

```
d: array(1..10, 1..10) of day_of_week;
```

or by supplying constraints to an unconstrained array type:

```
x: matrix(1..10, 1..10);
```

There is one exception to this rule. A constant array may be of an unconstrained type since its initialization provides the necessary constraint(s). For example:

```
x: constant matrix := (3..10 => (1..5 => 0));
```

is the same as

```
x: constant matrix(3..10, 1..5) := (3..10 => (1..5 => 0));
```

The following example gives no explicit range limits:

```
x: constant matrix := ((1,2,3), (4,5,6));
```

In this case, the aggregate's indices start at the minimum value for the index type given in the unconstrained array type declaration. For the type `matrix`, the index type for both dimensions is `positive`, whose minimum value is 1. Thus, the aggregate above is equivalent to this less readable declaration:

```
x: constant matrix := (1 => (1=>1, 2=>2, 3=>3),
                        (2 => (1=>4, 2=>5, 3=>6));
```

Note that if the index type is `integer`, the minimum value (integer'first) is a negative number of great magnitude.

10.7   ARRAY ATTRIBUTES

The following attributes may be applied to any constrained array type or object a:

```
a'first(n)    -- the lower bound of the nth index
a'last(n)     -- the upper bound of the nth index
a'length(n)   -- the number of values in the nth index
              --   (a'last(n) - a'first(n) + 1)
a'range(n)    -- the subtype defined by:
              --   a'first(n) .. a'last(n)
```

The index number n is optional. If it is present, n must be a static expression. If it is missing, the first index of the array type is used.

10.8   UNCONSTRAINED ARRAY PARAMETERS

Although all array objects must be constrained, the formal parameters to a subprogram may be of unconstrained array types, in which case the range of the array parameter is supplied by the actual array parameter when it is passed to the subprogram. Array attributes can be applied to unconstrained array parameters to determine the bounds of the actual parameters.

We now present an example of a procedure using unconstrained array parameters and array attributes. Recall the definition of matrix:

```
type matrix is
   array(integer range <>, integer range <>) of integer;
```

The following example includes a procedure to print any object of type matrix in a rectangular format.

```
procedure matprint_demo is
   type matrix is
     array(integer range <>, integer range <>) of integer;

   mat: matrix(1..2,1..3);

   procedure matprint(x: matrix) is -- print any "matrix"
   begin
     for i in x'range(1) loop      -- rows
       for j in x'range(2) loop    -- columns
         put(x(i, j), width => 4);
       end loop;
       new_line;
     end loop;
   end matprint;

begin
   mat := ((1 2 3) (4 5 6));
   matprint(mat);
end matprint_demo;
```

Execution of ''matprint_demo'' prints:

```
1    2    3
4    5    6
```

10.9   STRINGS

Character strings are a special case of arrays, selected by the positive numbers, whose components are members of the standard type character. The unconstrained array type string is predefined in Ada, using definitions of the following form:

```
subtype positive is integer range 1 .. integer'last;
type string is array(positive range <>) of character;
```

String literals are a special lexical form for character array aggregates; that is, the string literal

```
"abcd"
```

is equivalent to

```
(1=>'a',2=>'b', 3=>'c', 4=>'d')
```

Since string is declared as an unconstrained array type, a range constraint must be given in string object declarations:

```
name:  string(1..20);
```

However, the range constraint may be omitted from constant string declarations since it may be determined from the initial value:

```
x: constant string := "abcd";
```

As we have seen, the predefined procedure put works for character strings. The following procedure defines put for string objects:

```
procedure put(s: string) is
begin
  for i in s'range loop
    put(s(i));   -- uses "put" for characters
  end loop;
end put;
```

10.10   SLICES

A slice is a way of designating a section of an array. For example:

```
procedure slice_demo is
  type vector is array(integer range <>);
  a: vector(1..10);
begin
  a(3..7) := (5,4,3,2,1);
end slice_demo;
```

The expression a(3..7) has a type represented by vector(3..7). Its component values are those of the array a.

Slices appear most often in assignment statements, although they may appear anywhere that an array is permitted.

```
procedure slice_demo is
   type vector is array(integer range <>);
   a: vector(1..8);
   b: vector(1..5);

   procedure put(v: vector) is   -- "put" is overloaded
   begin
      for i in v'range loop
         put(v(i), 3);     -- uses "put" for integers
      end loop;
      new_line;
   end put;

begin
   a := (1,4,9,16,25,36,49,64);
   b := a(3..7);
   put(a);               -- prints:  1   4   9 16 25 36 49 64
   put(b);               -- prints:  9 16 25 36 49
   a(1..2) := b(4..5);
   put(a);               -- prints: 36 49   9 16 25 36 49 64
   a(3..7) := a(4..8);   -- overlapping slices
   put(a);               -- prints: 36 49   9 25 36 49 64 64
   put(b(2..4));         -- prints: 16 25 36
end slice_demo;
```

Slices follow the same rules for assignment as entire arrays. They must belong to the same array type, and must be the same length. In the last assignment above, notice that overlapping slices are assigned. There is no problem copying overlapping slices because the expression on the right hand side is evaluated before the assignment is performed.

Slices may only be used to select one-dimensional arrays. The following example is illegal:

```
procedure bad_slice is -- illegal
   p: matrix(1..10, 1..10);
begin
   matprint(p(1..5, 1..5));       -- Incorrect expression!!
end bad_slice;
```

This illegal slice expression hopes to select the upper left hand corner of the matrix p. This is not permitted by Ada.

Finally, the following example illustrates the distinction between an array component and a one-element slice.

```
procedure slice_type_demo is
   a: vector(1..10);
   n: integer;
begin
   n := a(2);              -- this is ok
   n := a(2..2);           -- this is illegal
end slice_type_demo;
```

The type of a(2..2) is vector(2..2) and the type of a(2) is integer.

10.11   DYNAMIC ARRAYS

Ada's arrays may be *dynamic*. That is, the range limits in an array declaration need not be constant:

```
procedure p(n: integer) is
   a: array(1..n) of integer;      -- size of a varies for
begin                              -- different calls to p
   for i in 1..n loop
      . . .
   end loop;
end p;
```

Each time procedure p is called, an array object a is created. The upper bound of a corresponds to the value of the parameter n, so the size of a is different for different values of n. For example, if p is called with an actual parameter value 5, the range of a is 1..5. If p is called again, but with n equal to 1000, the bounds on a are 1..1000. In general, the bounds of an index type may be expressions. Of course, the types of the bounds must be compatible.

The following function is equivalent to the standard string concatenation operator &.

```
function concat(x, y: string) return string is
   z: string(1 .. x'length + y'length);
begin
   z(1 .. x'length) := x;
   z(x'length+1 .. z'length) := y;
   return z;
end;
```

The declaration of the local dynamic array object z defines the array bounds in terms of the lengths of the parameters x and y, creating an array object whose size is appropriate for the function result.

10.12   OPERATIONS ON ARRAYS

The concatenation operator & has already been discussed in relation to the predefined type string which is an unconstrained array type. While concatenation is most useful for string values, the concatenation operation is defined for all array types. For example:

```
procedure concat_demo is
   a: vector(1..10);
   b: vector(1..5);
begin
   b := (1,2,3,4,5);
   a := b & b;              -- a is (1,2,3,4,5,1,2,3,4,5)
end concat_demo;
```

The operands to & must be compatible (that is, the types of the operands must be subtypes of the same unconstrained array type).

The operators = and /= are available for every type in Ada. Equality of two arrays corresponds to equality of the elements of the arrays. Equality is defined for two different instances of an unconstrained array type even if the arrays are of different lengths. Two array objects of different lengths are never equal.

The ordering operators (<, <=, > and >=) may be applied to one dimensional arrays. These operations are most useful for arrays of characters, where they correspond to alphabetical ordering.

```
"abc" < "ada"    -- true
"123" < "abcd"   -- true (uses underlying ASCII values)
"Zap" < "ab"     -- true ('Z' < 'a' in ASCII)
""  < "abc"      -- true (empty string less than anything)
```

These operations can also be used with any one-dimensional array whose component type is discrete. For such arrays, the ordering is defined in a manner analogous to the alphabetic ordering used for character arrays.

The logical operators and, or, and xor may each be applied to compatible one-dimensional arrays whose component type is boolean. The appropriate operation is performed on a component-by-component basis and the result is an array value of the same array type. Consider this example:

```
procedure logical_array_op_demo is
   type b5 is array(1..5) of boolean;
   a, b, c: b5;
begin
   a := (1 | 3 | 5 => true, others => false);
   b := (3 | 4 | 5 => true, others => false);
   c := a or b;  -- (1 | 3 | 4 | 5 => true, other => false)
   c := a and b; -- (3 | 5 => true, others => false)
   c := a xor b; -- (1 | 4 => true, others => false)
end logical_array_op_demo;
```

10.13   FORMAL SYNTAX

Notice that the productions object-declaration, type-definition, and type-indication are updated below.

object-declaration =
    identifier-list: -- Chapter 5
       [**constant**] type-indication
             [:= expression] ;
    | identifier-list:
       [**constant**] constrained-array-definition
             [:= expression] ;

type-definition =
    enumeration-type-definition   -- Chapter 9
    | array-type-definition
    | ...

array-type-definition=
    constrained-array-definition
    | unconstrained-array-definition

constrained-array-definition =
    array index-constraint **of** type-indication

index-constraint =
    (discrete-range {, discrete-range})

unconstrained-array-definition =
    array unconstrained-indices **of** type-indication

unconstrained-indices =
    (unconstrained-index {, unconstrained-index})

unconstrained-index =
    type-name **range** <>

type-indication =
    type-name   -- Chapter 4
    | type-name range-constraint   -- Chapter 9
    | type-name index-constraint
    | ...

The syntax for array-valued expressions (slices and aggregates) and array indexing is defined here. The production name is updated to include these definitions.

```
name =
      simple-name                              -- Chapter 4
    | attribute                                -- Chapter 9
    | indexed-component
    | slice
    | ...

range =
      simple-expression .. simple-expression   -- Chapter 4
    | range-attribute

indexed-component =
    prefix ( expression {, expression} )

slice = prefix ( discrete-range )

primary =
      name                                     -- Chapter 4
    | numeric-literal                          -- Chapter 4
    | string-literal                           -- Chapter 4
    | ( expression )                           -- Chapter 4
    | type-conversion                          -- Chapter 4
    | function-call                            -- Chapter 7
    | aggregate
    | ...

aggregate =
    ( component-association {, component-association} )

component-association =
    [choice {| choice} =>] expression
```

chapter 11

Record types

A *record* is used to group logically related data objects into a single data structure and, like an array, forms a composite type. Unlike the array, a record may group objects of different types. The components of a record are selected by specifying a *field* name. Record types may be defined in Ada, and objects of these types may be declared. For example:

```
type months is
   (jan, feb, mar, apr, may, jun, jul, aug, sep, oct, nov, dec);

type date is
  record
    month: months;
    day: integer range 1..31;
    year: integer range 1900..2100;
  end record;
```

This declaration creates a new data type date which may be used to declare record objects representing dates:

```
today: date;
holidays: array(1..10) of date;
```

Individual components of a record object may be selected by following the record variable with a dot . and a record field identifier. For example:

```
today.month := dec;
holidays(i).day := 25;
put(today.year);
```

11.1   RECORD AGGREGATES

A record value may be specified by a *record aggregate*. For example:

```
today := (jul, 4, 1776);
```

Field values may be specified positionally (that is, in the order in which the fields appear in the record type declaration) as shown above, or by specifying field names, as in this aggregate:

```
today := (month => jul, day => 4, year => 1776);
```

Note that record aggregates have the same appearance as subprogram arguments. As with parameter names in subprogram arguments, named record aggregate fields may appear in any order:

```
today := (day => 4, month => jul, year => 1776);
```

The two modes may be mixed provided the positional aggregate components precede the named components:

```
today := (jul, 4, year => 1776);
today := (month => jul, day => 4, 1776); -- illegal
```

The second example is illegal because a positional parameter (the year) is written following the named parameters. In general, we find "mixed" mode to be less clear than either all positional or all named record aggregate components.

Record types may be fields in larger records. For example:

```
type soc_sec_num is
  record
    f1: integer range 0..999;
    f2: integer range 0..99;
    f3: integer range 0..9999;
  end record;

type person is
  record
    last_name: string(1..10);
    ssn: soc_sec_num;
    birthday: date;
  end record;
me, you: person;
```

In this record type, two of the fields (`birthday` and `ssn`) are themselves records. With the objects declared above, all of the following are plausible constructions:

```
me. ssn  : = (123, 45, 6789) ;
me. birthday. month  : = nov;
you  : = ("yourname   ",  (987, 65, 4321) ,  (mar,  1,  1960) ) ;
```

11.2   DEFAULT FIELD VALUES

A record declaration may include a default initial value for any of its
fields. This expression is evaluated each time an object of the record type is
created. The following example illustrates the consequences of this rule.
The default value for the record field is the value of n, which may change
during program execution.

```
procedure init_demo is
  n:  integer  : = 4;

  type rec is
    record
      val:  integer  : = n;
    end record;

  x:  rec;       -- default value is 4

  procedure proc is
    y:  rec;       -- default value is 6 (see init_demo below)
  begin
    put (y. val) ; -- prints 6
  end;

begin
  put (x. val) ;    -- prints 4
  n  : = 6;         -- change value of n
  proc;
  put (x. val)      -- still 4
end init_demo;
```

If no initial value is specified for a field, the initial value of the field is
undefined, and must be set by the programmer before it is used. An aggregate for a record with field initializations must specify all fields, even those
with default initial values.

11.3   DISCRIMINANTS

Often, it is desirable to declare an array whose length can vary during
program execution. Unconstrained array types provide a mechanism for
allowing arrays of different lengths to belong to the same array type, but

each object of the unconstrained array type must be constrained to a fixed size when it is declared. Once we declare the following object:

```
name: string(1..10);
```

the object name must contain exactly 10 characters. The assignment below is illegal:

```
name := "abc";    -- illegal
```

We must instead write the following:

```
name := "abc      ";
```

In a string processing application, padding string literals with blanks could become quite tedious. Fortunately, Ada provides a mechanism for overcoming this difficulty. A record type may contain *discriminants*. A discriminant can be thought of as a parameter for the record type. The types of fields within the record may depend upon a discriminant value. For example, consider the following definition:

```
type text(len: integer range 0..256 := 0) is
   record
      value: string(1..len);
   end record;
```

We may now declare objects of type text. If an object declaration for a discriminant record specifies values for the discriminants in the record (called a *discriminant constraint*) then the record is said to be constrained.

The value of a discriminant of a constrained record object may not be changed:

```
procedure constrained_rec_demo is
   x: text(len => 7);
   y, z: text(len => 5);
begin
   x.value := "abcdefg";
   y := (5, "abcde")
   z := x;          -- illegal
end constrained_rec_demo;
```

If a discriminant record object declaration does not contain a discriminant constraint, it is said to be unconstrained. In this case, the default initial value specified in the type declaration is used as the initial value of the discriminant. If there is no default initial value, there can be no unconstrained objects for the type. The discriminants of an unconstrained object may be changed during the life of the object.

In the case of type text, the following object declaration:

```
a: text;
```

creates an object a whose initial length is 0, but whose length may vary during the life of the object. This value is given in the type declaration (0 for text). A discriminant can be thought of as a field of the record, but it cannot be assigned a value directly. The only way a discriminant can be changed is by assigning an entire record value. The following example illustrates the use of unconstrained objects:

```
procedure unconstrained_demo is
   x,y: text; -- initial length is 0
begin
   x := (4, "abcd");
   y := (10, "1234567890");
   y := x;  -- size of y changes
end;
```

An unconstrained object of type text may contain an array object whose length may range from 0 to 256. If the length is not in this range a constraint error occurs because the compiler ensures that discriminant constraints are not violated.

The presence or absence of a discriminant constraint appears analogous to default parameters in subprograms. There is an important difference however. A missing discriminant constraint not only causes the default value to be used, it also causes the object to be unconstrained. If a discriminant record type has more than one discriminant constraint, either all or none of the discriminant parameters must be given in a discriminant constraint.

The boolean attribute constrained can be applied to discriminant record objects. It returns true if the object was declared with a discriminant. If a subprogram parameter is declared to be an unconstrained record object, then the attribute applies to the actual argument to the subprogram.

```
with ada_io; use ada_io;
procedure constrained_demo is
   x: text;
   y: text(7);

   procedure put(b: boolean) is   -- overloading put
   begin
      put(boolean'image (b));   -- uses put for string
   end;

   procedure p(z: text) is
   begin
      put(z'constrained); -- output varies
   end;
```

```
begin
   put (x'constrained) ;      -- prints FALSE
   put (y'constrained) ;      -- prints TRUE
   p (x) ;                    -- prints FALSE
   p (y) ;                    -- prints TRUE
end constrained_demo;
```

The constrained attribute of a discriminant record object is the same throughout the lifetime of the object.

Most programs that require any string processing will probably use a type like text. The following example is a simple text package that defines the type text and several operations on text and string objects. It is used in subsequent examples. Notice that the declaration of the type text appears in the interface of the package. This allows users of the package to declare objects of type text.

```ada
with ada_io;
package text_handler is
  type text(len: integer range 0..256 := 0) is
    record
      value: string(1..len);
    end record;

  procedure set(x: out text; y: string);
  procedure get(x: out text);     -- is overloaded
  procedure put(x: in text);      -- is overloaded
end text_handler;

package body text_handler is
  use ada_io;

  procedure set(x: out text; y: string) is
  begin
    x := (y'length, y);
  end set;

  procedure get(x: out text) is -- overloaded
    t: string(1..256);
    i: integer := 0;
  begin
    while not end_of_line loop
      i := i + 1;
      get(t(i));   -- uses get for characters
    end loop;
    skip_line;
    x :=(i, t(1..i)); -- constraint error possible if x'
                      -- constrained and i not right for x
  end get;

  procedure put(x: in text) is  -- overloaded
  begin
    put(x.value);  -- uses put for string
  end put;
end text_handler;
```

The procedures get and put overload the declarations in the package ada_io. (There are several get and put procedures in ada_io.) A call to get using a text object as an argument will invoke the procedure defined above. The function end_of_line (from ada_io) returns a boolean value which is true if the end of the input line has been reached.

The following program illustrates a simple use of the package text_handler:

```
with text_handler;
procedure text_use_demo is
   x: text_handler.text;   -- dot notation for types
   use text_handler;
begin
   get(x);                 -- x is unconstrained
   put(x);
   set(x, "abcd");
   put(x);
end text_use_demo;
```

11.4   VARIANTS

Often, the contents of a record may vary depending upon the value of other fields in the record. In Ada, the *variant record* is used for this purpose. The person description record type given below has a variant part that depends upon the marital status of the person.

```
type marital_status is
   (single, married, divorced, widowed);

type person(m_stat: marital_status := single) is
 record
   name: string(1..10);
   ident: soc_sec_num;
   birthdate: date;
   case m_stat is
     when single =>
       null;
     when married =>
       spouse: soc_sec_num;
       marriage_date: date;
     when divorced | widowed =>
       end_date; date;
   end case;
 end record;
```

The variant record type person has a discriminant of type marital_status. The value of this discriminant determines which of the record fields may be accessed at runtime. Only those fields corresponding to a particular discriminant constraint value are accessible at runtime. If a constraint is given in the declaration of a variant record object, then the record object is said to be constrained and the constraint is constant throughout the lifetime of the object. If a constraint is not given, then the object is said to be unconstrained and the discriminant value may be changed by a record assignment at runtime.

```
procedure variant_demo is
  x: person(single);          -- constrained, single
  y: person;                  -- unconstrained, initially single
begin
  x.name   := "Smith    ";
  x.ident  := (123,45,6789);
  x.birthday := (Jul,4,1950);
  y := x;                     -- y is single
  y := (mstat => divorced,    -- discriminant given in aggregate
       name => "Jones    ",
       ident => (987,6543,21),
       end_date => (Dec, 25, 1976)); -- y is divorced now
  y.spouse := x.ident;        -- constraint error
                              -- no spouse field for divorced
end variant_demo;
```

The final assignment in this example is illegal because the field spouse is not accessible when the discriminant value is divorced. A constraint error is generated if this assignment is attempted at runtime.

The field names must be distinct, even between different variants. For example, the names of the fields marriage_date and end_date must be distinct, even though the two fields may never exist simultaneously in a record object.

As with case statements, the values specified in the when clauses must be distinct, and must include all values of the type of the case selector (the discriminant). For this reason, an others clause may be used. The when clauses may be simple values, discrete ranges or alternatives separated by a vertical bar | .

11.5   FORMAL SYNTAX

The productions type-declaration and type-definition are updated to incorporate record types. The type-indication production is changed to include discriminants.

```
type-declaration =
    type identifier is type-definition ;
  | type identifier discriminant-part is type-definition ;
  | ...

type-definition =
    enumeration-type-definition   -- Chapter 9
  | array-type-definition         -- Chapter 10
  | record-type-definition
  | ...
```

discriminant-part =
   (discriminant-decl {; discriminant-decl})

discriminant-decl =
   identifier-list : type-name [:= expression]

record-type-definition =
   record
     component-list
   end record

component-list =
   component-declaration {component-declaration}
  | {component-declaration} variant-part
  | **null** ;

component-declaration =
   identifier-list : type-indication [:= expression] ;

variant-part =
   case simple-name **is**
     variant
    { variant}
   end case

variant =
   when choice {| choice-list} =>
     component-list

choice =   -- Chapter 6
   simple-expression
  | discrete-range
  | **others**

type-indication =
   type-name   -- Chapter 4
  | type-name range-constraint   -- Chapter 9
  | type-name index-constraint   -- Chapter 10
  | type-name discriminant constraint
  | ...

discriminant-constraint =
   (discriminant-spec {, discriminant-spec})

discriminant-spec =
   [simple-name {| simple-name} =>] expression

chapter 12

Access types

Until now, all the objects we have seen have been explicitly declared. Such objects are created when the scope in which they are declared is entered, and destroyed when it is exited. *Access types* provide a mechanism for creating objects dynamically during the execution of a program. These objects have arbitrary lifetimes, independent of the point at which they are created and can be dynamically connected with other objects to form larger structures such as lists and trees. The values of an access type are often called pointers. Consider the following declarations:

```
procedure access_demo is
  type pair is
    record
      a, b: integer;
    end record;

  x: pair;

  type pair_ptr is
    access pair;

  p: pair_ptr;
begin
  ...
end access_demo;
```

The object x is created when access_demo is called. Its size is sufficient to hold the two integer values specified in the record type pair. The object p is not of type pair. No object of type pair is created when the declaration is seen. The object p is an access object: it is used to provide *access* to an object of type pair. Such an object must be explicitly created by an allocator and assigned to the access object:

```
p := new pair;
```

An allocator consists of the keyword **new** followed by the name of a type, called the *base type*. Once this allocation is done, the record object referred to by p may be referenced in the same way as an explicitly declared object:

```
x.a := 37;
p.b := 73;
```

An access object is always initialized to the value null (except when an explicit initialization is given in the declaration of the object). The value null indicates that an access object provides access to no object at all. Any access object may be compared with or assigned the value null. Any reference through an access object whose value is null is erroneous. For example, if p had not been given a value above, the reference p.b would be erroneous because there would be no object of type pair from which to select field b. Access checks are done to insure that attempts to reference through null access objects cause constraint errors.

The only operations available for access objects are assignment, comparison for equality, and selection. Arithmetic operations, for example, are not permitted for access objects.

More than one access object may refer to the same allocated object. The following example illustrates this important distinction:

```
procedure access_demo is
   x,y: pair;
   p,q: pair_ptr;
begin
   x.a := 1;
   x.b := 2;
   y := x;
   x.a := 3;      -- now x /= y

   p := new pair;
   p.a := 1;
   p.b := 2;
   q := p;
   p.a := 3;      -- p = q still true
end access_demo;
```

The first set of assignment statements initializes the record object x and then assigns its value to the record object y. In the second set of assignments, the access object p is given access to a new record object, which is then initialized. Then, the access object q is assigned the value of the access object p. Figure 12-1 illustrates this state of affairs.

Note the distinction between the relations x=y and p=q. The value of x is equal to the value of y, but they are distinct objects. For example, if the value of x.a is changed, x and y will no longer be equal. The access objects p and q are equal because they refer to the same record object. If the value p.a is changed, p and q are still equal because they refer to the same object. Such a change would change the value q.a as well.

12.1   LIST STRUCTURES

One common usage for access types is for building *list structures*. A list can be represented as a collection of records. An access object commonly called the *head* of the list refers to the first record in a list. Each record.has a *link* field that provides access to the next record. The final record in a list has a null link field. When the value of the head is null, a list is said to be *empty*.

The following declarations define types that are used to build lists of integers:

```
type element;    -- an incomplete type definition

type list is access element;

type element is
  record
    value: integer;
    link: list;
  end record;

head: list;
```

The record type element defines a single element of a list, and the access type list defines a mechanism for linking list elements together.

Notice that the types list and element are mutually dependent; type element contains a field of type list, and type list provides access to type element. Since all types in Ada must be defined before they are used, an *incomplete type declaration* must be provided for use as the base type of list. The declaration

```
type element;
```

says that element is a type that will be defined later. An incomplete type may only be used as the base type of an access type until the type is made complete by a subsequent declaration.

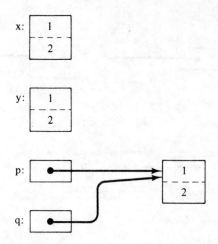

Figure 12-1. Equality of access objects.

The following procedure attaches a given integer to the front of a given‣ list:

```
procedure put_on_front (head:  in out list;  n:  integer)  is
   p:  list;
begin
   p : = new element;        -- make new list element
   p.value  : = n;           -- set its value
   p.link  : = head;         -- point it at current head
   head  : = p;              -- fix up list head
end put_on_front;
```

The procedure put_on_front contains a local access object p which is given access to a newly created record object of type element. The field value of the record is set to the integer parameter n and the field link is set to the value of the access object head. Finally, the object p is made the new head of the list. Figure 12-2 illustrates this operation. The procedure take_off_front is even simpler. It simply sets the head of the list to the link field of the first element of the list:

```
procedure take_off_front (head:  in out list)  is
begin
   if head /= null then
      head  : = head.link;
   end if;
end take_off_front;
```

Initial value of "head"

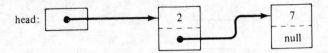

p := new element;
p. value := N:

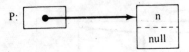

p. link := head

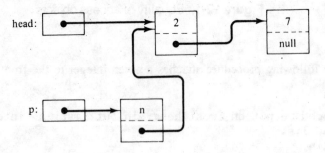

head := p;

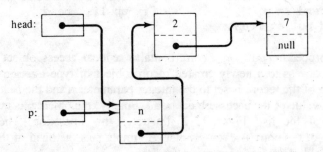

Figure 12-2. Execution of put_on_front.

Figure 12-3 illustrates the changes in the list structure caused by execution of `take_off_front`. If the element removed from the front of the list was not referred to by any other access object, the space for the object becomes inaccessible and is available for *garbage collection*. Some Ada implementations may reclaim this space and use it in subsequent allocations, but the language does not require that space be reclaimed. Programmers should consult the reference manual for the local implementation of Ada to determine the disposition of inaccessible storage.

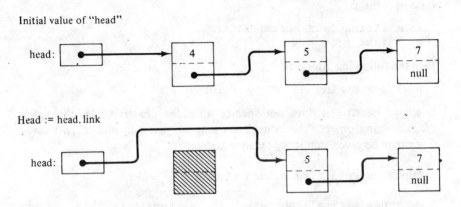

Figure 12-3. Execution of take_off_front.

12.2   ALLOCATORS

In the simplest case, an allocator consists of the reserved word **new** and a type name for the base type of an access type:

```
p := new element;
```

The type of the allocator is access element, which is the same as list; thus, the allocator is compatible with the object p and the assignment is allowed.

An allocator may optionally specify initialization for the allocated object, in which case the reserved word **new** is followed by an allocator initialization clause. Using this sort of allocator, the body of the procedure put_on_front can be reduced to a single statement:

```
head := new element'(n, head);
```

or using named aggregate notation:

```
head := new element'(value => n, link => head);
```

Recall that the expression on the right hand side of an assignment statement is evaluated before the left hand side. Therefore, the value of head used in the new element object is the value before the assignment operation is executed.

If the base type for an allocator has default initial values, these implicit initializations are done automatically. This applies to record types with field initializations or to any composite type with access components (whose default value is always null).

If the base type for an access type is an unconstrained type, the allocator must specify constraints for the base type. For example, if we define a new type string_p:

```
type string_p is access string;
p: string_p;
```

then the following allocator

```
p : = new string;        -- illegal
```

is illegal because it does not specify an index constraint for the newly created string object. The constraints may be given in one of two ways. They may be given implicitly by an initializer:

```
function getstring return string;
...
p : = new string' ("abcde");      -- length is 5
p : = new string' (getstring);    -- length of result string
```

or the allocator may contain an index constraint:

```
p : = new string (1..5);
```

Note that the type name in an allocator is the type of the object being allocated (in this case, string) not the type of the access object (in this case, string_p).

If an allocator for a record type with discriminants specifies a discriminant constraint, the created object is constrained. If not, the newly created record object is unconstrained and the default discriminant value is used. The following program fragment illustrates the use of allocators for the discriminant record type person.

```
type marital_status is
   (single, married, divorced, widowed);

type person (m_stat marital_status := single) is
   record
      name: string (1..10);
      ident: soc_sec_num;
      birthdate: date;
      case m_stat is
```

```
    when single =>
      null;
    when married =>
      spouse: soc_sec_num;
      marriage_date: date;
    when divorced | widowed =>
      end_date: date;
    end case;
  end record;

ype person_ref is access person;
                                -- can refer to any person
ype married_person_ref is access person(married);
                                -- can only refer to married
: person_ref;                   -- persons
np: married_person_ref;

) := new person(divorced);      -- constrained, always divorced
) := new person;                -- unconstrained, initially singl
np := new person;               -- constrained, always married
```

In the third statement, the type of the allocator is married_person_ref
(the same type as mp) so the allocated object person is constrained to always
be married.

12.3   REFERENCING ACCESS OBJECTS

As we have seen, when an access object refers to a record object, the
fields of that record can be selected directly. If we want to refer to the entire
record object, the reserved word **all** is used as if it were a selector:

```
procedure all_demo is
  n: integer;
  x: pair := (3, 7);
  p: pair_ptr;
begin
  p := new pair;
  p := x;               -- this is illegal
  p.all := x;           -- this is ok (copies both fields)
  n := p.b;
  n := p.all.b;         -- correct but strange
end all_demo;
```

When an access object referring to a record is selected, the effect is as
though there is one implicit .all. The type of the expression p.all is

pair (not pair_ptr) which means that the two selections of field b are equivalent.

If an access object refers to an array object, the array object can be indexed directly (there is an implicit .all).

```
procedure array_access_demo is
   type string_p is access string;
   sp:  string_p := new string'("Hello...");
   ch:  character;
begin
   ch := sp(3);            -- implicit ".all"
   ch := sp.all(3);        -- correct but unnecessary
   put(sp.all);            -- uses "put" for string
   put(sp);                -- illegal, no implicit ".all"
end array_access_demo;     --   and no put defined for string_p
```

In a fashion analogous to the record example given above, the two array references given here are equivalent. The two calls to put illustrate that the implicit all is only done in an array index or record field selection.

12.4   TREES

One of the more common data structures used for computer problem solving is the *tree*. A tree consists of a collection of *nodes*, one of which is designated the *root*. Figure 12-4 illustrates the simplest of trees: a tree with a single node.

With the exception of the root, each node in a tree has a *parent*. Figure 12-5 depicts another simple tree. Arrows are drawn from a parent to immediate descendants. The arrows define the relationship between the nodes of a tree. A node may have more than one immediate descendant, as shown in Figure 12-6. A more complex tree may be organized into many levels. Figure 12-7 illustrates a tree with multiple levels.

In addition, placing restrictions on the maximum number of immediate descendants a node may have allows us to define classes of trees. For example, a tree with at most two descendants from each node is called a binary tree; at most three descendants, a trinary tree; at most *n* descendants, an n-ary tree. The nodes of a tree that have no descendants are called *leaves* of the tree. A *subtree* of a tree is the tree that results from choosing any node and designating it a new root node.

The relationship between the nodes of a tree, depicted as arrows in the figures below, is one of the most important pieces of information required to define or use a tree data structure. In the example on page 112, package tree_handler, this relationship is the alphabetical ordering defined between strings of characters. For example, the string Ada is alphabetically

Figure 12-4. A single-node tree.

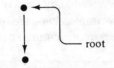

Figure 12-5. A dual node tree.

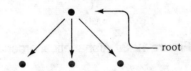

Figure 12-6. Multiple descendants.

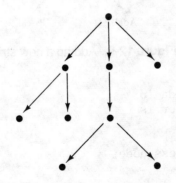

Figure 12-7. A multi-level tree.

less than Lisp, so we can construct a tree using this ordering (see Figure 12-8).

The node Lisp is the root of this tree. If we want to add something to the tree thus created, we use the same ordering relationship—start at the root of the tree and apply the comparison "less than" to the string to be added and the current node. Adding the string Pascal to the tree of Figure 12-8 results in the tree given in Figure 12-9.

The string Pascal is not less than Lisp, so we add it to the tree in a different way from Ada. Using a binary tree, descendants to the left of a node are alphabetically less than the node itself. Descendants to the right are alphabetically greater than the node. Since "less than" is inherently a binary operation, it is represented quite naturally by a binary tree. Other operations might be better represented by trees of greater magnitude.

The example given below implements the problem just discussed. A binary tree consisting of nodes representing strings is manipulated in various ways.

Figure 12-8. Alphabetical ordering.

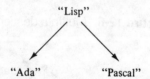

Figure 12-9. Adding a new string.

```
with ada_io; use ada_io;
package tree_handler is
  type node;

  type tree is access node;

  type node is
    record
      value: string_p;
      left: tree;
      right: tree;
    end;

  procedure insert(p: in out tree; s: string);
  function is_in_tree(p: tree; s: string) return boolean;
  procedure put(p: tree);   -- overloaded
end tree;
```

```
package body tree_handler is
   procedure insert(p: in out tree; s: string) is
   begin
      if p = null then            -- insert node here
         p := new node'(new string'(s), null, null);
      elsif s < p.value.all then
         insert(p.left, s);       -- search left subtree
      elsif s > p.value.all then
         insert(p.right. s);      -- search right subtree
      -- else string already in tree
      end if;
   end insert;

   function is_in_tree(p: tree; s: string) return boolean is
   begin
      if p = null then
         return false;                    --isn't in tree
      elsif s < p.value.all then
         return is_in_tree(p.left, s);  -- search left subtree
      elsif s > p.value.all then
         return is_in_tree(p.right, s); -- search right subtree
      else
         return true;                     -- found it
      end if;
   end is_in_tree;

   procedure put(p: tree) is  -- overloaded
   begin
      if p /= null then        -- if there's something to do
         put(p.left);          -- print left subtree
         put(p.value.all);     -- uses put for strings
         new_line;
         put(p.right);         -- print right subtree
      end if;
   end put;
end tree_handler;

with ada_io; use ada_io;
with tree_handler; use tree_handler;
procedure tree_demo is
   t: tree;         -- automatically initialized to null
begin
   insert(t, "Jefferson");
   insert(t, "Washington");
   insert(t, "Franklin");
   insert(t, "Madison");
   put(t);
end tree_demo;
```

Nodes in the trees manipulated by tree_handler contain two access objects used to designate immediate descendants and other object to access the string value of a node. Notice that the subprograms insert, is_in_tree, and put are recursive. The regular structure of trees with well-defined terminating conditions (that is, null indicates no descendant) makes recursion the most natural solution to problems involving trees.

Figure 12-10 illustrates the tree built by tree_demo.

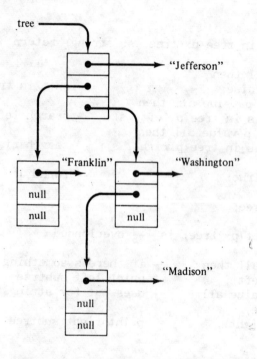

Figure 12-10. Tree from tree_demo.

12.5   FORMAL SYNTAX

Type-declaration is updated to include incomplete type declarations. The selector, type-definition, and primary productions are updated.

```
type-declaration =
     type identifier is type-definition ;    -- Chapter 9
   | incomplete-type-declaration
   | ...
incomplete-type-declaration =
     type identifier [discriminant-part] ;

selector =
     simple-name                 -- Chapter 11
   | all
   | ...

type-definition =
     enumeration-type-definition     -- Chapter 9
   | array-type-definition          -- Chapter 10
   | record-type-definition         -- Chapter 11
   | access-type-definition
   | ...

access-type-definition =
     access type-indication

primary =
     name                    -- Chapter 4
   | numeric-literal         -- Chapter 4
   | string-literal          -- Chapter 4
   | ( expression )          -- Chapter 4
   | type-conversion         -- Chapter 4
   | function-call           -- Chapter 7
   | aggregate               -- Chapter 10
   | null
   | allocator
   | ...

allocator =
     new type-name
   | new type-name index_constraint
   | new type-name discriminant-constraint
   | new allocator-initialization

allocator-initialization
     type-name ' ( expression )
   | type-name ' aggregate
```

chapter 13
Operator overloading

It is often clearer to express a function call in terms of an operator, such as +, rather than using conventional functon call notation. Ada provides a facility for declaring operators as functions. Since all operators already have at least one standard meaning, this facility is called *operator overloading*.

13.1   EXAMPLES OF OPERATOR OVERLOADING

The operator + has several predefined meanings. The following function specifications give two of these meanings:

```
function "+"(x,y: integer) return integer;
function "+"(x,y: float) return float;
```

As we said earlier, Ada does not normally permit mixing types integer and float in arithmetic expressions without explicit type conversions. If we desire such a facility, we can overload the operators to allow it. For +, the following two functions allow mixing of integer and float expressions:

```
function "+"(x: integer; y: float) return float is
begin
   return float(x) + y;
end "+";

function "+"(x: float; y: integer) return float is
begin
   return x + float(y);
end "+";
```

These functions can be called by simply writing + with arguments of the appropriate types.

```
procedure op_ovl_demo is
  i: integer := 5;
  f: float := 3.7;
begin
  put(i + f);          -- 8.7, call to first function
  put(f + i);          -- 8.7, call to second function
  put(f + i + i);      -- 13.7, two calls to second function
                       -- ("+" groups left-to-right)
  put(f + (i + i));    -- 13.7, one call to second function
end op_ovl_demo;       -- and one call to predefined "+"
```

It often makes sense to define functions of user-defined types as operators. For example, consider the following program fragment:

```
type vector is array(integer range<>) of integer;
...
function vector_add(x, y: vector) return vector is
  z: vector(x'range);
begin
  -- assumes x'range same as y'range
  for i in z'range loop
    z(i) := x(i) + y(i);
  end loop;
  return z;
end vector_add;
```

The type vector is an unconstrained array type whose component type is integer. If we wish to add two vectors, element by element, we can call the function vector_add. The function vector_add can be called as shown below:

```
procedure vector_add_demo is
  a, b: vector(1..5);
begin
  a := (1, 2, 3, 4, 5);
  b := vector_add(b, (1, 3, 5, 7, 9)):
end vector_add_demo;
```

The usage above is somewhat awkward. It is much clearer to express the statement above as:

```
b := b + (1, 3, 5, 7, 9);
```

This can be achieved by giving the function named vector_add the operator name +:

```
function "+"(x,y: vector) return vector is
  z: vector(x'range);
begin
  -- assumes x'range same as y'range
  for i in z'range loop
    z(i) := x(i) + y(i);
  end loop;
  return z;
end "+";
```

The use of operator overloading can improve readability greatly in complicated expressions. For example, the expression

```
vector_add(vector_add(a, b), c)
```

can be simplified by using the + function defined for vectors:

```
a + b + c
```

The left-to-right grouping, which has to be stated explicitly in function call notation, is implicit when using overloaded operators.

The concatenation operator & is defined for one dimensional arrays. It might also be convenient to overload & for lists. Recall the definition list for lists of integers:

```
type element;    -- an incomplete type definition

type list is access element;

type element is
  record
    value: integer;
    link: list;
  end record;
```

Here is the definition of & for two lists.

```
function last(ls: list) return list is
  p: list := ls;
begin
  while p.link /= null loop  -- search for end of list
    p := p.link;
  end loop;
  return p;
end last;
```

```
function "&"(l1, l2: list) return list is
   p: list;
begin
   if l1 = null then
     return l2;
   else
     last(l1).link := l2;
     return l1;
   end if;
end "&";
```

As is the case with the predefined concatenation operator, we would like to allow either of the operands to be of the component type. Here are functions to concatenate two integers, an integer and a list, and a list and an integer:

```
function "&"(i1, i2: integer) return list is
begin
   return new element'(i1, new element'(i2, null));
end "&";

funtion "&"(i: integer; ls: list) return list is
begin
   return new element'(i, ls);   -- put i on front of list
end "&";

function "&"(ls: list; i: integer) return list is
   p: list;
begin
   if ls = null then
     return new element'(i, null);   -- one-element list
   else
   ￪ last(ls).link := new element'(i,null);
     return ls;                       -- put i on end of list
   end if;
end "&";
```

The following example demonstrates the use of the functions defined above. In an actual application, we would probably want to build lists of more complicated element types.

```
with ada_io; use ada_io;
procedure list_concat_demo is
  p,q: list;
begin
  put("concat for strings" & " still works");
  p := 1 & 2 & 3;    -- p is <1,2,3>
  q := 4 & p & 5;    -- q is <4,1,2,3,5>
  p := p & q;        -- p is <1,2,3,4,1,2,3,5>
end list_concat_demo;
```

The operator overloading facility does not provide the programmer with any new programming capability, but it does provide new expressive power. If used wisely, operator overloading can greatly improve the readability of a program.

13.2   RULES FOR OPERATOR OVERLOADING

All of the predefined operators may be overloaded, except for the short-circuit operators (and then and or else) and the membership operators (in and not in). Operators may only be defined as functions, and must have the same number of parameters as in their predefined versions (+ and − may have one or two parameters). Default parameter values are not allowed. There are no restrictions on the parameter or result types of an overloaded operator function.

The relational operators <, <=, >, >= may be overloaded as described above. Overloading the relational operators does not change the meaning of the fundamental comparison operations defined by the language; for example, overloading <= and/or >= does not affect the membership operations.

The inequality operator /= may never be explicitly overloaded. It is implicitly overloaded when the equality operator = is overloaded; the value of /= being the complement of =. However, the rules governing overloading = are so restrictive as to almost never permit overloading of this operator. The concepts necessary to describe why this is so are not yet available; when we discuss the relevant concepts, we will present the rules for overloading =.

If an overloaded operator definition is declared in more than one package interface using the same parameter and return types, it may be necessary to use the dot notation to reference this operator. When this situation arises, it is necessary to use normal function call notation:

```
ls := list_package. "&"(1, 3);
```

This state of affairs should be avoided whenever possible because the notation is confusing. (It may not be possible to avoid if the packages involved have been produced by other programmers.)

If an operator is overloaded using the same parameter and return types as those given by one of the predefined operators, the predefined operator will be hidden. Consider this example:

```
function "+"(m, n: integer) return integer is
begin    -- can't use + here because it's a recursive call
   return standard."+"(m, n) mod 12;   -- time arithmetic
end "+"
```

This definition of the operator + hides the definition of + given in package standard and it is necessary to use normal function call notation to access the usual meaning of + for integers.

13.3   FORMAL SYNTAX

The productions designator and name are updated to reflect the specification of operator symbols as function names.

```
designator =
    identifier              -- Chapter 7
    | operator-symbol
name =
    simple-name             -- Chapter 4
    | attribute             -- Chapter 9
    | indexed-component     -- Chapter 10
    | slice                 -- Chapter 10
    | selected-component    -- Chapter 11
    | operator-symbol
    | ...
operator-symbol =
    string-literal
```

chapter 14

Overloading enumeration literals

The same enumeration literal may appear in more than one enumeration type definition. In this case, the enumeration literal is said to be overloaded. For example:

```
type hair_color is (blonde, brown, black, red);
type eye_color is (brown, green, blue);
```

The enumeration literal brown is a member of both enumeration types in this example. The two identifiers have nothing in common (except for the accident of having the same name). They are in no sense equal.

14.1   RESOLVING AMBIGUITIES

It is almost always the case that the type of an overloaded enumeration literal can be determined from the context in which it is used. Consider this example:

```
procedure resolution_demo is
   subtype x is brown .. red;        -- brown is a hair_color
   y: eye_color := brown;            -- brown is an eye_color
   z: x;
begin
   for i in brown .. blue loop       -- type of brown (and
      y := i;                        -- therefore of i) is
   end loop;                         -- eye_color
   z := brown;                       -- brown is a hair_color
end resolution_demo;
```

Each use of an overloaded enumeration literal in this example is unambiguous.

Under certain circumstances, the type of an overloaded enumeration literal cannot be determined by context. As an example, consider these (overloaded) procedure declarations:

```
procedure put (h: hair_color);
procedure put (e: eye_color);
```

Using these definitions, the procedure call

```
put (brown);
```

is illegal because the type of the enumeration literal brown cannot be determined (and neither can the identity of the overloaded procedure put).

There are several ways to resolve this ambiguity:

```
put (h => brown);
put (e => brown);
put (hair_color' (brown));
```

The first two alternatives uniquely determine the type of brown by using named parameter notation. The parameter name distinguishes between the two procedures named put, and once the procedure is known, the argument type can be determined. In the third example, a *qualified expression* is used to identify the type of brown. A qualified expression consists of a type name, followed by a single-quote ', followed by an expression enclosed in parentheses. Note that a qualified expression does not (and cannot be used to) change the type of an expression, it merely clarifies the type. For a qualified aggregate, only one set of parentheses is required:

```
v : = vector' (1, 2, 3);
```

(Recall that vector is an unconstrained array type defined in previous chapters.)

14.2   CHARACTER LITERALS IN ENUMERATIONS

Character literals may be used in enumeration type declarations. Since all character literals already have one meaning (literals of the standard type character), character literals are always overloaded when they appear in enumeration types. The following example defines an enumeration type with character literals:

```
type roman is ('I', 'V', 'X', 'L', 'C', 'D', 'M');
```

This declaration overloads the meaning of some of the literals of the standard type character. As with the overloaded literal brown above, the roman literal 'I' has nothing in common with the character literal 'I' except the accident of the same name. The value of roman'pos('I') is not the same as the value of character'pos('I'). One must take care that the type of these character literals is uniquely determined, either by context, or by use of one of the explicit measures mentioned above.

The standard type character can be thought of as a predefined enumeration type. However, it is not really an enumeration because unprintable characters are not represented in the enumeration.

(In general, we find that character literals in enumerations are confusing and not very useful. If someone comes up with a good use for this feature, we'd like to hear about it so we can put it in the next edition.)

14.3   FORMAL SYNTAX

The enumeration-literal production is changed to include overloaded character literals. The primary production is updated for qualified expressions.

```
enumeration-literal =
      identifier                  -- Chapter 9
    | character-literal

primary =
      name                        -- Chapter 4
    | numeric-literal             -- Chapter 4
    | string-literal              -- Chapter 4
    | ( expression )              -- Chapter 4
    | type-conversion             -- Chapter 4
    | function-call               -- Chapter 7
    | aggregate                   -- Chapter 10
    | null                        -- Chapter 12
    | allocator                   -- Chapter 12
    | qualified-expression

qualified-expression =
      type-name ' ( expression )
    | type-name ' aggregate
```

chapter 15

Derived types

A *derived type* declaration creates a completely new type which *inherits* all of the features of the *parent type*, but is not compatible with the parent type. Derived types provide additional protection against unwanted mixing of types; for example, programs should not add lengths and weights to each other (since the "units" aren't compatible). If length and weight are declared as subtypes of integer, such operations are allowed. As derived types of integer, expressions mixing lengths and weights are forbidden.

Consider the following declarations:

```
type length is new integer;    -- derived type
subtype count is integer;      -- subtype

x: length;
c: count;
i: integer;
```

The type length is a new, distinct derived type that has all of the features of the parent type integer, such as integer literals and subprograms defined at the point of the derived type declaration that have integer parameter types. Thus, all of the following statements are legal:

```
x := 7;          -- 7 is length literal as well
x := x + 2;      -- integer operations are defined for length
x := x + x;      -- operands and result are of type length
x := x * x;      -- same in this example
put(x);          -- uses put for integers
```

However, the following statements are illegal:

```
x := i;            -- assignment type clash
x := x + i;        -- "+" operand types are not compatible
```

The second statement above is illegal because the function + is implicitly derived by replacing all occurrences of the type integer in the specification of + with type length.

Notice that equivalent statements using c in place of x are legal:

```
c := i;            -- No type clash here
c := c + i;        -- nor here
```

These examples illustrate the distinction between subtypes and derived types. A subtype merely provides a new name for an existing type (perhaps with additional constraints), while a derived type actually defines a new type with the same characteristics as an existing type. In accordance with this rule, the objects c and x are not compatible.

Unfortunately, Ada's derived type mechanism does not provide complete protection against incorrect combinations of units. Notice that this operation:

```
x := x * x;
```

is permitted by the language even though it makes no sense to multiply two lengths to obtain a third length.

15.1   USE OF DERIVED TYPES

The programmer may use type conversion to defeat the strict type checking provided by Ada for derived types. A type conversion is written as a type-name followed by an expression in parentheses. For example, the illegal statements given in the previous section could be legitimized by writing:

```
x := length(i);
x := x + length(i);
```

This notation forces the programmer to realize that normally incompatible types are being used together. Type conversions may only be used to change a derived type to its parent type, a parent type to one of its derived types, or a derived type to another type derived from the same parent type. Arbitrary type conversions are not allowed.

Note the distinction between a type conversion and a qualified expression. A type conversion is written without the single-quote mark and changes the type of an expression from a parent type to a derived type or from a derived type to a parent type. A qualified expression does not change the type of an expression, it simply clarifies the type:

```
x := length(i);            -- type conversion
z := hair_color'(brown);   -- qualified expression
```

Using type conversions, we can solve the problem of multiplying two lengths together. We would like the result of such an operation to be an area, not a length. If we define area as a new derived integer type, the following example contains a subprogram that computes the product of two lengths giving an area:

```
procedure derived_demo is
    type length is new integer;
    l1, l2: length := 3;
    type area is new integer;
    a: area;

    function "*" (x, y: length) return area is  -- overloaded
    begin
        return area(integer(x) * integer(y));
    end "*";

begin
    a := l1 * l2;      -- uses "*" for length
    put(a);            -- uses original put for integers
end derived_demo;
```

The function * is overloaded, providing a definition that is meaningful when multiplying two length values. Care must be taken when writing the body of the function *. The following statement does not cause a compile time error but is erroneous nevertheless:

```
 return area(x * y);
```

Because x and y are both of type length, the expression x * y causes a recursive call to the function being defined. With nothing to halt the recursion, any use of this function will result in an error at run time.

15.2   DERIVED TYPES WITH CONSTRAINTS

The following definition (which includes a range constraint) is allowed by Ada:

```
type weight is new integer range 0..500;
```

It is equivalent to the following definitions:

```
type xxx is new integer;
subtype weight is xxx range 0..500;
```

where xxx does not appear anywhere else in the program. This construction is provided as a shorthand for those times when the programmer wishes to define a derived type that has an additional constraint not provided by the parent type.

15.3   FORMAL SYNTAX

The type-definition production is updated to include derived type definitions.

```
type-definition =
    enumeration-type-definition     -- Chapter 9
    | array-type-definition          -- Chapter 10
    | record-type-definition         -- Chapter 11
    | access-type-definition         -- Chapter 12
    | derived-type-definition
    | ...

derived-type-definition =
    new type-indication
```

chapter 16
Real types

The type integer discussed earlier is used for exact computation within a bounded set of whole numbers. Real types, on the other hand, are used for computation of approximate values. Use of real types is most often appropriate in applications that involve measurement of physical quantities—such as temperature or altitude—because the devices used to perform such measurements have inherent accuracy limitations. Accuracy limitations of this nature are the result of many factors, such as the inability of engineers to produce more accurate devices (which is often an economic consideration). The real data types in Ada are designed to accommodate the approximate computations involved in measuring the real world.

Literals for the real types were discussed earlier in the introduction to the predefined type float (see Chapter 3, Predefined Types and Operations). There is no implicit conversion of integer literals (or variables) to an appropriate real type in any context. Numeric values in all contexts must be compatible; however, explicit type conversion can be used to convert reals to integers and integers to reals. Real conversion to integer involves rounding.

There are two classes of real types in Ada: *fixed point* and *floating point*. Fixed point values are represented using a fixed number of digits before the decimal point and a fixed number of digits after the decimal point. Floating point values are represented using a fixed number of significant digits and an exponent defining the magnitude of the value. Real types are not discrete types.

The predefined operations available for real types include the relational operators (such as = and <), the predefined operator abs, and the arithmetic operators (including +, −, *, /, and **). Several attributes are also defined for use with the real types; these are discussed below.

16.1   FLOATING POINT

In Chapter 3, we discussed the primitive type float which is used in much the same manner as real data types defined in other languages. The attributes of float are (conveniently) chosen to correspond to characteristics of the target computer. An implementation may define other floating point types such as short_float or long_float, if the target machine is able to support different floating point data objects. The programmer should consult the reference manual for the local Ada compiler to determine which predefined floating point types are available.

In addition to these predefined floating point types, Ada permits the programmer to define additional floating point types that are implicitly derived from the predefined floating point types. New floating point types are defined by giving a relative error bound consisting of the number of significant decimal digits for values of the type and an optional range constraint which gives the upper and lower bounds on values of the type. The programmer specifies a minimum required precision for a floating point type; the actual precision is determined by the characteristics of the target machine. In particular, the accuracy of the new type may exceed that requested by the type definition. Consider this type definition:

```
type altitude is digits 8 range -100.0 .. 100_000.0;
```

The compiler compares the requirements specified in the type definition with the characteristics of the predefined floating point type(s). If these requirements cannot be satisfied by any of the predefined floating point types, then the definition is illegal. Otherwise, the compiler chooses the most appropriate predefined type to represent the new type.

As an example, consider a machine which implements the following floating point types:

```
type float is
   digits 7 range -2.9 * 10**(-39) .. 1.7 * 10**38;

type long_float is
   digits 16 range -2.9 * 10**(-39) .. 1.7 * 10**38;
```

Using these definitions, the type altitude defined above would employ the predefined type long_float as its underlying data representation because the predefined type float does not have sufficient precision to represent digits 8 as required.

All three of the values given in a floating point type definition are available through language defined attributes:

```
altitude'first        -- is -100.0
altitude'last         -- is 100_000.0
altitude'digits       -- is 8
```

The digits value given for a floating point type must be a static integer expression greater than zero. The floating point attributes of the predefined floating point types reveal the characteristics of the target computer.

The range constraint in a floating point type definition is optional. If it is not given, the range is taken from the (possibly implicit) parent type. For example, the following type definition:

```
type real_numbers is digits 6;
```

derives its range of values from the predefined type float and is therefore equivalent to:

```
type real_numbers is new float digits 6;
```

Of course, the programmer may use other floating point types in derived type or subtype declarations, as illustrated in these examples:

```
type short_reals is
   new real_numbers digits 4;
subtype temperature is
   real_numbers digits 4 range 0.0 .. 100.0;
```

The type short_reals is explicitly derived from real_numbers and inherits the range of values from real_numbers but has a different precision constraint. The subtype temperature is compatible with real_numbers but defines a different range of values from that of real_numbers which is presumably meaningful for an application involving temperature measurements (using, for example, the Celsius scale).

It is possible to determine the base type of a floating point type using another attribute.

```
real_numbers'base          -- equivalent to "float" (but
                           -- only used with other attributes)
real_numbers'base'digits   -- = float'digits = 7
real_numbers'base'first    -- = float'first = -29*10**(-39)
real_numbers'base'last     -- = float'last = 1.7*10**(38)
```

The language defines several other attributes specific to floating point types which are less often used. These may be found in Appendix VI.

Programs that have accuracy constraints and that are also intended to be portable should always specify the precision of floating point types explicitly. The explicit use of predefined floating point types might result in sufficient accuracy when moved to a machine with relatively less hardware floating point precision than required. If precision has been specified explicitly, the Ada compiler will provide an indication to the programmer when insufficient precision is available. Of course, since not all computers support floating point operations, some implementations may not implement floating point types at all.

16.2   FIXED POINT

While floating point types were defined by giving a relative error bound, fixed point types are defined by giving an absolute error bound. The term *absolute* is used to emphasize that errors resulting from computations using a fixed point type are required to be within a specified bound, called the *delta* of the type. A fixed point type definition also includes a range constraint specifying the upper and lower bounds on values for the type. These types may be used on target machines that do not have floating point capability or with data gathering applications that employ measurement devices that provide data in fixed point formats. To get a better idea of the meaning of absolute error bounds, consider this example:

```
type volts is delta 0.1 range -5.0 .. 5.0;
```

This type definition might be used to represent voltage in tenth-volt increments between −5 and 5 volts, inclusive. There are several facts about this example which should be explored.

The error bound on type volts is given as 0.1 which means that values of this type are accurate to within one-tenth. For example, the value 1.1 might not be represented exactly using this type definition because the compiler chooses a representation for values that is convenient for computation to the target machine. Instead, 1.1 might be represented by the value 1.125 because 1.125 can be easily represented on most computers (it doesn't really matter why) and is within the required error bound.

The *actual delta* is a fixed-point type (that is, the actual increment between successive values of the type) is chosen by the compiler and must be less than or equal to the specified delta. In the case of the type volts, the actual delta might be 0.0625, which leads to the representation of 1.125 given above. Incremental values of the type are at least as accurate as specified by the programmer; however, the programmer is not certain of the actual values represented by a fixed-point type.

All three programmer-specified values in the definition of type volts are accessible using language defined attributes.

```
volts'first        -- is -5.0
volts'last         -- is 5.0
volts'delta        -- is 0.1
```

The value given for the delta of a fixed-point type must be a static real expression greater than zero.

The usual arithmetic operations are available or fixed point types; however, there are some unique restrictions on multiplication and division of fixed point values. These restrictions are necessary because the arithmetic capabilities of most computers are limited in ways that make fixed point arithmetic difficult. The rules for fixed point multiplication are:

1. An integer value multiplied by a fixed point value gives a fixed point result value whose type is the same as the fixed point value:

```
x: volts;
i: integer;
...
x := x * i;
x := i * x;
```

2. A fixed point value multiplied by another fixed point value results in a value whose type is an anonymous fixed point type for which no operations are available. The type of such an operation must be explicitly given by a type conversion:

```
x, y: volts;
...
y := volts(x * y);   -- explicit conversion to "volts"
```

Conversion is required because of the properties of fixed point multiplication which make it necessary to give the precision of the result of such an operation. For example:

```
2.1 * 1.5 = 3.15
```

Intuitively, since the result has more decimal places than the operands, it is necessary to tell the compiler how many decimal places are required in the result. In the example given above, the type of y is volts, so the multiplication of x by y must be scaled to the proper number of decimal places for an object of type volts.

There are similar rules for fixed point division.

1. Division of a fixed point value by an integer value yields a fixed point result whose type is the same as the fixed point value. Division of an integer value by a fixed point value is not allowed.

2. Division of a fixed point value by another fixed point value yields a fixed point value whose type is anonymous. Explicit conversion of such a result is required as for multiplication of fixed point values.

It is possible to specify the actual delta for a fixed point type. For example, consider the following fixed point type:

```
type dollars is delta .01 range 0.0..1_000_000.0;
```

For computations involving dollars, we want exact results. This is indicated by specifying that the actual delta for dollars should be 0.01 using a fixed point representation specification:

```
for dollars'small use 0.01;
```

The representation specification should appear immediately after the type declaration for dollars. Fixed point operations are usually more expensive when the programmer specifies the actual delta, because the compiler normally chooses an actual delta that allows efficient fixed point operations.

16.3   FORMAL SYNTAX

The syntax of real type definitions is defined as follows. Notice that the type-definition and type-indication productions are updated here.

```
type-definition =
    enumeration-type-definition      -- Chapter 9
  | array-type-definition            -- Chapter 10
  | record-type-definition           -- Chapter 11
  | access-type-definition           -- Chapter 12
  | derived-type-definition          -- Chapter 15
  | real-type-definition

real-type-definition = accuracy-constraint

accuracy-constraint =
    fixed-point-constraint
  | floating-point-constraint

fixed-point-constraint =
    delta static-simple-expression [range-constraint]

floating-point-constraint =
    digits static-simple-expression [range-constraint]

type-indication =
    type-name                          -- Chapter 4
  | type-name range-constraint         -- Chapter 9
  | type-name index-constraint         -- Chapter 10
  | type-name discriminant-constraint  -- Chapter 11
  | type-name accuracy-constraint
```

chapter 17

More on packages

In Chapter 8, Packages, we described the fundamental features of Ada packages. In this chapter, we describe some more advanced facilities associated with packages.

17.1 TYPES IN PACKAGE SPECIFICATIONS

Type declarations may appear in package specifications. Often, type declarations cause the definition of several identifiers. For example, the declaration of an enumeration type definition defines the literals of the enumeration. In the following package specification, those identifiers that are visible to the user of the package are underlined:

```
package calendar is
   type months is
      (jan, feb, mar, apr, may, jun, jul, aug, sep, oct, nov, dec);
   type yeardate is
   record
      month: months;
      day: integer range 1..31;
   end record;
   christmas: constant yeardate := (dec, 25);
end calendar;
```

This package specification does not require a corresponding body because there are no subprogram specifications in the package specification.

The following example shows how the package calendar is used:

```
with calendar;
procedure package_demo is
  d: calendar.yeardate;
begin
  d := calendar.christmas;
  d.month := calendar.jul;
end package_demo;
```

The type yeardate, the object christmas, and the enumeration literal jul are all defined in the package specification calendar, so they must be preceded by the package name when referenced outside the package. The field identifier month is also defined in package calendar, but the name d.month does not need to specify calendar since that was already done in the declaration of the object d.

17.2   PRIVATE TYPES

Recall the package we defined to generate unique numbers such as employee ID numbers:

```
package id is
  function make return integer;
end id;

package body id is
  next: integer := 0;

  function make return integer is
  begin
    next := next + 1;
    return next;
  end make;
end id;
```

There are still some problems with this package. One improvement is to define the employee ID type as a derived type, which prevents the user of the package from mixing ID numbers with other integer values. The package interface now looks like this:

```
package id is
  type number is new integer;
  function make return number;
end id;
```

This is better, but the type of the ID number is still known to the users of the package as a derived integer type. ID numbers can be added or printed.

The type number should be declared as a *private type*. Private types may only appear in package specifications. Outside the package, the only operations available for objects of private types are assignment, tests for equality, and those operations defined by subprograms in the package specification. Within the corresponding package body, the representation of a private type is known, so all operations are available for objects of the type.

A package specification with private types includes a private part which describes the representation of the types. Using private types, the package id looks like:

```
package id is
   type number is private;
   function make return number;
private -- separates visible from private declarations
   type number is new integer;
end id;
```

The keyword **private** is used to separate the visible part of the package from the private declarations; there is only one occurrence of the keyword **private** even if more than one private declaration is given. Every private type declared in the visible part of a package interface must subsequently be completely defined in the private declaration part of the interface.

Package id is used just as it was before, but now it is impossible to perform any unauthorized operations on ID numbers. They may be declared, assigned, compared for equality, or returned from the function make. The fact that an ID number is represented as an integer is hidden completely from the user of the package id.

This is as it should be. One of the main criticisms of computers has been that they turn people into numbers. It is necessary, of course, to represent people in this way, but the package specification above emphasizes that this is only a representation. It ensures that the representation of people as numbers is confined to the body of package id.

The private part of a package appears in the specification because an Ada compiler needs to know about certain properties of the private types (how much memory the object requires, for example). Users of a package should consider the private part of the package interface to be part of the implementation of the package.

A private type may be declared *limited* as well:

```
type x is limited private;
```

The only difference between a limited private type and a private type is that assignment and tests for equality are not available for limited private objects.

The equality operator = may be overloaded in the interface of package if the package defines a limited private type and if the parameters to = are of that limited private type. This is the only situation in which overloading of equality is permitted. The result type of = must be boolean. Recall that overloading the equality operator implicitly overloads the inequality operator /=.

Limited private types can be useful when the programmmer wants or requires complete control over references to objects of a given type. The only operations available for limited types are defined by the subprograms declared in the corresponding package specification.

17.3   DEFERRED CONSTANTS

Private types may not be used to declare variable objects in a package interface; however, a package interface may contain constant objects of a private type. In our ID number example, we might want to have a constant object null_id which represents the absence of an ID number. A *deferred constant* declaration is used to declare such a constant. The specification of package id is modified as follows:

```
package id is
   type number is private;
   null_id: constant number;
   function make return number;
private
   type number is new integer;
   null_id: constant number := -1;
end id;
```

The actual value of the constant is given in the private part of the interface, which, as we said before, should be considered by the user to be part of the implementation of the package.

Except as default parameter values, deferred constants cannot be used until their declaration has been completed.

17.4   PACKAGE INITIALIZATION

A package may include initialization statements in the package body. In this case, the keyword **begin** and a sequence of statements precede the keyword **end** in the same fashion as a subprogram.

```
package body id is
   next: integer;   -- initialization below
```

```
function make return integer is
begin
   n := next;
   next := next + 1;
end make;

begin                  -- start of initialization statement(s)
   next := 0;
end id;
```

The example above illustrates a simple use of package initialization; the initialization of next has been moved from the declaration to the package initialization. This example does not really make use of the power of initialization, which is especially useful if loops, subprogram calls, or other more complex actions are necessary for initialization. (The initialization of the object next is probably clearer when associated with the declaration.)

17.5   DATA ABSTRACTION

The term *data abstraction* refers to the encapsulation of a data structure and the operations associated with that data structure. Using this concept, a data structure is defined entirely in terms of the operations available upon it—the actual structure of the data is hidden. Packages are a convenient mechanism for implementing data abstraction.

For example, consider the following package interface:

```
package person_table is
   type string_p is access string;
   type person;
   type person_ref is access person;
   type person is
     record
       name: string_p;
       soc_sec_num: integer;
       birthdate: date;
       link: person_ref;
     end record;
   procedure enter(p: person_ref);
   function lookup(name: string) return person_ref;
end person_table;
```

This package interface completely describes an abstract data structure for storing and retrieving person records. Knowledge of its implementation is not required.

One possible implementation of the body of the package person_table is to simply keep all the person records in a list:

```
package body person_table is
  head: person_ref;                    -- recall default
                                       -- initialization to null

  procedure enter(p: person_ref) is
  begin
    p.link := head;
    head := p;
  end enter;

  function lookup(name: string) return person_ref is
    p: person_ref := head;
  begin
    while p /= null loop          -- search list
      if p.name.all = name then
        return(p);
      end if;
      p := p.link·
    end loop;
    return null;
  end lookup;
end person_table;
```

This implementation is rather inefficient because, on the average, half the elements in the list must be inspected for every lookup operation. For a large number of person records this cost could be prohibitive.

A simple modification of this package body can greatly improve the efficiency of the lookup operation. In the package body below, 26 lists of person records are kept in an array. Records are entered based on the first character of the name field. This improves lookup efficiency by a factor of about 26 (less because the distribution of last initials is not uniform; for example there are more T's than X's).

```
package body person_table is
  hash_table: array('A'..'Z') of person_ref;

  procedure enter(p: person_ref) is
    ch: character := p.name(1);
  begin
    p.link := hash_table(ch);
    hash_table(ch) := p;
  end enter;
```

```
function lookup(name: string) return person_ref is
  p: person_ref := hash_table(name(1));
begin
  while p <> null loop
    if p.name.all = name then
      return p;
    end if;
    p := p.link;
  end loop;
  return null;
end lookup;
end person_table;
```

Person records could also be kept in a binary tree (as in Chapter 12). There are as many possible data structures as there are books on the subject of data structures. The important point here is that the implementation of a data structure can be entirely hidden by an Ada package.

17.6   FORMAL SYNTAX

The private part of a package specification is added to the package-specification production. The production type-declaration is updated to include private types.

```
package-specification =
    package identifier is
        {declaration}
    [ private
      {declaration} ]
    end [simple-name]

type-declaration =
    type identifier is type-definition ;      -- Chapter 9
    | incomplete-type-declaration             -- Chapter 12
    | private-type-declaration

private-type-declaration =
    type identifier [discriminant-part] is
        [limited] private;

deferred-constant-declaration =
    identifier-list : constant type-name ;
```

chapter 18

More on statements

In Chapter 6, the fundamental statement forms most commonly found in Ada programs were described. There are, however, several less frequently used, but nevertheless useful, statement forms.

18.1 LABELED LOOPS

Any loop may be preceded by a loop identifier that may be specified in an exit statement to cause termination of a particular enclosing loop. This is particularly useful when the loop to be terminated is not the immediately enclosing loop, but is at some higher level of statement nesting. The following examples illustrate the use of loop identifiers.

```
this_loop:
  loop
    -- some initial statements
    exit this_loop when n > m;
    -- more statements
  end loop this_loop;
...
outer_loop:
  for n in 1 ..10 loop
    inner_loop:
      while m < n loop
        -- some statements
        exit outer_loop when m = maxvalue;
      end loop inner_loop;
  end loop outer_loop;
```

The first example simply illustrates the use of a loop identifier. The label this_loop need not be specified in the exit statement; the meaning of the statement would be unchanged. In the second example, a while loop is nested inside a for loop. The exit statement specifies that when m = max value the loop labeled outer_loop (the for loop) is to be terminated.

Loop labels may appear only in loop statements. Whenever a loop label is given for a loop, it must also appear following the **end loop** tokens for that loop. Labeled loops should be used sparingly, because program readability can suffer if control structures are too complex.

18.1.1   Formal Syntax

```
statement =
      assignment-statement        -- Chapter 6
    | if-statement                -- Chapter 6
    | case_statement              -- Chapter 6
    | loop-statement              -- Chapter 6
    | null-statement              -- Chapter 6
    | exit-statement
    | procedure-call-statement    -- Chapter 7
    | return-statement            -- Chapter 7
    | labeled-loop-statement
    | ...

labeled-loop-statement =
      identifier :
        [iteration-clause] loop
          sequence-of-statements
        end loop simple-name;

exit-statement =                  -- Chapter 6
      exit [when boolean-expression]
    | exit simple-name [when boolean-expression]
```

18.2   BLOCKS

Declarations can be associated with a sequence of statements by using a block, which may appear anywhere a statement may appear. All block declarations may be used only within the text of the block itself and may not be referred to by statements or declarations outside the block. The following simple example illustrates a block with a related declaration:

```
swapexample:
   declare
      swaptemp: integer;
   begin
      swaptemp := i;
      i := j;
      j := swaptemp;
   end swapexample;
```

This example exchanges the values of two integers, i and j, using a temporary variable, swaptemp, which is associated with the block.

The keyword **declare** introduces the declarative part of the block; the keywords **begin** and **end** surround the statement part of the block. An optional block identifier may precede the block, terminated by a colon. If a block identifier appears, it must also appear following the block **end** as well. Block identifiers serve no purpose other than to provide additional information to a human reader.

The declarative part of a block may contain declarations of all kinds, including constants, types, variables, subprograms, and so forth. However, using blocks for anything other than very simple operations like swapexample is not recommended. Complex operations involving new types or subprograms are more readable when written using subprograms.

18.2.1   Formal Syntax

```
block-statement =
  [identifier :]
  [declare declarative-part]
  begin
     sequence-of-statements
  end [simple-name] ;

statement =
     assignment-statement        -- Chapter 6
   | if-statement                -- Chapter 6
   | case-statement              -- Chapter 6
   | loop-statement              -- Chapter 6
   | exit-statement
   | null-statement              -- Chapter 6
   | procedure-call-statement    -- Chapter 7
   | return-statement            -- Chapter 7
   | labeled-loop-statement
   | block-statement
   | . . .
```

18.3   GOTO STATEMENT

A goto statement is used to alter the normal sequential execution of a program. However, since the use of gotos can often make code difficult to understand, Ada provides a rich set of structured control forms (such as the exit statement, short-circuit operations, and the return statement). In addition, Ada places restrictions on the more flagrant abuses of the goto statement. Thus, the goto statement, which is very common in other programming languages, is almost entirely unnecessary in Ada. We urge the programmer to use gotos only in uncommon situations not covered by any of the other Ada control forms. It is as hard to read gotos as it is easy to write them.

Any statement may be labeled by an identifier enclosed in double angle brackets << >>. A label is implicitly declared at the beginning of the enclosing scope and therefore the same label name may appear in two different scopes. It is permissible to define more than one label for a single statement as long as different identifiers are used. Some examples of labeled statements:

```
<<here>>    a := 5;
<<more>> <<than>> <<one>> null;
...
goto here;        -- transfers to assignment
goto more;        -- to null statement
goto one;         -- transfers to same statement
                  -- as "goto more"
```

The goto statement can be used to transfer control to a labeled statement; however, there are some restrictions on the use of goto.

• A goto may not attempt to transfer control outside of the current subprogram or package body.

• A goto may not be used to transfer control from one sequence of statements to another sequence of statements in the same enclosing statement. For example, a goto may not be used to transfer from the then part of an if statement to a labeled statement in the else part of the same if statement.

• Finally, a goto may not attempt to transfer control from outside of a structured statement into the body of a structured statement. That is, a goto may not transfer to a labeled statement inside an if statement, case statement, block, or other such statement. Thus, the following is not permitted.

```
if n < 0 then
  n := 0;
<<a_label>>
  m := 1;
end if;
goto a_label;    -- Ada does NOT permit this!!
```

18.3.1   Formal Syntax

```
label = << identifier >>

goto-statement =
    goto simple-name ;

statement =
    assignment-statement          -- Chapter 6
    | if-statement                -- Chapter 6
    | case-statement              -- Chapter 6
    | loop-statement              -- Chapter 6
    | null-statement              -- Chapter 6
    | exit-statement
    | procedure-call-statement    -- Chapter 7
    | return-statement            -- Chapter 7
    | labeled-loop-statement
    | block-statement
    | goto-statement
    | ...
```

chapter 19
Generics

template

pass "types" as arguments

In Ada, a program unit (that is, a subprogram or package) can be *generic*. A generic program unit is not called directly. Instead, a generic program unit defines a template from which other kinds of program units can be created. The process of creating a program unit from a generic program unit is called *generic instantiation*. Generic program units may have types as parameters and when the unit is instantiated, types are passed as arguments. Thus, a generic program unit may be used to create a class of similar program units whose only differences are based on the types upon which they operate.

Those programmers familiar with macros will notice that generics provide similar capabilities.

19.1   GENERIC SUBPROGRAMS

A very common action to take in a program is to swap the values of two variables. Since Ada is a strongly typed language, it is not possible to write a single procedure that can be used to swap two values of arbitrary type. We can, however, define a generic procedure to do the job. The following example gives the specification for a generic procedure from which specific swapping procedures can be instantiated.

```
generic
   type elem is private;   -- private means generic param
procedure exchange (u, v:  in out elem);
```

The generic procedure exchange has one formal parameter, elem, which is the type of the two objects to be swapped. The formal parameter must be

147

described as a private type because any type may replace it. We may make no assumptions about the representation of the type. This type is used in the procedure specification as the type of the two procedure parameters u and v;

The procedure body for the generic procedure exchange (given below) repeats the subprogram specification given in the generic specification and defines the actions of the generic. A local variable t of type elem is declared for storing the intermediate value during the swap.

```
procedure exchange (u, v: in out elem) is
   t: elem;
begin
   t : = u;
   u : = v;
   v : = t;
end exchange;
```

A generic procedure cannot be called directly; it defines a template from which actual procedures can be generated. If we need to exchange values of type integer, we can instantiate the generic procedure exchange with the type integer as an argument:

```
procedure swap is new exchange (integer);
```

This declares a procedure swap which swaps the values of two integer objects. The procedure swap behaves exactly as if it had been declared like this:

```
procedure swap (u, v: in out integer);
```

A generic instantiation is a declaration, not a statement. It may only appear in the declarative part of a program unit.

The following example further illustrates the declaration and use of the generic procedure exchange defined above.

```
with ada_io; use ada_io;
procedure generic_demo is
   x, y: integer;
   generic
      type elem is private;
   procedure exchange (u, v:  in out elem) ;

   procedure exchange (u, v:  in out elem)  is
      t:  elem;
   begin
      t  : = u;
      u  : = v;
      v  : = t;
   end exchange;

   procedure swap is new exchange (integer) ;

begin
   x  : = 1;
   y  : = 2;
   swap (s, y) ;
   put (x) ;          -- prints 2
   put (y) ;          -- prints 1
end generic_demo;
```

The generic exchange is instantiated for integers as procedure swap. Execution of procedure swap on integer objects interchanges the values of the objects.

A generic procedure can be instantiated many times. For example, if we want to swap boolean values as well, we can instantiate a second procedure:

```
procedure bswap is new exchange (boolean) ;
```

The procedure bswap can now be called to swap boolean values. We might have called this procedure swap as well, which would have resulted in two overloaded procedures called swap. These procedures would be distinguishable in a call because their parameter types are different.

19.2   GENERIC PACKAGES

Packages may be generic as well. As with subprograms, they define a template from which actual packages may be created. There is an important distinction, though. If a package has object declarations, either in its specification or in the top level of its body, then every time that package is instantiated, new objects are created. For example, consider the following generic package:

```
generic
package counter is
  function value return integer;
  procedure bump;
end counter;

package body counter is
  x: integer := 0;

  function value return integer is
  begin
    return x;
  end value;

  procedure bump is
  begin
    x := x + 1;
  end bump;
end counter;
```

This generic package implements a counter. The object in which the counter is kept (the object x) is hidden within the body of the package. The only operations available on the counter are getting its value and incrementing it. This is good programming practice because it emphasizes that the object is used only for the purpose of counting something. A simple integer object would work just as well as a counter, but such an object could be modified in unintended ways.

If we instantiate two such packages, we get two distinct counters. Once this is done, the two packages (byte_count and page_count, below) can be thought of simply as counters. The counters can be incremented using the procedure bump, and their value can be examined using the function value:

```
with ada_io; use ada_io;
procedure counter_demo is
  package byte_count is new counter;      -- first counter
  package page_count is new counter;      -- second counter
begin
  put (byte_count.value);  -- prints 0
  put (page_count.value);  -- prints 0
  byte_count.bump;
  page_count.bump;
  put (byte_count.value);  -- prints 1
enter counter_demo:
```

The value of byte_count.value is 1 in the last statement because each time the generic package counter is instantiated, a distinct object x is created inside the body of that package.

19.3   GENERIC LIST HANDLING PACKAGE

The linked list is a very common data structure. In Chapter 12, Access Types, we defined several types and subprograms for manipulating lists of integers. Using instantiations of the following generic package, lists of any type can be manipulated. The list element type is a generic parameter.

```
generic
   type elem is private;  -- private means generic param
package list_package is
   type cell is private;  -- private means private type
   type pointer is access cell;

   type arr is array(integer range<>) of elem;
   function make(a: arr) return pointer;

   function front(p: pointer) return elem;
   function rest(p: pointer) return pointer;
   function add_on(e: elem; p: pointer) return pointer;
private
   type cell is
     record
       value: elem;
       link: pointer;
     end record;
end list_package;
```

The type elem is a generic formal parameter. When the package is instantiated, the desired element type from which lists are to be constructed is passed as an argument:

```
type person is       -- from Chapter 11
   record
     last_name: string(1..10);
     ssn: soc_sec_num;
     birthday: date;
   end record;

package person_list is new list_package(elem => person);

package int_list is new list_package(elem => integer);
```

The package person_list is used to manipulate lists of person records and the package int_list is used to manipulate lists of integers.

The type cell is a private type for the generic package list_package; it is used internally by package list_package to describe a single element of a list. The two instantiations above created two distinct private types: person_list.cell and int_list.cell. Note that although the declarations of elem and cell look the same, they are really quite different. The type elem is a generic formal parameter, and the type cell is a private type for the (generic) package counter.

The type pointer is an access type that refers to the private type cell. This type is used outside package list_package to refer to a list. Since it is an access type, it is compatible with null and null is its default value. A declaration of an access object meant to hold a list of integers is written as in this example:

```
P: int_list.pointer;   -- default value is null
```

The actual structure of a list is hidden from the user of the package. The private part of the package specification gives the structure of a cell; a record with a field of type elem and a field of type pointer.

The type arr is an unconstrained array type whose component type is the generic parameter elem. Its primary purpose is to allow the declaration of the function make, which can be passed an array aggregate whose components are of type elem. The components of the aggregate are used to construct a new list structure. The first component of the aggregate becomes the first element of the list. The following function call returns a four-element list:

```
p := int_list.make((1,2,3,4));
```

The function front returns the first element of the given list argument. The function rest returns a list consisting of all but the first element of the given list. The function add_on returns a list built by inserting the given element on the front of the given list. (For those programmers familiar with LISP, these functions correspond to car, cdr, and cons.)

The following procedure illustrates the use of the generic list handling package:

```
procedure list_demo is
   package int_list is new list_package(integer);
   p: int_list.pointer;
begin
   p := int_list.make((1,2,3,4));
   p := int_list.add_on(5, p);
   while p /= null loop    -- loop through list
      put(int_list.front(p), width => 2);
      p := int_list.rest(p);    -- next element
   end loop;
end list_demo; -- prints 5 1 2 3 4
```

This is body of the generic package list_package:

```
package body list_package is
  function make(a: arr) return pointer is
    p: pointer;      -- initialized to null by default
  begin
    for i in reverse a'range loop
      p := add_on(a(i), p);
    end loop;
    return p;
  end make;

  function front(p: pointer) return elem is
  begin
    return p.value;
  end front;

  function rest(p: pointer) return pointer is
  begin
    return p.link;
  end rest;

  function add_on(e: elem; p: pointer) return pointer is
  begin
    return new cell'(e, p);
  end add_on;            -- note: copying e may be expensive
end list_package;        -- if elem is a large composite type
```

The implementation of the function make is interesting. A local list object p (initially null) is used to construct a list. We proceed through the array *backwards* putting elements on the front of the list p. When the loop completes, we have built a list whose first element is the first component of the array parameter.

Notice that the use of an initializer in an allocator greatly simplifies the body of function add_on. But it also obscures the fact that a value of type elem must be copied into each initialized access object. If the package list_handler is instantiated with a scalar type like integer, this copying operation is relatively inexpensive. If, however, the package is instantiated with a large composite type (for example an employee information record with 20 or 30 fields) the cost of this copying operation for every record could be prohibitive. A more efficient solution is to instantiate the list handling package with an access type whose base type is the employee record type. In this case, only the access value is copied, not the whole record.

19.4   GENERIC FORMAL PARAMETER TYPES AND MATCHING RULES

In the previous examples, all of the generic formal parameters were specified as private types, meaning that they could be instantiated using almost any type. Often, a generic formal parameter is restricted to a certain class of types. Ada provides a method for describing different classes of generic formal parameter types. If a type satisfies the restrictions placed on the formal generic parameter type, it is said to *match* the formal parameter type. This section describes the different classes of generic parameter types and their corresponding matching rules.

If a generic formal parameter is a limited private type, it may be matched by any type other than an unconstrained array type. If the generic formal type is a private type (not limited), the actual type can be any type for which assignment and tests for equality are available. If the generic formal parameter type has discriminants, the actual type must have the same discriminants. Within the generic, there are no operations available for limited private types and only assignments and tests for equality are available for private types.

If a generic formal parameter has the following form:

```
type discrete_elem is (<>);
```

then it is matched by any discrete type. Recall that discrete types include integer types and enumeration types. Within the generic, the attributes for discrete types are available, including pos, val, first, last, succ, pred, and image. For example consider the following generic function:

```
with random_integer;
generic
   type rng is (<>);
function random return rng;

function random return rng is
   rand: integer := random_integer.next;
   length: integer := rng'last - rng'first + 1;
begin
   return rng'val((rand mod length) + rng'pos(rng'first));
end random;
```

This generic function is instantiated with a discrete type, creating a function that returns values in the range specified by the discrete type. Since the generic type parameter is known to be a discrete type, the attributes for discrete types may be applied to the generic type parameter rng. The package random_integer is used by this function to generate random integer values. It is specified in Appendix I. Some examples of the use of random:

```
function random_day is new random(day_of_week);
subtype small is integer range 1..10;
function random_small is new random(small);
```

The first function generates random values of the enumeration type day_of_week. The second one generates integer values in the range 1..10. Notice that the subtype small must be defined because generic type parameters must be type names—they may not include constraints.

If a generic formal parameter is an array type definition,

```
type array_elem is array(discrete_elem) of elem;
```

the array type may depend upon previous generic formal parameter types. If the component type or any index type for the array type is a generic formal parameter itself, the actual type is substituted in the array type. After this substitution is done, the actual array type matches only if the two array types are the same. Within the generic, all facilities available for array types are available. For example, if the formal parameter is an unconstrained array type, a constrained array object of this type could be declared within the generic.

If a generic formal parameter is an access type definition, such as

```
type ptr_elem is access array_elem;
```

the access type may also depend upon previous generic formal parameter types. If the type referred to by the access type is a generic parameter, the actual type is substituted. If the formal access type refers to the same type as the actual access type, the two types match. Within the generic, all facilities available for access types are available (for example, allocators and compatibility with null).

19.5   GENERIC FORMAL OBJECTS

A generic may have objects as parameters. This usage is analogous to subprogram parameters. The modes in and in out are permitted, but the mode out is not. For example, the following generic package implements a stack whose size is given as a generic parameter:

```
generic
  size: integer;
  type elem is private;
package stack is
  procedure push(e: elem);
  function pop return elem;
end stack;

package body stack is
  space: array(1..size) of elem;
  index: space'range := 1;

  procedure push(e: elem) is
  begin
    space(index) := e;
    index := index + 1;
  end push;

  procedure pop return elem is
  begin
    index := index - 1;
    return space(index);
  end pop;
end stack;
```

19.6   GENERIC FORMAL SUBPROGRAMS

A generic may specify a subprogram as a formal parameter. The generic parameter is specified by the reserved word **with** followed by a subprogram specification. The actual generic parameter must be a subprogram with the same type and number of arguments, and the same return value (if any). For example, we might want to write a generic procedure to sort arrays of arbitrary type. The greater-than operation is not defined for all types, so it must be specified as a generic formal function parameter.

```
generic
  type elem is private;
  type vector is array(integer range <>) of elem;
  with function ">"(x, y: elem) return boolean;
procedure sort(a: in out vector);
```

This generic procedure is instantiated as shown below:

```
procedure generic_demo is
  type int_vector is
    array(integer range <>) of integer;
  a: int_vector(1..10) := (4,7,10,2,5,8,1,2,6,9);
  procedure int_sort is
    new sort(integer, int_vector, ">");
begin
  int_sort(a);
  for i in a'range loop
    put(i, 4);
  end loop;
end generic_demo;
```

The body of the procedure sort could implement any of several popular sorting algorithms (no class of algorithm has been studied more than sorting has). Here we present the simplest (and least efficient) sorting algorithm, a simple insertion sort:

```
procedure sort(a: in out vector) is
  procedure swap is
    new exchange(elem);
begin
  for i in a'range loop
    for j in i+1 .. a'last loop
      if a(i) > a(j) then
        swap(a(i), a(j));
      end if;
    end loop;
  end loop;
end sort;
```

A more complicated body for this generic procedure which uses quick sort can be found in Appendix I.

19.7   FORMAL SYNTAX

The declaration production is updated to include generics and generic instantiations.

```
declaration =
    object-declaration          -- Chapter 5
    | subprogram-declaration    -- Chapter 7
    | package-declaration       -- Chapter 8
    | use-clause                -- Chapter 8
    | type-declaration          -- Chapter 9
    | subtype-declaration       -- Chapter 9
    | deferred-constant-declaration  -- Chapter 17
    | generic-declaration
    | generic-instantiation
    | ...

generic-declaration =
    generic-specification ;

generic-specification =
    generic-formal-part subprogram-specification
    | generic-formal-part package-specification

generic-formal-part =
    generic {generic-parameter-declaration}

generic-parameter-declaration =
    identifier-list : [in [out]] type-name [:= expression] ;
    | type identifier [discriminant-part]
        is generic-type-definition
    | private-type-declaration
    | with subprogram-specification ;

generic-type-definition =
    (<>) | array-type-definition | access-type-definition

generic-instantiation =
    generic-package
    | generic-procedure
    | generic-function

generic-package =
    package identifier is
        new generic-package-name [generic-actual-part];

generic-package-name = name

generic-procedure =
    package identifier is
        new generic-procedure-name [generic-actual-part];
```

generic-procedure-name = name

generic-function =
    package identifier is
      new generic-function-name [generic-actual-part];

generic-function-name = name

generic-actual-part =
    (generic-association {, generic-association})

generic-association =
    [generic-formal-parameter =>] generic-actual-parameter

generic-formal-parameter =
    simple-name | operator-symbol

generic-actual-parameter =
    expression | name

chapter 20

Tasking

— concurrent programs

The concept of independent but interacting activities is familiar to everyone. For example, consider the activities of a bank teller and a customer. When we visit a bank we frequently stand in a line that is serviced by a number of tellers. Each teller interacts with a single customer at a rate appropriate to the service requested by the customer. When there are fewer customers than tellers, some tellers wait for customers to arrive. When there are more customers than tellers (alas, the more usual scenario), then customers wait for tellers to be available. The key point is that the activities of the customer and the teller are independent of one another except while they are interacting.

Similar situations are frequently encountered in computer systems. Most resources, for example, must be managed so as to make them available to all users. Printers and databases are good examples of such resources. The integrity of databases is insured by disallowing write access to records in the database by more than one user at a time. In order to accomplish this, a database server (for a bank's database, for example) must intercept write requests and process them one at a time.

Ada provides a mechanism, called *tasking*, for implementing independent but interacting activities, called *tasks*. Tasks are program components that may operate in parallel with other program components.

20.1   SOME CONCEPTS

Most collections of interacting tasks are organized in such a way that individual tasks can be classified according to their function in the system of which they are a part. In particular, from a given frame of reference most tasks will be broadly categorized as either *servers* or *requestors*. For instance, in the banking example mentioned above, tellers are servers; that is, they exist to provide services to customers. The customer, who uses the services of the teller, is a requestor.

Usually, requestors are the active elements of a system of cooperating tasks. They use servers to accomplish certain well-defined functions. Servers are generally passive, reacting only to the external requests generated by requestors. This characterization does not prohibit a server, such as a teller, from requesting the services of yet another server (such as the bank's database). From this new frame of reference, the teller becomes a requestor and the database a server. If we examine any system closely enough, we will discover that the components of the system are related in myriad ways; however, most of the individual interactions can be broken down into this server/requestor model. The Ada tasking mechanism permits the programmer to define such relationships.

Any Ada task that is to provide a service has a task specification which defines a number of *entries* to the task. These entries, which syntactically are very similar to subprogram specifications, define the functions or services that the task provides. A requestor task initiates or requests a service by making an *entry call*. A server task indicates readiness to provide a service by executing an *accept statement*. When both these actions have occurred, the requestor and server are synchronized for the duration of the service provided. If a server is able to provide any one of several services, the *select statement* is used to implement this concept. Once a server is finished with a request, the requestor and server are both free to continue their independent activities asynchronously.

The tasking mechanism does not define a mapping onto physical processors. A collection of tasks may be executed on one or more processors, constrained by the number of physical processors and the Ada implementation. If fewer processors are available than there are tasks to be run (probably a common situation), then the implementation will alternate tasks between the available processors. The important point is that the execution of a task is independent of other tasks.

In this chapter, we develop an Ada program that uses tasking to simulate the operations of a bank. With this example program, we illustrate all the basic features of tasking in Ada. Our bank simulation contains four major components:

1. A collection of customer tasks.
2. A collection of teller tasks.
3. A single task to set up new bank accounts.
4. A single task to manage the bank's database.

Figure 20-1 illustrates the various components of the model and their interactions.

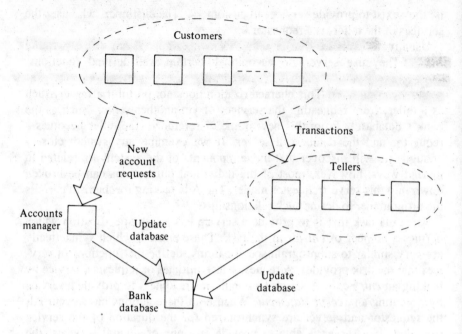

Figure 20-1. Bank simulation tasks.

20.2   TASK SPECIFICATIONS

Tasks are program components that may operate in parallel with other program components. A task specification, like a package specification, defines the interface which other (related) program components use to interact with the task. The interface consists of entry declarations that are not unlike the subprogram declarations in a package specification.

For example, consider a task specification for a task that simulates the activity of a (novice) bank teller:

```
-- global types used throughout chapter
type money is new integer range 0..integer'last;
type status is (success, insufficient_funds, bad_cust_id);
type cust_id is new integer range 0..number_of_customers;
...
task single_teller is
  -- entries to do simple transactions and return status
  entry deposit(id: cust_id; val: money; stat: out status);
  entry withdraw(id: cust_id; val: money; stat: out status);
  entry balance(id: cust_id; val: out money; stat: out status)
end single_teller;
```

The entry deposit is used to deposit val dollars into a customer's account. The entry withdraw is used to withdraw money from a customer's account. Entry balance returns a customer's current balance. It is the responsibility of the teller task to control access to the bank's database to ensure that the integrity of the customer's account is maintained. However, the manner in which this is done is not of interest to the customer, so the details are hidden in the task body in just the same way that the implementation details of packages are hidden in a package body. The task may interact with other tasks or use other packages to accomplish its purpose, but the task user need not be aware of these subsidiary interactions.

20.3   TASK TYPES

In addition to the definition of tasks as described above, Ada also permits the definition of task types. Since most banks have more than one teller, it is appropriate to define a task type teller which is used in another data structure that defines the number of tellers a particular bank employs.

```
task type teller is
   -- entries to do simple transactions and return status
   entry deposit(id: cust_id; val: money; stat: out status);
   entry withdraw(id: cust_id; val: money; stat: out status);
   entry balance(id: cust_id; val: out money; stat: out status);
end teller;
```

For our bank simulation, an array of teller tasks is used:

```
tellers: array(1..10) of teller;
```

This declares 10 distinct tasks of type teller.

Single task definitions as described above (task single_teller) are equivalent to the definition of an anonymous task type followed immediately by the declaration of an object of the anonymous type. However, the number of tasks of the anonymous type is restricted to one. The object declaration

```
single_teller: teller;
```

defines an object that is equivalent to the previous declaration of the single task single_teller.

Task types may be used to declare task objects, or as components of other types (such as array or record types), or as the target of an access type. The following types could be used to build linked lists of teller tasks:

```
type teller_cell;

type teller_list is access teller_cell;

type teller_cell is
  record
    tell: teller;
    link: teller_list;
  end record;
```

All task types are implicitly limited types and, therefore, there are no language-defined operations defined on objects of a task type (such as the elements of the array tellers). However, if, for example, it is necessary to distinguish one task object from another, a task object can be the target of an access object. Equality and assignment are available for such access objects.

```
type teller_ptr is access teller;
p: teller_ptr : = new teller;
q: teller_ptr : = p;
```

Since task types are always limited, the use of task objects in subprogram calls is restricted. Task objects can be used as **in** parameters to subprograms, but not as **in out** or **out** parameters.

It is not necessary for a task to define any entry definitions. Some tasks simply may execute asynchronously, without the interaction of entry calls. For example,

```
task type customer;
```

defines a task type that has no entries. Customers in our scenario do not require entry definitions because the actions of a customer are controlled by forces external to the banking simulation, which corresponds to the real world. Tellers generally do not know why a customer deposits or withdraws money, just that the transaction is taking place.

20.4.   ENTRY CALLS

An entry call to a task resembles a procedure call. Task entries may not be functions, but the same effect can be achieved using out parameters. The task entry name is preceded by the name of a task object, and a dot:

```
id: cust_id;
amount: money;
stat: status;
...
single_teller.deposit(id, amount, stat);
tellers(4).withdraw(id, amount, stat);
teller_list.tell.balance(id, amount, stat);
p.all.deposit(id, amount, stat);
```

The first statement calls the entry deposit of the task single_teller. The second statement calls the entry withdraw of the fourth task in the teller task array tellers. The third statement calls the entry balance of the first element of the task list teller_list. The fourth statement calls the entry deposit of the task object designated by the access object p.

20.5   THE DELAY STATEMENT

The delay statement is used to suspend the task requesting the delay for a specified period. For example,

```
delay 60.0;
```

This statement causes the executing task to be suspended for at least 60 seconds. The language does not insure that the task executing a delay statement will immediately begin execution when the delay period has expired.

The argument to delay is specified using a predefined fixed point type duration. The language specifies that duration must be capable of representing at least 86400 seconds (one day) and its accuracy must be at least 20 milliseconds. Duration represents signed values, but a delay statement with a negative argument has no effect.

20.6   TASK BODIES

The body of a task looks like the body of a package except that a sequence of statements must appear to define the actions of the task. The entry definitions in the task specification are used in conjunction with accept statements in the task body to control the actions of the task.

Here is an outline for the task body for the entry-less task type customer:

```
task body customer is
   -- local type
   type transaction is (deposit, withdraw, balance);
   -- functions to create random values for simulation
   function random_transaction is ...
   function random_teller is ...
   function random_amount is ...
   function random_time_between_visits is ...
   -- local variables
   id: cust_id;
   amount: money;
   stat: status
begin
   accounts_manager.new_account(id); -- get new cust id
   loop
      delay duration(random_time_between_visits);
                                   -- simulate customer away
                                   -- from bank
      case random_transaction is    -- pick random transaction
       ‘when deposit =>
          tellers(random_teller).deposit(id, random_amount, stat)
         when withdraw =>
          tellers(random_teller).withdraw(id, random_amount, stat
         when balance =>
          tellers(random_teller).balance(id, amount, stat);
      end case;
      -- note: stat is ignored in this simple example
   end loop;
end customer;
```

A customer task first opens an account with the bank by calling the new_account entry of the task accounts_manager which returns a unique customer ID. (The accounts_manager task is described in the next section.) After delaying a random amount of time (simulating the time a customer spends outside of the bank), a customer picks a teller and transaction at random and makes an entry call. A customer task loops indefinitely, making entry calls to random tellers.

20.7   ACCEPT STATEMENTS

Every accept statement corresponds to an entry declaration in a task specification. Associated with each accept statement is a sequence of statements that is executed when the corresponding entry is called. The parameters defined in the corresponding entry declaration are visible to this sequence of statements, but not elsewhere. More than one accept statement for the same entry is permitted.

The `accounts_manager` task is responsible for allocating unique customer ID numbers to different customer tasks. Its specification and body are as follows:

```
task accounts_manager is
  -- opens accounts, establishes new customer id's
  entry new_account (new_id:  out cust_id) ;
end;

task body accounts_manager is
  next: cust_id := 0;
begin
  loop
    accept new_account (new_id:  out cust_id) do
      new_id : = next;
      -- enter "next" in bank's databases
      next : = next + 1;
    end new_account;
  end loop;
end accounts_manager;
```

The task `accounts_manager` manages the local object next so that each customer task gets a unique customer ID. The accept statement for the entry `new_account` is repeated indefinitely. If several tasks make calls to the entry `new_account`, they are processed one at a time. The object next may only be accessed within the body of the task `accounts_manager`.

If the object next were a global variable, each customer task could access it directly. This, however, could cause serious problems. For example, the declaration

```
customers: array (1..10) of customer;
```

causes 10 customer tasks to begin execution at about the same time. Each task first attempts to allocate a customer ID. Task `customer (1)` could get the value of next, then `customer (2)` could get the value of next, and then task `customer (1)` could increment the value of next. This would result in two customers with the same ID. The use of such shared variables is permitted by Ada, but should be avoided whenever possible. Tasks should be used to manage shared data.

Accept statements and the actions associated with them are very similar to procedures; however, there is one crucial difference. When a procedure call is executed, the actions associated with the procedure declaration are executed immediately. When an entry call is executed, the actions associated with the entry are only executed when the task is ready to accept the entry call. An entry call and a corresponding accept statement are said to be *synchronized*; the manner in which synchronization is achieved differs based upon the order of execution of the entry call and accept statement.

• If the entry call is executed prior to the corresponding accept statement, then the calling task is suspended until the accept statement is reached.

• If the accept statement is executed prior to the corresponding entry call, then the accepting task is suspended until the proper entry call is executed.

Once synchronization has been achieved, the statements associated with the accept statement in the called task are executed while the calling task is suspended. This interaction, regardless of the order in which the entry call and accept statement are executed, is called a *rendezvous*. Once the rendezvous is complete (that is, once the statements associated with the accept have been executed), the called and calling tasks are free to continue parallel execution. Figures 20-2 and 20-3 illustrate the steps involved in a rendezvous.

20.8   EXECUTION STATES

There are a number of important events in the life of a task. The definition of the task interface (the task specification) and the definition of the actions to be performed by the task (the task body) have already been discussed. In addition to these events, tasks are activated, executed, suspended, completed, and terminated.

A task is *activated* when a corresponding task object is created. Activation consists of initialization of any implementation-defined tasking data structures (which are not visible to the programmer) and any initialization defined by the declarative part of the task body. All tasks declared in the declarative part of a block, subprogram body, package body, or task body are said to *depend* on that program unit. Tasks are activated prior to execution of the first statement of the program unit on which the task is dependent.

The task body is *executed* in parallel with other program components once activation is complete.

Tasks are *suspended* as necessary to accomplish rendezvous with other tasks or to share a limited number of processors among many tasks.

A program component has *completed* execution when it reaches the end of the sequence of statements that defines the body of the component being considered. When a program component has completed execution, it waits for the termination of dependent tasks.

A task is normally *terminated* when it reaches the end of the sequence of statements that defines the task body and has no dependent tasks still executing. Abnormal termination of tasks is discussed below.

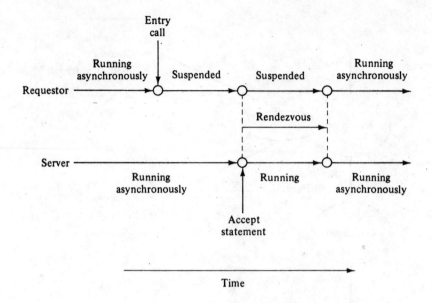

Figure 20-2. Stages of a rendezvous (entry call first).

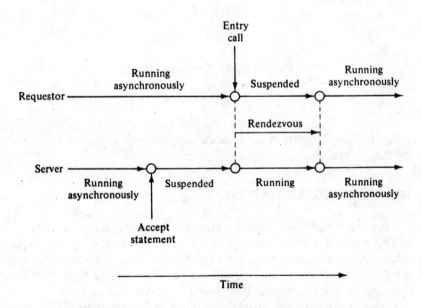

Figure 20-3. Stages of a rendezvous (accept first).

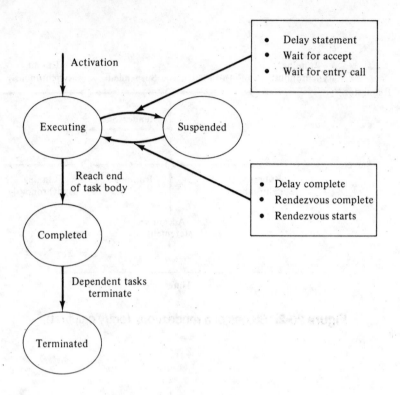

Figure 20-4. Execution states.

Figure 20-4 illustrates the execution state transitions that may occur during the life of a task.

20.9   SELECTIVE WAITING

It is often the case in concurrent programs that the order in which requests will be received is not or cannot be known at program development time. In order to react to externally changing conditions, it must be possible to accept entry calls in arbitrary order sometimes based on internally recorded state information. The selective wait statement is used for this purpose.

The selective wait statement permits the programmer to define several accept alternatives to be selected among. Since a selective wait contains accept statements, it may only appear in the body of a task. A task of type teller may accept entry calls for transactions in any order; the body of the task type teller consists of a select statement inside an indefinite loop:

```
task body teller is
   current_balance: money;
   valid: boolean;
   function random_transaction_time is ...
begin
   loop
      select    -- wait for any transaction request
         accept deposit(id: cust_id;
                           val: money; stat: out status) do
            bank_database.verify_cust_id(id, valid);
            if not valid then
               stat := bad_cust_id;
            else
               bank_database.deposit(id, val);
               stat := success;
            end if;
         end deposit;
      or
         accept withdraw(id: cust_id;
                           val: money; stat: out status) do
            bank_database.verify_cust_id(id, valid);
            if not valid then
               stat := bad_cust_id;
            else
               bank_database.balance(current_balance);
               if current_balance < val then
                  stat := insufficient_funds;
               else
                  bank_database.withdraw(cust_id, val);
                  stat := success;
               end if;
            end if;
         end withdraw;
      or
         accept balance(id: cust_id;
                           val: out money; stat: out status) do
            bank_database.verify_cust_id(id, valid);
            if not valid then
               stat := bad_cust_id;
            else
               bank_database.balance(id, val);
               stat := success;
            end if;
         end balance;
      end select;
      delay duration(random_transaction_time);
   end loop;                          -- simulate transaction time
end teller;
```

A task of type `teller` accepts entry calls for any of its three services in any order. It makes entry calls to the single task `bank_database` to update the bank's database. (The definition of `bank_database` is given in the next section.) Teller tasks act as both a requestor and a server. A teller task acts as a server when it accepts an entry call from a customer, and acts as a requestor when it makes an entry call to the task `bank_database` to record the transaction.

20.10   BANK SIMULATION EXAMPLE

In this section, we present the complete, executable bank simulation program we have been developing. The details left out of the earlier discussion are filled in here. A programmer who understands how this program works is well on the way to an understanding of Ada tasking.

The task `bank_database` is analogous to the task `accounts_manager` in that it is used to manage access to data. Since `bank_database` has several entries, a select statement is used to selectively wait for a database entry call. This task also prints a transaction log as database requests are processed.

The generic function `random` is used in many places to create random values for our simulation. But we don't want to imply that the use of random values is somehow directly related to the use of tasking. The random values are required because our program is a simulation, not because it uses tasking.

```
with ada_io; use ada_io;
with random; use random;
procedure bank_simulation is
   -- these 2 constants can be altered to change
   -- the behavior of the simulation
   number_of_tellers: constant integer := 4;
   number_of_customers: constant integer := 10;

   -- these 2 ranges can be altered to change
   -- the behavior of the simulation
   subtype transaction_time_range is integer range 1..10;
   subtype time_between_visits_range is integer range 1..100;

   -- global types
   type money is new integer range 0..integer'last;
   type status is (success, insufficient_funds, bad_cust_id);
   type cust_id is new integer range 0..number_of_customers;

   -- task specifications

   task type customer;    -- requestor task type, has no entries
   task type teller is
      -- entries to do simple transactions and return status
      entry deposit(id: cust_id; val: money; stat: out status);
```

```
  entry withdraw(id: cust_id; val: money; stat: out status);
  entry balance(id: cust_id; val: out money; stat: out status);
  end teller;

task accounts_manager is
  -- opens accounts, establishes new customer id's
  entry new_account(new_id: out cust_id);
end accounts_manager;

task bank_database is
  -- maintains bank's internal data about open accounts and balances
  entry enter_cust_id(id: cust_id);
  entry verify_cust_id(id: cust_id; legal: out boolean);
  entry deposit(id: cust_id; amount: money);
  entry withdraw(id: cust_id; amount: money);
  entry balance(id: cust_id; amount: out money);
end bank_database;

-- arrays of tasks
tellers: array(1..number_of_tellers) of teller;
customers: array (1..number_of_customers) of customer;

task body teller is
  current_balance: money;
  valid: boolean;
  -- instantiation of the generic function "random"
  function random_transaction_time is
    new random(transaction_time_range);
begin
  loop
    select    -- wait for any transaction request
      accept deposit(id: cust_id; val: money; stat: out status) do
        bank_database.verify_cust-id(id, valid);
        if not valid then
          stat := bad_cust_id;
        else
          bank_database.deposit(id, val);
          stat := success;
        end if;
      end deposit;
    or
      accept withdraw(id: cust_id; val: money; stat: out status) do
        bank_database.verify_cust_id(id, valid);
        if not valid then
          stat := bad_cust_id;
        else
          bank_database.balance(current_balance);
          if current_balance < val then
            stat := insufficient_funds;
          else
            bank_database.withdraw(cust_id, val);
            stat := success;
```

```
                end if;
              end if;
          end withdraw;
       or
          accept balance(id: cust_id; val: out money; stat: out status) d
            bank_database.verify_cust_id(id, valid);
              if not valid then
                stat := bad_cust_id;
              else
                bank_database.balance(id, val);
                stat := success;
              end if;
          end get_balance;
        end select;
        delay duration(random_transaction_time);
      end loop;                        -- simulate transaction time
    end teller;

    task body customer is
      -- local type
      type transaction is (deposit, withdraw, balance);
      -- instantiations of generic function "random"
      function random_transaction is
        new random(transaction);
      function random_teller is
        new random(tellers'range);
      subtype money_range is money range 1..1000;
      function random_amount is
        new random(money_range);
      function random_time_between_visits is
        new random(time_between_visits_range);
      -- local variables
      id: cust_id;
      amount: money;
    begin
      accounts_manager.new_account(id);    -- get new cust id
      loop
        delay duration(random_time_between_visits) -- customer lives life
        case random_transaction is          -- pick random transaction
          when deposit =>
            tellers(random_teller).deposit(id,random_amount,stat);
          when withdraw =>
            tellers(random_teller).withdraw(id, random-amount, stat);
          when balance =>
            tellers(random_teller).balance(id, amount, stat);
        end case;
        -- note: stat is ignored in this simple example
      end loop;
    end customer;

    task body accounts_manager is
      next: cust_id := 0;
```

```
begin
  loop
    accept new_account(new_id: out cust_id) do
      new_id := next;
      bank_database.enter_cust_id(next);
      next := next + 1;
    end new_account;
  end loop;
end accounts manager;

task bank_database is
  -- in real situations, more elaborate data structures are needed
  balances: array(cust_id) of money;
  valid_id: array(cust_id) of boolean := (others => false);
begin
  loop
    select
      accept enter_cust_id(id: cust_id) do
        valid_id(id) := true;
        balances(id) := 0;
        put("open account #"); put(id); new_line;
      end enter_cust_id;
    or
      accept verify_cust_id(id: cust_id; legal: out boolean) do
        legal := valid_id(id);
        put("verify account #"); put(id); new_line;
      end verify_cust_id;
    or
      accept deposit(id: cust_id; amount: money) do
        balances(id) := balances(id) + amount;
        put("deposit for account #"); put(id); new_line;
      end deposit;
    or
      accept withdraw(id: cust_id; amount: money) do
        balances(id) := balances(id) - amount;
        put ("withdraw for account#"); put(id); new_line;
      end withdraw;
    or
      accept balance(id: cust_id; amount: out money) do
        amount := balances(id);
        put("balance for account #"); put(id); new_line;
      end balance;
    end select;
  end loop;
end bank_database;

begin -- main body of bank_simulation
  -- Activation of customer and teller task collections
  -- and bank_database and accounts_manager tasks occurs here.
  null;
  -- This program runs forever.
  -- procedure bank_simulation is completed but not terminated
end bank_simulation;
```

20.11   MORE ABOUT SELECTIVE WAITING

In the simple selective wait statements presented so far, all of the select alternatives have been accept statements. The selective wait statement does, however, include several more advanced features.

Each select alternative may include an optional condition that must be true for the alternative to be selected:

```
select
  when not on_coffee_break =>
    accept deposit ...
or
  ...
end select;
```

If the boolean variable on_coffee_break is true, the alternative deposit cannot be selected.

The select statement may contain an optional else clause which is executed if none of the accept alternatives have outstanding entry calls.

```
select
  accept deposit ...
or
  accept withdraw ...
or
  accept balance ...
else
  -- clean up desk
end select;
```

In this example, if there are any tasks waiting for entry calls to be accepted, one of them is accepted, otherwise, the else clause is executed.

An alternative may be a sequence of statements beginning with a delay statement. The meaning of this is similar to the else clause. If no task has made an entry call when the select starts, and no entry calls are made within the duration specified in the delay statement, then the statements after the delay are executed.

```
select
  accept deposit ...
or
  accept withdraw ...
or
  accept balance ...
```

```
or
   delay 5 * 60.0;
   -- check if open sign is up
end select;
```

A select alternative may consist simply of a terminate alternative. In this case, if there are no outstanding entry calls when the select is executed, the task terminates.

```
select
   accept deposit ...
or
   accept withdraw ...
or
   accept balance ...
or
   terminate;
   -- quit to find more interesting job
end select;
```

As soon as there are no outstanding entry calls requesting a transaction, the teller task containing the above select statement terminates.

There must be at least one accept alternative in a select statement. Only one of the special alternative forms (the else clause, the delay alternative, and the terminate alternative) may appear in a select statement.

The algorithm used to select which of several accept alternatives to execute is not defined by the language. A programmer who becomes familiar with how a particular compiler chooses select alternatives may be tempted to use this information in a program. But programs that use such information are erroneous because they may not execute properly when another compiler or operating system is used.

20.12   CONDITIONAL ENTRY CALLS

A conditional entry call statement issues an entry call if and only if a rendezvous is possible immediately upon execution of the statement. The syntax of a conditional entry call resembles a selective wait statement:

```
select
   single_teller.balance(my_name, current_balance);
   -- Verify balance against check book.
else
   null; -- Bank is crowded. Come back later.
end select;
```

If the rendezvous can be accomplished when the select statement is first entered, the entry call to balance is executed, followed by the (optional) sequence of statements following the entry call. Otherwise, the teller is busy, so the sequence of statements in the else alternative is executed.

20.13   TIMED ENTRY CALLS

A timed entry call executes an entry call if and only if the entry call can be accepted within a specified period. Its syntax also resembles a selective wait:

```
select
    single_teller.deposit(my_name, paycheck_amount);
    -- Record deposit in check register.
or
    delay 5 * 60.0; -- Wait 5 minutes for teller.
    -- Remember to come back tomorrow.
end select;
```

If the deposit entry call is accepted within 5 minutes, the optional sequence of statements following the entry call is executed. Otherwise, the statements following the delay alternative are executed.

20.14   TERMINATION

Tasks are terminated normally when the end of the task body is reached. Tasks may terminate abnormally by using the terminate alternative in a select statement or by using the abort statement.

When the terminate alternative is used in a select statement, that alternative may be chosen only if the block on which the task depends is waiting for termination of its dependent tasks.

The abort statement may be used to abnormally terminate any given task, including the task executing the abort statement. For example:

```
abort single_teller;
```

causes abnormal termination of the task single_teller or

```
abort tellers(4);
```

aborts the task represented by the fourth element of the tellers array. If the designated task has already been terminated, the abort statement has no effect. If the task being aborted has dependent tasks, the dependent tasks are aborted as well.

20.15   FORMAL SYNTAX

The declaration and body productions are updated.

```
declaration =
      object-declaration              -- Chapter 5
    | subprogram-declaration          -- Chapter 7
    | package-declaration             -- Chapter 8
    | use-clause                      -- Chapter 8
    | type-declaration                -- Chapter 9
    | subtype-declaration             -- Chapter 9
    | deferred-constant-declaration   -- Chapter 17
    | generic-declaration             -- Chapter 19
    | generic-instantiation           -- Chapter 19
    | task declaration
    | ...

task-declaration =
    task-specification ;

task-specification =
    task [type] identifier [is
        {entry-declaration}
    end [simple-name] ] ;

body =
      subprogram-body                 -- Chapter 7
    | package-body                    -- Chapter 8
    | task-body
    | ...

task-body =
    task body simple-name is
        [declarative-part]
    begin
        sequence-of-statements
    end [simple-name] ;

entry-declaration =
    entry identifier [formal-part] ;
```

The statement production is also updated to incorporate the several tasking-related statements:

```
statement =
    assignment-statement          -- Chapter 6
  | if-statement                  -- Chapter 6
  | case-statement                -- Chapter 6
  | loop-statement                -- Chapter 6
  | exit-statement                -- Chapter 18
  | null-statement                -- Chapter 6
  | procedure-call-statement      -- Chapter 7
  | return-statement              -- Chapter 7
  | labeled-loop-statement        -- Chapter 18
  | block-statement               -- Chapter 18
  | goto-statement                -- Chapter 18
  | entry-call-statement
  | accept-statement
  | delay-statement
  | abort-statement
  | select-statement
  | ...

entry-call-statement =
    entry-name [actual-parameter-part] ;

entry-name = name

accept-statement =
    accept simple-name [formal-part]
      [do sequence-of-statements
        end [simple-name] ] ;

delay-statement =
    delay simple-expression;

abort-statement =
    abort task-name {, task-name} ;

select-statement =
    selective-wait
  | conditional-entry-call
  | timed-entry-call

selective-wait =
    select
       select-alternative
    {or
       select-alternative}
    [else sequences-of-statements]
    end select;
```

select-alternative =
  [**when** condition =>]
  alternative-action

alternative-action =
    accept-alternative
  | delay-alternative
  | terminate-alternative

accept-alternative =
  accept-statement [sequence-of-statements]

delay-alternative =
  delay-statement [sequence-of-statements]

terminate-alternative =
  alternative ;

conditional-entry-call =
  select
    entry-call [sequence-of-statements]
  else
    sequence-of-statements
  end select;

timed-entry-call =
  select
    entry-call [sequence-of-statements]
  or
    delay-statement [sequence-of-statements]
  end select;

chapter 21

Exceptions

— error handling

Errors may occur in any program and may be the result of several different factors. The author of a program may make programming errors that are not syntactic in nature (and are therefore not discovered by the compiler). One very common error of this type is indexing an array beyond its defined bounds, which almost always results in incorrect actions when the program is run.

Another common error is incorrect input by a human operator of a program. For example, if a program requests an integer value in the range 1 . . 20 and an operator responds with the value 30, what is the program to do? One choice (the wrong one) is to use the data as though it were valid. Another is to always verify that such input is always within the proper bounds. Invalid data should be rejected.

Some programs may be able to detect inconsistencies in internal data and act upon them. Hardware failure is also a plausible source of many errors.

Whatever their source, most errors cannot be ignored (or they wouldn't be errors) and the program must respond by taking some action to correct the error or abort the program. For example, a space shuttle pilot would be less than happy to learn that an arithmetic overflow has just caused shutdown of the navigational computer systems 60 seconds into re-entry. The software (and hardware) for such critical systems must be as robust as possible—able to continue functioning in spite of fairly serious errors. But what mechanism should be used to report and handle hardware failures, or data inconsistencies, or improper input, or programming-related errors? In Ada, the mechanism is the *exception* and associated *exception handler*.

The designers of Ada defined the exception mechanism as a consistent approach to all kinds of error conditions. The philosophy behind the design of exceptions dictates that exceptions are not to be used in situations that may be considered normal program operation; they are intended to be used to report and handle unusual errors that are not expected to occur when a program is executing properly. Of course, the meaning of "normal" is somewhat subjective and programmers should exercise good judgment in the use of exceptions. The reasons for this approach will become clearer as we discuss exceptions in detail.

21.1 PREDEFINED EXCEPTIONS

There are several exceptions that are predefined by the language specification. These predefined exceptions are language-related errors that are detected at runtime and that are very useful during program development, especially the debugging cycle. The most familiar of these runtime errors, a numeric error, is usually detected by the processor on which an Ada program runs. For example, a numeric error occurs when a program attempts to divide by zero or when overflow occurs in a numeric operation such as addition. The Ada identifier numeric_error is used to refer to the numeric error exception. Reporting an exception is called *raising* the exception. An Ada compiler generates code that is responsible for raising the exception "numeric_error" when the processor detects such errors. (Since not all processors detect and report such errors, not all implementations of Ada are able to support this exception in precisely the same manner. Programmers should refer to the reference manual for the specific implementation of Ada that they use to determine how numeric_error is treated in their implementation.)

Several other exceptions are predefined in the language, including constraint_error, program_error, storage_error, and tasking_error. Of these, most programmers will encounter only constraint_error and possibly storage_error. More detail is given below.

constraint_error   In general, this exception is raised when a program violates some form of constraint, including range constraints, index constraints, or discriminant constraints. Some examples:

```
x: integer range 1..20;
a: array(1..10) of integer;
...
x := 30;
        -- constraint_error is raised if
        -- this assignment is attempted
x := a(x);
        -- constraint_error will be raised if:
        --    value of x not in range 1..10; or
        --    value of a(x) not in range 1..20
```

In addition, Ada compilers generate code to raise constraint_error if a program attempts to reference through an access object whose value is null.

program_error   This exception is a catch-all for a number of semantic errors that may be detected at runtime; the most likely cause is when none of the alternatives of a select statement are open. (It follows that the select statement had no else alternative.) Implementations may cause program_error to be raised if other erroneous conditions are detected, such as the use of uninitialized variables.

storage_error   This exception is raised when there is insufficient storage available to satisfy the runtime requirements of a program. This error is detected at runtime and is normally raised when there is not enough storage to satisfy a request made by an allocator.

tasking_error   This exception may be raised if an error occurs during attempts at inter-task communication. For example, tasking_error is raised if a task calls another task and the called task completes before the entry call is accepted.

The raise statement can be used to explicitly raise an exception. For example

```
raise numeric_error;
```

causes the predefined exception numeric_error to be raised when the statement is executed.

21.2   EXCEPTION HANDLERS

At this point we know about certain exceptions that are automatically reported or raised in Ada programs, but we don't know how to take any action based on the occurrence of an exception. This is called *handling* the exception and, not surprisingly, is written in Ada using exception handlers. An exception handler specifies the exception(s) to be handled and the action to be taken for each exception. Exception handlers may appear at the end of four different program units: a **begin . . . end** block or the body of a subprogram, package or task. Consider this example:

```
procedure exc_demo is
  x: integer range 1..20;
begin
  x := 43;
  x := 10;
exception
  when constraint_error =>
    put("Constraint Error Exception!!");
  when others =>
    put("Other Exception");
end;
```

The list of exception handlers is introduced by the keyword **exception**. The introduction of the exception handlers constitutes the normal end of the sequence of statements in the enclosing unit; that is, if no exception occurs during execution of the unit, the unit is exited when the keyword **exception** is reached just as though the exception handlers had not been present.

A particular exception handler begins with the keyword **when** and ends with the last statement in the sequence of statements following the => token. When the last statement of the exception handler is executed, the unit containing the exception handler is terminated.

When an exception occurs while executing the statements of a unit, none of the statements following the statement in which the exception occurred are executed. The execution of the corresponding exception handler *replaces* the remaining statements of the unit. In the contrived example above, this means that the second statement in procedure exc_handler will never be executed because the first statement will always raise constraint_error.

In a manner analogous to the case statement, the keyword **others** may be used alone and last in the list of exception handlers in order to handle any exceptions that have not been named in previous exception handlers.

21.3   EXCEPTION PROPAGATION

When an exception is raised in a unit that does not define a handler for that exception, execution of the unit is terminated and the exception is *propagated* to a unit that does contain the appropriate handler. Consider the following example.

```
procedure exc_demo is

   procedure raise_exc is
   begin
     put("    raise_exc");
     raise constraint_error;
     -- no exception handler here
     -- exception is propagated to caller
   end;

   procedure handle_exc is
   begin
     put("  handle_exc");
     raise_exc;
     -- more code here
   exception
     when constraint_error =>
       put("  constraint_error in handle_exc");
   end;

begin
   put("exc_demo: calling handle_exc");
   handle_exc;
   put("exc_demo: back from handle_exc");
exception
   when constraint_error =>
     put("  constraint_error in exc_demo");
end exc_example;
```

When this contrived example is executed, the procedure handle_exc calls raise_exc which raises constraint_error. However, raise_exc has no handler for constraint_error and the exception is propogated to the caller of raise_exc (namely, handle_exc). Since handle_exc does have a handler for constraint_error, the handler replaces the execution of any statements that follow the call to raise_exc. The program will output the following:

```
exc_demo: calling handle_exc
   handle_exc
     raise_exc
   constraint_error in handle_exc
exc_demo: back from handle_exc
```

This simple example illustrates the general principle of exception propagation: an exception is always propagated to the most recently activated exception handler. The phrase "most recently activated" is used with reference to the execution of statements at runtime; that is, when execution of the program enters the scope of an exception handler, that exception handler is *active*.

If an exception handler for constraint_error is defined in a **begin ... end** block inside a procedure that also defines a handler for con straint_error, then the proper exception handler is chosen based upon the statement that raises constraint_error.

```
procedure many_handlers (first_handler: boolean) is

   procedure might_raise_exc (should_raise_exc: boolean) is
   begin
     if should_raise_exc then
       raise constraint_error;
     end if;
   end;

begin
  begin
    -- code here
    might_raise_exc (first_handler);
    -- more code here
  exception
    when constraint_error =>
      put ("constraint_error in block");
  end;

  might_raise_exc (not first_handler);

exception
  when constraint_error =>
    put ("constraint_error in main body");
  when others =>
    put ("other exception in main body");
end;
```

When a **begin ... end** block containing an exception handler is entered, the exception handler is active as discussed above. Thus, if an exception occurs within the scope of the block, it may be handled by the block's exception handler and any statements remaining in the block are replaced by the statements in the corresponding exception handler. This occurs if we write:

```
many_handlers (first_handler => true);
```

With respect to exceptions, we should view execution of a **begin ... end** block as we do execution of a called procedure. If an exception is raised that has no corresponding exception handler in the block, the exception is propagated ''outward'' until an appropriate execution handler is found. In the example above, if an exception other than constraint_error were raised in the scope of the block, it would be propagated to the others handler in the main body of many_handlers. If we write:

```
many_handlers(first_handler => false);
```

no exception will be raised until execution of the block has completed. Thus, the exception handler in the block is no longer active and the exception generated by might_raise_exc is handled in the main body of many_handlers.

A special form of the raise statement can be used inside exception handlers to re-raise the exception currently being handled. This is especially useful when the name of the exception being handled is not known (as in an exception handler specifying the exception choice **others**). Consider this example:

```
begin
...
-- allocate some resource which
-- shouldn't be permanently
-- allocated
...
exception
  when others =>
    -- code might be here to clean up
    -- resources that were allocated
    -- in the enclosing unit
    raise;   -- re-raise exception
             -- being processed
end;
```

The unit in which an exception handler like the one above might appear probably doesn't care which exception has been raised. It may only be necessary to clean up so that the program can maintain consistent state information about allocated resources.

An exception which is re-raised in this manner is propagated to the next exception handler using the rules defined above. Of course, it makes no sense to re-raise an exception outside of an exception handler and this form of the raise statement is illegal except within an exception handler.

If an exception is propagated to the main body of a program and no exception handler is found at that point, the program is terminated. If an exception is propagated to the main body of a task and no exception handler is found, the task completes. This last action ensures that an error local to a task does not cause termination of an entire program.

The Ada language specification allows different implementations of composite-type **out** parameters of subprograms. This freedom can cause problems when arrays or records are used as out parameters in a program which also uses exceptions. Consider the following example.

```
procedure propagation_demo is
   type rec is
     record
       a,b: integer;
     end record;

   x: rec;

   procedure parameter_problem(m: out rec) is
   begin
     -- code sequence 1
     m.a := 4;
     -- code sequence 2
     m.a := 5;
     -- code sequence 3
   end;

begin
   x := (1, 2);
   parameter_problem(x);
end propagation_demo;
```

If an exception occurs during any code sequence, the value of the object x is indeterminate; however, only composite type parameters are affected by this problem. The value of a scalar or access type object passed as an out parameter always retains the value prior to a call of a subprogram in which an exception occurs. Any program that depends on the implementation of out parameters is erroneous. Therefore, it is important that the effect of exceptions be carefully considered during program design.

Ada has been carefully designed so that the work of handling exceptions can be placed entirely on the exception propagation mechanism, and little or no overhead is necessary during normal execution. This means that the programmer doesn't need to be afraid of defining ''too many'' exception handlers. On the other hand, the exception mechanism was designed for handling truly unusual conditions, and exceptions should not be used to handle conditions expected to occur during normal operation of a program. Placing the burden of exceptions on the propagation mechanism means that a great deal of overhead may be incurred when an exception is propagated.

21.4   EXCEPTION DECLARATIONS

In addition to the predefined exceptions discussed previously, the programmer is allowed to define new exceptions. This is done using an exception declaration as in these examples:

```
table_full: exception;
illegal_data: exception;
stack_overflow, stack_underflow: exception;
```

Programmer-defined exceptions behave in precisely the same manner as the predefined exceptions: exception handlers, propagation, and the raise statement are identical. In fact, the predefined exceptions are described using ordinary exception declarations:

```
numeric_error: exception;
constraint_error: exception;
program_error: exception;
storage_error: exception;
tasking_error: exception;
```

The only thing different about these exceptions is that an Ada compiler knows about them and automatically generates checks that can result in raising them.

The scope of an exception name is the same as the scope of other identifiers in a declaration. Since this implies that exception names are not visible everywhere in a program, the form of the raise statement used in an exception handler to re-raise the current exception is even more important. One can easily envision program structures in which exception names are not always visible. Consider the following example.

```
with ada_io; use ada_io;
procedure exception_scope_demo is
   e: exception; ←──────────────────────────────────────┐
                                                         │
   procedure p is                                        │
   begin                                                 │
     raise e;      -- means "exception_scope_demo.e"     │
   end;                                                  │
                                                         │
   procedure q is                                        │
      e: exception; ←───────────────────────────┐        │
   begin                                         │        │
     p;                                          │        │
   exception                                     │        │
     when e =>    -- means local exception "e"───┘        │
       put("handler for q.e");                            │
       new_line;                                          │
   end;                                                   │
                                                          │
 begin                                                    │
   q;                                                     │
 exception                                                │
   when e =>       -- means first exception "e"───────────┘
     put("handler for exception_scope_demo.e");
     new_line;
 end exception_scope_demo;
```

Since the scope of an exception name is the same as any other object name, this program prints "handler for exception_scope_demo.e." Exceptions are propagated through the dynamic chain of calls created by the execution of a program, but the exception to which a particular name refers is determined by the static appearance of the program text. The dynamic call chain up to the raise statement in procedure p is given below.

```
exception_scope_demo
  q
    p    -- raises "e"
```

Since procedure p does not have a handler for exception e, the exception is propagated to the caller (procedure q in the example). Procedure q does have a handler for an exception named e, but the name e referred to by q is not the same e referenced in p. Therefore, the exception is propagated again, this time to procedure exception_scope_demo. Another handler for e is found. This handler is the correct handler because the name e refers to the exception e which is visible in the scope of procedure p as well. This discussion should motivate the programmer to try to provide unique names for exceptions whenever possible.

21.5   FORMAL SYNTAX

Declaration and statement are updated to include exception-declaration and raise-statement, respectively.

```
declaration =
    object-declaration              -- Chapter 5
  | subprogram-declaration          -- Chapter 7
  | package-declaration             -- Chapter 8
  | use-clause                      -- Chapter 8
  | type-declaration                -- Chapter 9
  | subtype-declaration             -- Chapter 9
  | deferred-constant-declaration   -- Chapter 17
  | generic-declaration             -- Chapter 19
  | generic-instantiation           -- Chapter 19
  | task-declaration                -- Chapter 20
  | exception-declaration

exception-declaration =
    identifier-list : exception ;

exception-handler =
    when exception_choice {| exception_choice} =>
        sequence-of-statements

exception_choice =
    exception-name | others

statement =
    assignment-statement            -- Chapter 6
  | if-statement                    -- Chapter 6
  | case-statement                  -- Chapter 6
  | loop-statement                  -- Chapter 6
  | exit-statement                  -- Chapter 18
  | null-statement                  -- Chapter 6
  | procedure-call-statement        -- Chapter 7
  | return-statement                -- Chapter 7
  | labeled-loop-statement          -- Chapter 18
  | block-statement                 -- Chapter 18
  | goto-statement                  -- Chapter 18
  | entry-call-statement            -- Chapter 20
  | accept-statement                -- Chapter 20
  | delay-statement                 -- Chapter 20
  | abort-statement                 -- Chapter 20
  | select-statement                -- Chapter 20
  | raise-statement

raise-statement = raise [exception-name] ;

exception-name = name
```

Also, block-statement and subprogram, package, and task bodies are altered to include exception-handlers.

```
block-statement =
    [identifier :]
    [declare declarative-part]
    begin
        sequence-of-statements
    exception
        exception-handler
        {exception-handler}
    end [simple-name] ;

subprogram-body =
    subprogram-specification is
        declarative-part
    begin
        sequence-of-statements
    exception
        exception-handler
        {exception-handler}
    end [designator];

package-body =
    package body simple-name is
        declarative-part
    [begin
        sequence-of-statements
    exception
        exception-handler
        {exception-handler}]
    end [simple-name] ;

task-body =
    task body simple-name is
        [declarative-part]
    begin
        sequence-of-statements
    exception
        exception-handler
        {exception-handler}
    end [simple-name] ;
```

chapter 22

Program structure and separate compilation

In order to facilitate structured programming in general and programming-in-the-large (development of large, complex programs by many programmers) in particular, the Ada language includes powerful features that allow a program to be compiled in one or more pieces. As with much of Ada, the primary motivation behind these features is the effort to reduce the cost of developing and maintaining large complex programs (which should appeal to most organizations involved in software development).

The structure of an Ada program is defined by several different language features. The most important feature related to program structure, the package, has already been discussed (see Chapter 8). In general, packages are used to hide the implementation of a data structure or to group a set of logically related subprograms. Subprograms (Chapter 7) are the means whereby a programmer defines an algorithm (a set of logically related statements). Tasks (Chapter 20) are the unit of parallel execution. Generics (Chapter 19) define templates for packages or subprograms.

An Ada program is a collection of these *program units*. The simplest program consists of a single subprogram, while the most complex may include many instances of subprograms, packages, and tasks. When combinations of these program units are used to create a program, a single subprogram is designated the *main program* in the usual sense of this phrase and all other program units depend (in some way) on this main program.

Fortunately, not all of the program units that make up a complex program need be submitted to the Ada compiler in a single giant compilation. Ada permits separate compilation of several language elements. Apportioning the work involved in a large software project is greatly simplified by separate compilation since distinct program units (usually corresponding to packages) can be assigned to programmers for independent development.

Packages and subprograms may be compiled separately from the program units that use them and included in a *program library* that can be made available to subsequent compilations. Further, package and subprogram bodies may be compiled independently of the corresponding specifications. Ada also permits separate compilation of generics, which may also be included in a program library. Task bodies may also be compiled independently of the corresponding specifications. Each of these separately compilable language elements may be submitted to the compiler as a distinct *compilation unit*.

A program library is a collection of compilation units usually intended to support a single application. For example, a program library supporting a radar tracking system might include packages containing several trigonometric functions, display management routines, operator interface routines, and an aircraft identification and routing database manager.

The Ada compiler inserts a unit into the library when the unit is compiled. This is sufficient for most programmers, but special facilities for manipulating libraries are required. The langauge does not define the facilities used to support maintenance of program libraries, except to state that there must be some basic operations that apply to individual library units (such as insert, delete, update, and list). Programmers should refer to the reference manual for the local Ada compiler to determine how to use the library maintenance facilities.

22.1   CONTEXT SPECIFICATIONS

The *library units* (packages, subprograms, and so on) contained in a program library are not automatically visible to a compilation unit. As was briefly mentioned in Chapter 8, Packages, in order to make one of the units in the library visible, it is necessary to specify its name in a *context specification*. For example, in order to use the put and get I/O functions, the programmer must use the following context specification:

```
with ada_io;
```

which instructs the Ada compiler to retrieve the specification for package ada_io from the program library and make it visible. Using the context specification just given, references to routines in ada_io must use the dot notation to reference names in the package interface. For example,

```
ada_io.put("Don't forget the package name!");
```

In order to make the symbols directly visible, the context specification optionally may include a use clause:

```
with ada_io; use ada_io;
```

The use clause was presented in the discussion on packages (Chapter 8) and its meaning in this context is the same.

The context specification precedes the main body of the compilation unit as in this example (recall Chapter 2):

```
with ada_io; use ada_io;
procedure double is
   x,y: integer;
begin
   get(x);             -- read a number
   y := x * 2;         -- multiply it by 2
   put(y);             -- print the result
   new_line;           -- skip to next line
end double;
```

Several library unit names may appear in a single with clause (separated by commas). Several with clauses may appear in the context specification, each of which may include the optional use clause. If a library unit is mentioned more than once, the effect is as though it had been mentioned only once.

If a with clause mentions a library unit that is a subprogram, the subprogram may be called from the compilation unit affected by the with clause. If a with clause mentions a library unit that is a generic, then instances of that generic may be instantiated in the compilation unit containing the with clause.

When a compilation unit mentions a library unit in its context specification, then that compilation unit is said to be *dependent* on the library unit. It is not necessary for a compilation unit to mention any library units that it does not itself use. That is, if a library unit is mentioned in the context specification of a compilation and the library unit is dependent on a third library unit, it is not necessary for the compilation unit to mention that third library unit unless it requires that unit. Consider the following example:

```
package cipher is
   type cipher_value is private;
   function encrypt(str: string) return cipher_value;
   function decrypt(val: cipher-value) return string;
private
   type cipher_value is ... ;
end cipher;
```

```
package body cipher is
  -- code for cipher
end cipher;
```

```
with cipher, ada_io, text_handler;
function password_verified(user: string) return boolean is
              -- read password and verify that
              -- it is correct for the given
              -- user name
  password: text_handler.text;   -- recall Chapter 11
  proper_password: cipher.cipher_value;
begin
  ada_io.put("password: ");
  text_handler.get(password);

  -- read password file and get
  -- proper (encrypted) password

  return encrypt(password.value) = proper_password;
end password_verified;
```

```
with ada_io, text_handler, password_verified;
procedure command_processor is
  user_name: text_handler.text;
begin
  loop
    ada_io.put("login: ");
    ada_io.get(user_name);      -- get a text object
    exit when password_verified(user_name.value); -- pass
                                                    -- a string
  end loop;

  loop
    -- read a command
    -- execute it
  end loop;
end command_processor;
```

This example illustrates the relationship between several different kinds of
compilation units. (In the example, the dashed lines represent the division of
the text in the example into potentially separate compilation units.) In particular, the procedure command_processor does not require use of package
cipher as password_verified does, so it is not necessary for cipher
to be mentioned in the context specification for command_processor.

In addition, package ada_io is required by password_verified and command_processor, but cipher is not dependent on any other library unit. Figure 22-1 graphically illustrates these dependencies.

Notice that the body of a package may be compiled separately from the corresponding specification. The items declared in the package specifications are visible within the separately compiled body. In the example above, the type cipher_value is visible within the separately compiled body of the package cipher.

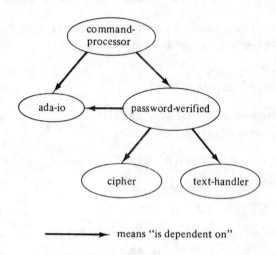

means "is dependent on"

Figure 22-1. Dependencies in the Command_Processor example.

22.2 SUBUNITS

The body of a subprogram, package, or task can be extracted from within a larger scope and separately compiled. Such a body is called a *subunit* of the compilation unit in which the subunit is declared. Consider the following program fragments:

```
with ada_io; use ada_io;
procedure visibility_demo is
   factor: integer := 3;
   function multiply(n: integer) return integer is separate;
begin
   put(multiply(7));
end visibility_demo;
```

```
separate(visibility_demo)          -- mention parent unit
function multiply(n: integer) return integer is
begin
    put("In body of multiply");    -- ada_io visible
    return factor * n;             -- factor visible
end multiply;
```

Within the procedure visibility_demo, the body of the function multiply is represented by a *body stub*, indicated by the keyword **separate** in place of the body of the function. The separately compiled function multiply is preceded by the keyword **separate** and the name of the *parent unit* (that is, the name of the compilation unit in which the corresponding body stub appears).

The important fact about subunits is that the visibility of names in the subunit corresponds to the visibility at the point where the body stub is declared in the parent unit. This means that objects, types, or subprograms declared before the body stub will be visible in the subunit, but anything declared following the body stub is not visible—just as though the body were given in the parent unit. In this respect, the semantics of subunits is similar to the semantics of the "include file" as defined by many compilers for other languages.

Within the body of the separately compiled function multiply, the construct

```
separate(visiblity_demo)
```

makes the package ada_io and the variable factor visible because those names existed at the point where the body stub was declared.

A subunit is a compilation unit and may be preceded by a context specification. The context specification of a subunit may mention library units not mentioned in the parent unit; however, as indicated in the previous paragraph, it need not mention any library unit given in the parent's context specification.

Package bodies and task bodies may also be separately compiled by writing body stubs (the reserved word **separate**) in place of corresponding bodies and giving the **separate** parent unit with the text of the body. Since subunits are compilation units, nothing prohibits writing subunits which themselves have subunits and so on. The programmer should use common sense when building programs with complex separate compilation structures.

22.3   COMPILATION

When an Ada compiler is executed, the programmer supplies the text of the compilation unit(s) to be compiled and an optional program library. The language specification does not define the manner in which this information is passed to the compiler; this action is implementation specific. Since it is intended that there be only one library associated with a compilation, most development projects will involve management of a single application library. There is no restriction on libraries whose contents overlap; that is, two or more libraries may contain the same library unit. Library management is the responsibility of the development organizations and is not covered by the Ada language.

In addition to the text of declarations, statements, and so on, program source text may include compiler directives called *pragmas*. Pragmas are used to affect various aspects of the compilation process, including generation of constraint checks, null access checks, and composite type storage compaction. The pragmas predefined by the language are discussed in Appendix VII.

Since program units are often dependent on other program units, Ada defines several simple rules governing the order in which related program units are compiled.

1. A program unit must be compiled *after* any program units listed in any of its with clauses.
2. The body of a subprogram or package must be compiled *after* the declaration of the subprogram or package.
3. A program unit that has subunits must be compiled *before* any of the subunits.

These rules are intended to maintain the consistency of the visibility rules and do not refer specifically to separate compilation, but rather to compilation in general. The programmer is free to compile program units in any order that does not violate these rules.

Re-compilations are subject to similar rules.

1. A subunit may be affected by changes in its parent unit.
2. Any changes in the program library may affect compilation units that mention the changed portions of the library.

If a given implementation is able to determine that a unit that has been changed will not actually affect a compilation unit dependent on that unit, then re-compilation may not be necessary.

22.4   FORMAL SYNTAX

The syntax for the language elements discussed in this chapter is given as
follows. Note that the production body is updated to include a body-stub.

```
compilation = {compilation-unit}

compilation-unit =
      context_specification subprogram-declaration
   |  context_specification subprogram-body
   |  context_specification package-declaration
   |  context_specification package-body
   |  context_specification generic-declaration
   |  context_specification subunit

context-specification =
      {with-clause [use-clause]}

with-clause =
      with simple-name {, simple-name} ;

subunit =
      separate (simple-name) subprogram-body
      separate (simple-name) package-body
      separate (simple-name) task-body

body =
      subprogram-body          -- Chapter 7
   |  package-body             -- Chapter 8
   |  task-body                -- Chapter 20
   |  body-stub

body-stub =
      subprogram-specification is separate;
   |  package body simple-name is separate;
   |  task body simple-name is separate;
```

Appendices

appendix I
Sample Ada programs

This Appendix contains several simple Ada programs intended to provide the reader with some additional examples of the use of Ada:

I.1   RANDOM NUMBER GENERATOR

```
-- this package contains a single function "next" which
-- returns a (sort of) random integer value
-- there are far better random number generators,
-- but this one is very simple, and is required
-- by a couple of examples in the text.
package random_integer is
   function next return integer is
end random_integer;

package random_integer is
   x: integer := 737;      -- this is why it's a package, this value
                           -- is used to generate random values
   function next return integer is
      n: integer;
   begin
      x := x * 29 + 37;  -- perform random operations
      n := x;            -- save result
      x := x mod 1000;   -- insure that next multiply doesn't overflow
      return n;          -- return result
   end next;
end random_integer;
```

I.2   SORTING

```
-- this generic sort routine uses the popular "quicksort"
-- algorithm, which partitions the array and calls itself
-- recursively on both partitions
generic
   type elem is private;
   type vector is array(integer range <>) of elem;
   with function ">"(x, y: elem) return boolean;
procedure sort(v: in out vector);

procedure sort(v: in out vector) is
   i: integer := v'first;
   j: integer := v'last;
   x: elem := v((i+j)/2);
   procedure swap is new exchange(elem);
begin
   while i <= j loop              -- loop until partitioned
      while x > v(i) loop         -- find left-most one out of order
         i :- i + 1;
      end loop;
      while v(j) > x loop         -- find right-most one out of orde
         j := j - 1;
      end loop;
      if i <= j then
         swap(v(i), v(j));        -- swap out of order elements
         i := i + 1;
         j := j - 1;
      end if;
   end loop;
   if v'first < j then
      sort(v(v'first..j));        -- recursive call on left partitio
   end if;
   if i < v'last then
      sort(v(i..v'last));         -- recursive call on right partiti
end sort;
```

I.3   GENERIC STACK MANAGER

```ada
-- generic package to implement a stack of objects of type elem --
-- subprograms: push and pop                                    --
-- exceptions: overflow and underflow                           --
generic
  type elem is private;
package stack is
  procedure push (x: in elem);
  procedure pop(x: out elem);
  overflow, underflow: exception;
end stack;

package body stack is
  subtype srange is integer range 1..100; -- determines size of stack
  s: array(srange) of elem;               -- stack
  sp: srange := s' first;                 -- stack index

  procedure push (x: in elem) is          -- push elem on stack
  begin
    s(sp) := x;
    sp := sp + 1;           -- possible constraint error here
  exception
    when constraint_error =>
      raise overflow;       -- constraint error must be overflow
  end push;

  procedure pop(x: out elem) is
  begin
    sp := sp - 1;           -- possible constraint error here
    x := s(sp);
  exception
    when constraint_error =>
      raise underflow;      -- constraint error must be underflow
  end pop;
end stack;
```

I.4   SIMPLE CALCULATOR

```ada
-- stack oriented desk calculator
with text_io; use text_io;
with stack;
procedure calculator is
  package int_io is new integer_io(integer);
  package istack is new stack(integer);    -- integers only
  use int_io, istack;
  ch: character;
  done: exception;

  function getint(first_digit: character) return integer is
    n: integer := 0;
    ch: character := first_digit;
  begin
    loop
      n := n * 10 + character'pos(ch) - character'pos('0');
      exit when end_of_line;
      get(ch);
    end loop;
    return n;
  end;

  procedure process_command(ch: character) is
    a, b: integer;
  begin
    case ch is
      when '0'..'9' =>            -- number
        push(getint(ch));
      when 'p' | 'P' =>           -- print
        pop(a);
        put(a);
        new_line;
      when '-' =>                 -- subtract
        pop(a);
        pop(b);
        push(b - a);
      when '+' =>                 -- add
        pop(a);
        pop(b);
        push(b + a);
      when 'q' | 'Q' =>           -- quit
        raise done;
      when others =>
        put_line("bad command");
    end case;
```

```
   exception
     when overflow =>
       put_line ("stack overflow");
     when underflow =>
       put_line ("stack underflow");
   end process_command;

begin
   loop
     put (">  ");
     get (ch);
     process_command (ch);
     skip_line;
   end loop;
exception
   when done =>
     skip_line;
end calculator;
```

appendix II

Notes for Pascal programmers

The design of Ada is based, at least in part, on Pascal and since there are an increasing number of Pascal programmers, this appendix has been prepared to acquaint the Pascal programmer/reader with similar Ada constructs, accelerating the Pascal programmer's acquisition of Ada. The sections in this appendix have the same titles as the corresponding chapters in the main text. Particularly where some of the more advanced Ada constructs are concerned, no corresponding Pascal analogy exists and it is necessary to build on knowledge of Ada already acquired. The *Pascal User Manual and Report* by Kathleen Jensen and Nicklaus Wirth is used as the basis for Pascal analogies.

CHAPTER 3, PREDEFINED TYPES AND OPERATIONS

The correspondences between the predefined types in Ada and Pascal are given by this table:

Ada	Pascal
integer	integer
boolean	boolean
character	char
float	real

CHAPTER 4, EXPRESSIONS

Ada's expressions provide a number of advanced features not available in Pascal. These features are described in the main text.

CHAPTER 5, OBJECT DECLARATIONS

Object declarations in Ada are similar to **var** declarations in Pascal. The major differences are the declaration of constants and the Ada extension which permits initialization of objects. The specific differences are:

1. The Pascal keyword **var** is not used in Ada object declarations.

2. Pascal has a separate syntax for constant declarations, while Ada constant declarations are simply a variation on object declarations.

3. Pascal does not permit initialization of variables in declarations.

4. In Pascal, the constant declarations must precede the variable declarations, while in Ada, the two may be interspersed.

The following examples illustrate these differences:

```
        Ada                             Pascal

x:  integer;                    const y = 1000;
y:  constant integer : = 1000;
z:  integer : = 73;             var x, z:  integer;
    .
    .
    .
    .                               .
begin                           begin
    .                             z : = 73;
    .                               .
    .
```

An Ada object initialization is equivalent to a Pascal declaration and an assignment at the start of the block to which the object is local. Constant declarations differ only in their syntax.

CHAPTER 6, BASIC ADA STATEMENTS

Assignment Statement

The syntax and semantics of Ada assignment statements are nearly identical to Pascal. Ada has some additional data structuring mechanisms that permit the programmer to name fairly complex items; however, for those types and structures that are the same, Ada and Pascal both use the same syntactic form for assignment.

If Statement

The differences between Pascal and Ada if statements are syntactic rather than semantic.

1. Pascal does not permit more than one statement to appear in any of the if clauses, although the use of the compound (**begin ... end**) statement permits the equivalent of the Ada sequence of statements.

2. Pascal does not provide an **elsif** syntax; however, the same effect can be achieved by the use of nested if statements. For example:

Ada	Pascal
if a < b then	if a < b then
a: = 1;	begin
b: = a;	a := 1;
elsif b < c then	b := a
b := 1;	end
else	else if b < c then
c := 1;	b := 1
end if;	else c := 1;

These two statements are equivalent in the respective languages.

3. Pascal does not use the **end if** token sequence to terminate an if statement.

Case Statement

The Pascal case statement is very similar to the Ada case statement, with a few important exceptions.

1. Pascal has no equivalent of the **others** clause.

2. In Pascal, a range may not be used as a case label.

3. In Pascal, the programmer need not provide an exhaustive list of choices and the effect is not defined if a choice is selected which is not listed. Ada requires that all choices for a given selector type be present.

4. Pascal uses the keyword **end**, rather than **end case**, to indicate the end of the final choice.

Loop Statements

There are a number of differences between the Ada loop statements and the corresponding Pascal statements, most of which are simply syntactic.

There are, however, some semantic differences in the for statement.

1. There is no basic loop in Pascal but it can be simulated with a label and a goto statement. The following examples are equivalent:

```
      Ada                      Pascal

loop                    1:
   --statements              (* statements *)
end loop;               goto 1;
```

The Pascal label ''1'' must be declared in the declaration part of the enclosing block.

2. The Ada while loop is identical to the Pascal while loop, except for minor syntactic variations.

3. The Ada for loop is different from the Pascal for loop in several ways:

- The Pascal for loop control variable must be local to the block in which the for loop apears. The Ada for loop control variable is declared by the for loop itself, and any other definition using the same name is hidden from the statements inside the for loop.

- There are several syntactic differences between Pascal and Ada for statements, as illustrated in these examples:

```
      Ada                         Pascal

for i in 1..n loop         for i := 1 to n
   -- statements                (* statements *);
end loop;
```

In addition, the use of the keyword reverse in Ada corresponds to the use of downto in Pascal.

4. There is no **exit** construct in Pascal. But it may be simulated with a goto and a label. The repeat construct in Pascal is equivalent to an Ada basic loop with an **exit when** as its last statement:

```
      Ada                         Pascal

loop                       repeat
   -- statements                (* statements *)
   exit when x < 10;         until x < 10;
end loop;
```

5. Pascal does not permit more than one statement to appear in the body of a loop, although the use of the compound (**begin . . . end**) statement per-

mits the equivalent of the Ada sequence of statements.

6. Ada uses the **end loop** token sequence to terminate a loop statement.

Null Statement

Pascal does not define an explicit null statement, although it is possible to specify an empty statement sequence. For example, the following fragments are equivalent:

```
       Ada                                    Pascal

while boolean_function loop            while boolean_function do;
   null;
end loop;
```

The readability of Ada is improved by the use of the null statement.

CHAPTER 7, SUBPROGRAMS

Pascal defines both procedure and function subprograms, using essentially the same semantics as Ada, although the syntax differs slightly. There is no return statement in Pascal, although the same effect can be achieved by an assignment to the function variable and a goto which transfers to the end of the procedure of function.

Pascal parameter access modes differ in subtle ways from those in Ada. Ada **in** parameters are similar to Pascal value parameters, but in Pascal a value parameter acts as a local temporary variable which can be assigned a value. Ada **in out** and **out** parameters are the same as Pascal var parameters except when an Ada subprogram terminates abnormally (more about this later).

Pascal does not permit default parameter values or named parameter passing.

CHAPTER 9, USER-DEFINED TYPES

Enumeration Types

Ada enumerations are quite similar to Pascal enumerations; however, a significant difference is that in Ada, all enumeration types must be declared in type statements. Pascal permits enumeration type definitions in VAR statements. For example,

```
var x: (red, yellow, blue);
```

is legal Pascal, but a similar declaration is not permitted in Ada.

Attributes

The Pascal intrinsics succ, pred, and ord are analogous to the Ada attributes succ, pred, and pos. The Pascal intrinsics are called directly with expressions of different types. In Ada, distinct functions for each type are named using the attribute notation. There is no Pascal intrinsic analogous to the Ada attribute val, although the instrinsic chr has the same effect for the Pascal type char. The following examples should clarify the differences:

Ada	Pascal
day_of_week'succ(wed)	succ(wed)
integer'pred(i)	pred(i)
day_of_week'pos(thu)	ord(thu)
day_of_week'val(4)	(* not allowed *)
character'val(5)	chr(5)

CHAPTER 10, ARRAY TYPES

Pascal arrays are equivalent to constrained arrays in Ada. Ada provides many more array handling facilities than does Pascal, but those facilities provided by Pascal are semantically the same as the corresponding Ada constructions. The differences are:

1. Ada uses parentheses for indexing, Pascal uses square brackets.

2. In Pascal, there is no difference between an array of arrays and a two-dimensional array. In Ada, these are different types.

3. Pascal has no slices, unconstrained arrays, or dynamic arrays.

4. Standard Pascal has no String types, although most implementations of Pascal provide some extension for string types.

Pascal's set types can be simulated in Ada using the logical operations defined on boolean arrays. The following program fragments give the Ada constructs that correspond to Pascal's set operations:

Ada	Pascal
| ```
type day_set is
  array(day_of_week) of boolean;
``` | ```
type day_set =
  set of day_of_we
``` |

Ada	Pascal
| ```
x,y: day_set;
...
x := (others => false);
x := (sat|sun => true, others => false);
x := (mon..fri => true, others => false);
x := x or y;
y := y and x;
if x(mon) then ...
``` | ```
var x,y: day_set;
...
x := [];
x := [sat, sun];
y := [mon..fri];
x := x + y;
y := y * x;
if mon in x then
``` |

Pascal's set notation is more concise, but Ada gives equivalent power without introducing any additional constructs into the language.

CHAPTER 11, RECORD TYPES

Pascal does not provide default field values or discriminants, but basic Pascal records are completely equivalent to Ada records. The major differences have to do with variant records. Ada's variant record facility provides a greater degree of protection against abuse of variant records. In Pascal, the case tag field is optional, so the variant record does not necessarily contain a value indicating which variant the record is. Ada requires that discriminant values always exist for a variant record, and a reference to a field in another variant causes a constraint error.

CHAPTER 12, ACCESS TYPES

Access types in Ada are very similar to pointer types in Pascal. The major differences are:

‾ 1. In Ada, each access type declaration creates a distinct type, even if the base types are compatible. In Pascal, two such types are compatible.

Ada	Pascal
| ```
-- incompatible
type p1 is access integer;
type p2 is access integer;
``` | ```
(* compatible *)
type p1 = ^integer;
type p2 = ^integer;
``` |

2. The Pascal intrinsic new provides essentially the same capabilities that Ada's allocators do. The major differences have to do with allocation of

variant records. In Ada, the allocation

```
p := new person(divorced);
```

constrains the allocated object to always be divorced. The Pascal allocation

```
new(p, divorced);
```

causes sufficient space to be allocated for a divorced person object, but does not constrain the object or initialize the variant tag field. Thus, it is possible to assign a complete record value to p^ which would not fit in the allocated space. Needless to say, this can cause grave problems. In Ada, no such problems are possible.

3. The ^ operator in Pascal is equivalent to the .all construct in Ada. However, in Pascal, the operation is always indicated explicitly:

```
    Ada              Pascal

p: pair_ptr;     var p:pair_ptr;
p                p
p.all            p^
p.b              p^.b
p.all.b          p^.b
```

CHAPTER 15, DERIVED TYPES

Pascal has no derived types. The declarations

```
type length = integer;
     area = integer;
```

are equivalent to Ada subtype declarations. They simply provide new names for the type integer and variables of these types may be freely mixed in expressions.

CHAPTER 18, MORE ON STATEMENTS

Pascal statement labels must be integers in the range 0 to 9999 and they must also be explicitly declared in the declaration part of the enclosing block. Ada statement labels may use any identifier and there is no requirement for declaration prior to use in a goto statement.

Pascal gotos may specify a jump out of the current subprogram; Ada gotos may not. Otherwise, the Pascal goto statement is identical to the Ada goto statement, syntactically and semantically.

appendix III

Syntactic definitions

III.1 EXPRESSIONS

name =
	character-literal	-- Chapter 3
		simple-name	-- Chapter 4
		indexed-component	-- Chapter 10
		slice	-- Chapter 10
		selected-component	-- Chapter 11
		attribute	-- Chapter 9
		operator-symbol	-- Chapter 13

simple-name = identifier

primary =
	name	-- Chapter 4
		numeric-literal	-- Chapter 4
		string-literal	-- Chapter 4
		(expression)	-- Chapter 4
		type-conversion	-- Chapter 4
		function-call	-- Chapter 7
		aggregate	-- Chapter 10
		null	-- Chapter 12
		allocator	-- Chapter 12
		qualified-expression	-- Chapter 15

type-conversion =
    type-name (expression)

type-name = name   -- like integer

expression =
        relation {**and** relation}
    | relation {**or** relation}
    | relation {**xor** relation}
    | relation {**and then** relation}
    | relation {**or else** relation)

relation =
    simple-expression [relational-op simple-expression]
    | simple-expression [**not**] **in** range

range =
    simple-expression .. simple-expression   -- Chapter 4
    | range-attribute   -- Chapter 10

simple-expression =
    [unary-op] term {adding-op term}

term =
    factor {multiplying-op factor}

factor =
    primary [** primary] | **abs** primary | **not** primary

relational-op =
    < | > | <= | >= | = | /=

adding-op =
    + | − | &

unary-op =
    + | −

multiplying-op =
    * | / | **rem** | **mod**

III.2   OBJECT DECLARATIONS

```
declaration =
    object-declaration              -- Chapter 5
    | subprogram-declaration        -- Chapter 7
    | package-declaration           -- Chapter 8
    | use-clause                    -- Chapter 8
    | type-declaration              -- Chapter 9
    | subtype-declaration           -- Chapter 9
    | deferred-constant-declaration -- Chapter 17
    | generic-declaration           -- Chapter 19
    | generic-instantiation         -- Chapter 19
    | task-declaration              -- Chapter 20
    | exception-declaration         -- Chapter 21

object-declaration =
    identifier-list :               -- Chapter 5
        [ constant ] type-indication
                        [ := expression ] ;
    | identifier-list :             -- Chapter 10
        [ constant ] constrained-array-definition
                        [ := expression ] ;

identifier-list = identifier { , identifier }

type-indication =
    type-name                        -- Chapter 4
    | type-name range-constraint     -- Chapter 9
    | type-name index-constraint     -- Chapter 10
    | type-name discriminant-constraint -- Chapter 11
    | type-name accuracy-constraint  -- Chapter 16
```

III.3   BASIC ADA STATEMENTS

```
sequence-of-statements =
    statement {statement}

statement =
    assignment-statement             -- Chapter 6
    | if-statement                   -- Chapter 6
    | case-statement                 -- Chapter 6
    | loop-statement                 -- Chapter 6
    | exit-statement                 -- Chapter 18
    | procedure-call-statement        -- Chapter 7
    | return-statement               -- Chapter 7
    | labeled-loop-statement         -- Chapter 18
    | null-statement                 -- Chapter 18
    | block-statement                -- Chapter 18
```

	goto-statement	-- Chapter 18
|	entry-call-statement	-- Chapter 20
|	accept-statement	-- Chapter 20
|	delay-statement	-- Chapter 20
|	abort-statement	-- Chapter 20
|	select-statement	-- Chapter 20
|	raise-statement	-- Chapter 21

assignment-statement =
    name := expression ;

if-statement =
    if boolean-condition **then**
      sequence-of-statements
    {**elsif** boolean-condition **then**
      sequence-of-statements}
    [**else** sequence-of-statements]
    end if ;

boolean-condition = expression

loop-statement = [iteration-clause] basic-loop ;

basic-loop =
    loop
      sequence-of-statements
    end loop

iteration-clause =
    for identifier **in** [**reverse**] discrete-range
    \| **while** boolean-condition

discrete-range =
    range   -- Chapter 6
    \| type-name [range-constraint]   -- Chapter 9

exit-statement =
    exit [**when** boolean-condition] ;

case-statement =
    case expression **is**
      {**when** choice {\| choice} =>
        sequence-of-statements}
    end case;

choice =
    static-simple-expression
    \| discrete-range
    \| **others**

null-statement = **null** ;

III.4   SUBPROGRAMS

```
subprogram-declaration =
    subprogram-specification ;

subprogram-specification =
    procedure identifier [formal-part]
  | function designator [formal-part]
        return type-indication

subprogram-body =
    subprogram-specification is
        declarative-part
    begin
        sequence-of-statements
    exception
        exception-handler
        {exception-handler}
    end [designator];

formal-part =
    ( parameter-declaration {; parameter-declaration} )

parameter-declaration =
    identifier list : mode type-name [:= expression]

mode = [ in ] | out | in out

designator =
    identifier              -- Chapter 7
  | operator-symbol         -- Chapter 13

declarative-part =
    { declaration }
    { body }

body =
        subprogram-body     -- Chapter 7
      | package-body        -- Chapter 8
      | task-body           -- Chapter 20
      | body-stub           -- Chapter 22

procedure-call-statement =
    procedure-name [actual-parameter-part] ;

procedure-name = name

return-statement =
    return [expression] ;

prefix =
    name                    -- Chapter 4
  | function-call           -- Chapter 7

function- call =
    function-name [actual-parameter-part]
```

function-name = name

actual-parameter-part =
    (parameter-association {, parameter-association })

parameter-association =
    [formal-parameter =>] actual-parameter

formal-parameter = simple-name

actual-parameter = expression

III.5   PACKAGES

selector =
    simple-name   -- Chapter 8
    | character-literal   -- Chapter 3
    | **all**   -- Chapter 12
    | operator-symbol   -- Chapter 13

package-declaration =
    package-specification ;

package-specification =
    package identifier **is**
        {declaration}
    [**private**
      {declaration}]
    end [simple-name]

package-body =
    package body simple-name **is**
        declarative-part
    [begin
        sequence-of-statements
    excepton
        exception-handler
        {exception-handler}]
    end [simple-name] ;

use-clause =
    use package-name { , package-name } ;

package-name = name

III.6   USER-DEFINED TYPES

```
type-declaration =
    type identifier is type-definition ;    -- Chapter 9
    | incomplete-type-declaration           -- Chapter 12
    | private-type-declaration              -- Chapter 17

type-definition =
    enumeration-type-definition             -- Chapter 9
    | array-type-definition                 -- Chapter 10
    | record-type-definition                -- Chapter 11
    | access-type-definition                -- Chapter 12
    | derived-type-definition               -- Chapter 15
    | real-type-definition                  -- Chapter 16

enumeration-type-definition =
    ( enumeration-literal {, enumeration-literal} )

enumeration-literal =
    identifier                              -- Chapter 9
    | character-literal                     -- Chapter 14

subtype-declaration =
    subtype identifier is type-indication ;

range-constraint =
    range simple-expression .. simple-expression

discrete-range =
    range                                   -- Chapter 6
    | type-name [range-constraint]

attribute =
    name ' attribute-designator

attribute-designator =
    simple-name
    | simple-name ( static-simple-expression)
```

III.7   ARRAY TYPES

```
array-type-definition =
    constrained-array-definition
    | unconstrained-array-definition

constrained-array-definition =
    array index-constraint of type-indication

index-constraint =
    ( discrete-range {, discrete-range} )

unconstrained-array-definition =
    array unconstrained-indices of type-indication
```

unconstrained-indices =
   (unconstrained-index {, unconstrained-index})

unconstrained-index =
   type-name **range** <>

indexed-component =
   prefix (expression {, expression})

slice = prefix (discrete-range)

aggregate =
   (component-association {, component-association})

component-association =
   [choice {| choice} =>] expression

III.8   RECORD TYPES

selected-component =
   prefix . selector

record-type-definition =
   record
     component-list
   end record

component-list =
   component-declaration {component-declaration}
  | {component-declaration} variant-part
  | **null** ;

component-declaration =
   identifier-list : type-indication [:= expression } ;

variant-part =
   case simple-name **is**
    variant
    {variant}
   end case

variant =
   when choice {| choice-list} =>
    component-list

discriminant-part =
   (discriminant-decl {; discriminant-decl})

discriminant-decl =
   identifier-list : type-name [:= expression]

discriminant-constraint =
   (discriminant-spec {, discriminant-spec})

discriminant-spec =
   [simple-name {| simple-name} =>] expression

III.9   ACCESS TYPES

access-type-definition =
    access type-indication

allocator =
    new type-name
    | **new** type-name index_constraint
    | **new** type-name discriminant-constraint
    |. **new** allocator-initialization

allocator-initialization =
    type-name ' (expression)
    | type-name ' aggregate

III.10   OPERATOR OVERLOADING

operator-symbol =
    string-literal

III.11   OVERLOADING ENUMERATION LITERALS

qualified-expression =
    type-name ' (expression)
    | type-name ' aggregate

III.12   DERIVED TYPES

derived-type-definition =
    new type-indication

III.13   REAL TYPES

real-type-definition = accuracy-constraint

accuracy-constraint =
    fixed-point-constraint
    | floating-point-constraint

fixed-point-constraint =
    delta static-simple-expression [range-constraint]

floating-point-constraint =
    digits static-simple-expression [range-constraint]

III.14   MORE ON PACKAGES

```
private-type-declaration =
    type identifier [discriminant-part] is
        [limited] private;
```

```
deferred-constant-declaration =
    identifier-list : constant type-name ;
```

III.15   MORE ON STATEMENTS

```
labeled-loop-statement =
    identifier :
        [iteration-clause] loop
            sequence-of-statements
        end loop simple-name ;
```

```
exit-statement =                        -- Chapter 6
    exit [when boolean-expression]
  | exit simple-name [when boolean-expression]
```

```
block-statement =
    [identifier :]
    [declare declarative-part]
    begin
        sequence-of-statements
    exception
        exception-handler
        {exception-handler}
    end [simple-name] ;
```

```
label = << identifier >>
```

```
goto-statement =
    goto simple-name ;
```

III.16   GENERICS

```
generic-declaration =
    generic-specification ;

generic-specification =
    generic-formal-part subprogram-specification
  | generic-formal-part package-specification

generic-formal-part =
    generic {generic-parameter-declaration}

generic-parameter-declaration =
    identifier-list : [in [out]] type-name [:expression} ;
  | type identifier [discriminant-part]
      is generic-type-definition
  | private-type-declaration
  | with subprogram-specification ;

generic-type-definition =
    (<>) | array-type-definition | access-type-definition

generic-instantiation =
    generic-package
  | generic-procedure
  | generic-function

generic-package =
    package identifier is
      new generic-package-name [generic-actual-part];

generic-package-name = name

generic-procedure =
    package identifier is
      new generic-procedure-name [generic-actual-part];

generic-procedure-name = name

generic-function =
    package identifier is
      new generic-function-name [generic-actual-part];

generic-function-name = name

generic-actual-part =
    ( generic-association {, generic-association} )

generic-association =
    [generic-formal-parameter =>] generic-actual-parameter

generic-formal-parameter =
    simple-name | operator-symbol

generic-actual-parameter =
    expression | name
```

III.17   TASKING

task-declaration =
  task-specification ;

task-specification =
  task [**type**] identifier [**is**
    {entry-declaration}
  end [simple-name]] ;

task-body =
  task body simple-name **is**
    [declarative-part]
  begin
    sequence-of-statements
  exception
    exception-handler
    {exception-handler}
  end [simple-name] ;

entry-declaration =
  entry identifier [formal-part] ;

entry-call-statement =
  entry-name [actual-parameter-part] ;

entry-name = name

accept-statement =
  accept simple-name [formal-part]
    [**do** sequence-of-statements
     end [simple-name]] ;

delay-statement =
  delay simple-expression;

abort-statement =
  abort task-name {, task-name} ;

select-statement =
  selective-wait
  | conditional-entry-call
  | timed-entry-call

selective-wait =
  select
    select-alternative
  {**or**
    select-alternative}
  [**else** sequence-of-statements]
  end select;

select-alternative =
  [**when** condition =>]
  alternative-action

alternative-action =
 accept-alternative
 | delay-alternative
 | terminate-alternative

accept-alternative =
 accept-statement [sequence-of-statements]

delay-alternative =
 delay-statement [sequence-of-statements]

terminate-alternative =
 alternative ;

conditional-entry-call =
 select
  entry-call [sequence-of-statements]
 else
  sequence-of-statements
 end select;

timed-entry-call =
 select
  entry-call [sequence-of-statements]
 or
  delay-statement [sequence-of-statements]
 end select;

III.18   EXCEPTIONS

exception-declaration =
 identifier-list : **exception** ;

exception_handler =
 when exception_choice {| exception_choice} =>
  sequence-of-statements

exception_choice =
 exception-name | **others**

exception-name = name

raise-statement = **raise** [exception-name] ;

III.19   PROGRAM STRUCTURE AND SEPARATE COMPILATION

compilation = {compilation-unit}

compilation-unit =
    context_specification subprogram-declaration
    | context_specification subprogram-body
    | context_specification package-declaration
    | context_specification package-body
    | context_specification generic-declaration
    | context_specification subunit

context-specification =
    {with-clause [use-clause]}

with-clause =
    with simple-name {, simple-name} ;

subunit =
    separate (simple-name) subprogram-body
    separate (simple-name) package-body
    separate (simple-name) task-body

body-stub =
    subprogram-specification **is separate;** |
    package body simple-name **is separate;** |
    task body simple-name **is separate;**

appendix IV

ASCII character representation

0 000 00	NUL		43 053 2B	+		86 126 56	V
1 001 01	SOH		44 054 2C	,		87 127 57	W
2 002 02	STX		45 055 2D	-		88 130 58	X
3 003 03	ETX		46 056 2E	.		89 131 59	Y
4 004 04	EOT		47 057 2F	/		90 132 5A	Z
5 005 05	ENG		48 060 30	0		91 133 5B	[
6 006 06	ACK		49 061 31	1		92 134 5C	\
7 007 07	BEL		50 062 32	2		93 135 5D	]
8 010 08	BS		51 063 33	3		94 136 5E	^
9 011 09	HT		52 064 34	4		95 137 5F	_
10 012 0A	LF		53 064 35	5		96 140 60	`
11 013 0B	VT		54 066 36	6		97 141 61	a
12 014 0C	FF		55 067 37	7		98 142 62	b
13 015 0D	CR		56 070 38	8		99 143 63	c
14 016 0E	SO		57 071 39	9		100 144 64	d
15 017 0F	S!		58 072 3A	:		101 145 65	e
16 020 10	DLE		59 073 3B	;		102 146 66	f
17 021 11	DC1		60 074 3C	<		103 147 67	g
18 022 12	DC2		61 075 3D	=		104 150 68	h
19 023 13	DC3		62 076 3E	>		105 151 69	i
20 024 14	DC4		63 077 3F	?		106 152 6A	j
21 025 15	NAK		64 100 40	@		107 153 6B	k
22 026 16	SYN		65 101 41	A		108 154 6C	l
23 027 17	ETB		66 102 42	B		109 155 6D	m
24 030 18	CAN		67 103 43	C		110 156 6E	n
25 031 19	EM		68 104 44	D		111 157 6F	o
26 032 1A	SUB		69 105 45	E		112 160 70	p
27 033 1B	ESC		70 106 46	F		113 161 71	q
28 034 1C	FS		71 107 47	G		114 162 72	r
29 035 1D	GS		72 110 48	H		115 163 63	s
30 036 1E	RS		73 111 49	I		116 164 74	t
31 307 1F	US		74 112 4A	J		117 165 75	u
32 040 20	SP		75 113 4B	K		118 166 76	v
33 040 21	!		76 114 4C	L		119 167 77	w
34 042 22	"		77 115 4D	M		120 170 78	x
35 043 23	#		78 116 4E	N		121 171 79	y
36 044 24	$		79 117 4F	O		122 172 7A	z
37 045 25	%		80 120 50	P		123 173 7B	{
38 046 26	&		81 121 51	Q		124 174 7C		
39 047 27	'		82 122 52	R		125 175 7D	}
40 050 28	(		83 123 53	S		126 176 6E	~
41 051 29	)		84 124 54	T		127 177 7F	DEL
42 052 2A	*		85 125 55	U			

appendix V
Lexical elements

2. Lexical Elements

The text of a program consists of the texts of one or more compilations. The text of a compilation   1
is a sequence of lexical elements, each composed of characters; the rules of composition are given
in this chapter. Pragmas, which provide certain information for the compiler, are also described in
this chapter.

References: character 2.1, compilation 10.1, lexical element 2.2, pragma 2.8   2

2.1 Character Set

The only characters allowed in the text of a program are the graphic characters and format effec-   1
tors. Each graphic character corresponds to a unique code of the *ISO* seven-bit coded character
set (*ISO* standard 646), and is represented (visually) by a graphical symbol. Some graphic
characters are represented by different graphical symbols in alternative national representations of
the *ISO* character set. The description of the language definition in this standard reference manual
uses the *ASCII* graphical symbols, the *ANSI* graphical representation of the *ISO* character set.

```
graphic_character ::= basic_graphic_character
    | lower_case_letter | other_special_character
```
                                                                                                  2

```
basic_graphic_character ::=
        upper_case_letter | digit
    |   special_character | space_character
```

```
basic_character ::=
        basic_graphic_character | format_effector
```

The basic character set is sufficient for writing any program. The characters included in each of the   3
categories of basic graphic characters are defined as follows:

(a) upper case letters   4
     A B C D E F G H I J K L M N O P Q R S T U V W X Y Z

(b) digits   5
     0 1 2 3 4 5 6 7 8 9

(c) · special characters
   " # & ' ( ) * + , - . / : ;· < = > _ |

(d) the space character

Format effectors are the *ISO* (and *ASCII*) characters called horizontal tabulation, vertical tabulation, carriage return, line feed, and form feed.

The characters included in each of the remaining categories of graphic characters are defined as follows:

(e) lower case letters
   a b c d e f g h i j k l m n o p q r s t u v w x y z

(f) other special characters
   ! $ % ? @ [\ ] ^ ` { } ~

Allowable replacements for the special characters vertical bar (|), sharp (#), and quotation (") are defined in section 2.10.

-*Notes:*

The *ISO* character that corresponds to the sharp graphical symbol in the *ASCII* representation appears as a pound sterling symbol in the French, German, and United Kingdom standard national representations. In any case, the font design of graphical symbols (for example, whether they are in italic or bold typeface) is not part of the *ISO* standard.

The meanings of the acronyms used in this section are as follows: *ANSI* stands for American National Standards Institute, *ASCII* stands for American Standard Code for Information Interchange, and *ISO* stands for International Organization for Standardization.

The following names are used when referring to special characters and other special characters:

symbol	name	symbol	name
"	quotation	>	greater than
#	sharp	_	underline
&	ampersand	|	vertical bar
'	apostrophe	!	exclamation mark
(	left parenthesis	$	dollar
)	right parenthesis	%	percent
*	star, multiply	?	question mark
+	plus	@	commercial at
,	comma	[	left square bracket
-	hyphen, minus	\	back-slash
.	dot, point, period	]	right square bracket
/	slash, divide	^	circumflex
:	colon	`	grave accent
;	semicolon	{	left brace
<	less than	}	right brace
=	equal	~	tilde

2.2 Lexical Elements, Separators, and Delimiters

The text of a program consists of the texts of one or more compilations. The text of each compilation is a sequence of separate lexical elements. Each lexical element is either a delimiter, an identifier (which may be a reserved word), a numeric literal, a character literal, a string literal, or a comment. The effect of a program depends only on the particular sequences of lexical elements that form its compilations, excluding the comments, if any.

In some cases an explicit *separator* is required to separate adjacent lexical elements (namely, when without separation, interpretation as a single lexical element is possible). A separator is any of a space character, a format effector, or the end of a line. A space character is a separator except within a comment, a string literal, or a space character literal. Format effectors other than horizontal tabulation are always separators. Horizontal tabulation is a separator except within a comment.

The end of a line is always a separator. The language does not define what causes the end of a line. However if, for a given implementation, the end of a line is signified by one or more characters, then these characters must be format effectors other than horizontal tabulation. In any case, a sequence of one or more format effectors other than horizontal tabulation must cause at least one end of line.

One or more separators are allowed between any two adjacent lexical elements, before the first of each compilation, or after the last. At least one separator is required between an identifier or a numeric literal and an adjacent identifier or numeric literal.

A *delimiter* is either one of the following special characters (in the basic character set)

    & ' ( ) * + , - . / : ; < = > |

or one of the following *compound delimiters* each composed of two adjacent special characters

    => .. ** := /= >= <= << >> <>

Each of the special characters listed for single character delimiters is a single delimiter except if this character is used as a character of a compound delimiter, or as a character of a comment, string literal, character literal, or numeric literal.

The remaining forms of lexical element are described in other sections of this chapter.

Notes:

Each lexical element must fit on one line, since the end of a line is a separator. The quotation, sharp, and underline characters, likewise two adjacent hyphens, are not delimiters, but may form part of other lexical elements.

The following names are used when referring to compound delimiters:

delimiter	name
=>	arrow
..	double dot
**	double star, exponentiate
:=	assignment (pronounced: "becomes")
/=	inequality (pronounced: "not equal")
>=	greater than or equal
<=	less than or equal
<<	left label bracket
>>	right label bracket
<>	box

References: character literal 2.5, comment 2.7, compilation 10.1, format effector 2.1, identifier 2.3, numeric literal 2.4, reserved word 2.9, space character 2.1, special character 2.1, string literal 2.6

2.3 Identifiers

Identifiers are used as names and also as reserved words.

    identifier ::=
       letter ([underline] letter_or_digit)

    letter_or_digit ::= letter | digit

    letter ::= upper_case_letter | lower_case_letter

All characters of an identifier are significant, including any underline character inserted between a letter or digit and an adjacent letter or digit. Identifiers differing only in the use of corresponding upper and lower case letters are considered as the same.

Examples:

    COUNT   X   get_symbol   Ethelyn   Marion

    SNOBOL_4   X1   PageCount   STORE_NEXT_ITEM

Note:

No space is allowed within an identifier since a space is a separator.

References: digit 2.1, lower case letter 2.1, name 4.1, reserved word 2.9, separator 2.2, space character 2.1, upper case letter 2.1

2.4 Numeric Literals

There are two classes of numeric literals: real literals and integer literals. A real literal is a numeric literal that includes a point; an integer literal is a numeric literal without a point. Real literals are the literals of the type *universal_real*. Integer literals are the literals of the type *universal_integer*.

    numeric_literal ::= decimal_literal | based_literal

References: literal 4.2, universal_integer type 3.5.4, universal_real type 3.5.6

2.4.1 Decimal Literals

A decimal literal is a numeric literal expressed in the conventional decimal notation (that is, the base is implicitly ten).

    decimal_literal ::= integer [.integer] [exponent]

    integer ::= digit ([underline] digit)

    exponent ::= E [+] integer | E - integer

Lexical Elements

An underline character inserted between adjacent digits of a decimal literal does not affect the value of this numeric literal. The letter E of the exponent, if any, can be written either in lower case or in upper case, with the same meaning.

An exponent indicates the power of ten by which the value of the decimal literal without the exponent is to be multiplied to obtain the value of the decimal literal with the exponent. An exponent for an integer literal must not have a minus sign.   4

Examples: 5

| 12 | 0 | 1E6 | 123_456 | -- | integer literals |

| 12.0 | 0.0 | 0.456 | 3.14159_26 | -- | real literals |

| 1.34E-12 | 1.0E+6 | -- | real literals with exponent |

Notes:

Leading zeros are allowed. No space is allowed in a numeric literal, not even between constituents of the exponent, since a space is a separator. A zero exponent is allowed for an integer literal.   6

References: digit 2.1, lower case letter 2.1, numeric literal 2.4, separator 2.2, space character 2.1, upper case letter 2.1   7

2.4.2 Based Literals

A based literal is a numeric literal expressed in a form that specifies the base explicitly. The base must be at least two and at most sixteen.   1

```
based_literal ::=
    base # based_integer [.based_integer] # [exponent]

base ::= integer

based_integer ::=
    extended_digit [[underline] extended_digit]

extended_digit ::= digit | letter
```
2

An underline character inserted between adjacent digits of a based literal does not affect the value of this numeric literal. The base and the exponent, if any, are in decimal notation. The only letters allowed as extended digits are the letters A through F for the digits ten through fifteen. A letter in a based literal (either an extended digit or the letter E of an exponent) can be written either in lower case or in upper case, with the same meaning.   3

The conventional meaning of based notation is assumed; in particular the value of each extended digit of a based literal must be less than the base. An exponent indicates the power of the base by which the value of the based literal without the exponent is to be multiplied to obtain the value of the based literal with the exponent.   4

Examples: 5

2#1111_1111#	16#FF#	016#0FF#	--	integer literals of value 255
16#E#E1	2#1110_0000#		--	integer literals of value 224
16#F.FF#E+2	2#1.1111_1111_111#E11		--	real literals of value 4095.0

References: digit 2.1, exponent 2.4.1, letter 2.3, lower case letter 2.1, numeric literal 2.4, upper case letter 2.1   6

2.5   Character Literals

A character literal is formed by enclosing one of the 95 graphic characters (including the space) between two apostrophe characters. A character literal has a value that belongs to a character type.

    character_literal ::= 'graphic_character'

Examples:

    'A'   '*'   '''   ' '

References: character type 3.5.2, graphic character 2.1, literal 4.2, space character 2.1

2.6   String Literals

A string literal is formed by a sequence of graphic characters (possibly none) enclosed between two quotation characters used as *string brackets*.

    string_literal ::= "{graphic_character}"

A string literal has a value that is a sequence of character values corresponding to the graphic characters of the string literal apart from the quotation character itself. If a quotation character value is to be represented in the sequence of character values, then a pair of adjacent quotation characters must be written at the corresponding place within the string literal. (This means that a string literal that includes two adjacent quotation characters is never interpreted as two adjacent string literals.)

The *length* of a string literal is the number of character values in the sequence represented. (Each doubled quotation character is counted as a single character.)

Examples:

    "Message of the day:"

    ""   -- an empty string literal
    " "   "A"   """"   -- three string literals of length 1

    "Characters such as $, %, and } are allowed in string literals"

Note:

A string literal must fit on one line since it is a lexical element (see 2.2). Longer sequences of graphic character values can be obtained by catenation of string literals. Similarly catenation of constants declared in the package ASCII can be used to obtain sequences of character values that include nongraphic character values (the so-called control characters). Examples of such uses of catenation are given below:

    "FIRST PART OF A SEQUENCE OF CHARACTERS " &
    "THAT CONTINUES ON THE NEXT LINE "

    "sequence that includes the" & ASCII.ACK & "control character"

References: ascii predefined package C, catenation operation 4.5.3, character value 3.5.2, constant 3.2.1, declaration 3.1, end of a line 2.2, graphic character 2.1, lexical element 2.2

2.7 Comments

A comment starts with two adjacent hyphens and extends up to the end of the line. A comment   1
can appear on any line of a program. The presence or absence of comments has no influence on
whether a program is legal or illegal. Furthermore, comments do not influence the effect of a
program; their sole purpose is the enlightenment of the human reader.

Examples: 2

— the last sentence above echoes the Algol 68 report

end; -- processing of LINE is complete

-- a long comment may be split onto
-- two or more consecutive lines

--------------- the first two hyphens start the comment

Note:

Horizontal tabulation can be used in comments, after the double hyphen, and is equivalent to one   3
or more spaces (see 2.2).

References: end of a line 2.2, illegal 1.6, legal 1.6, space character 2.1   4

2.8 Pragmas

A pragma is used to convey information to the compiler. A pragma starts with the reserved word   1
pragma followed by an identifier that is the name of the pragma.

```
pragma ::=
    pragma identifier [(argument_association {, argument_association})];

argument_association ::=
       [argument_identifier =>] name
    | [argument_identifier =>] expression
```

Pragmas are only allowed at the following places in a program: 3

● After a semicolon delimiter, but not within a formal part or discriminant part.   4

● At any place where the syntax rules allow a construct defined by a syntactic category whose   5
  name ends with "declaration", "statement", "clause", or "alternative", or one of the syntactic
  categories variant and exception handler; but not in place of such a construct. Also at any
  place where a compilation unit would be allowed.

Additional restrictions exist for the placement of specific pragmas.   6

Some pragmas have arguments. Argument associations can be either positional or named as for   7
parameter associations of subprogram calls (see 6.4). Named associations are, however, only possible if the argument identifiers are defined. A name given in an argument must be either a name
visible at the place of the pragma or an identifier specific to the pragma.

The pragmas defined by the language are described in Annex B: they must be supported by every   8
implementation. In addition, an implementation may provide implementation-defined pragmas,
which must then be described in Appendix F. An implementation is not allowed to define pragmas
whose presence or absence influences the legality of the text outside such pragmas. Consequently,
the legality of a program does not depend on the presence or absence of implementation-defined
pragmas.

A pragma that is not language-defined has no effect if its identifier is not recognized by the (current) implementation. Furthermore, a pragma (whether language-defined or implementation-defined) has no effect if its placement or its arguments do not correspond to what is allowed for the pragma. The region of text over which a pragma has an effect depends on the pragma.

Examples:

```
pragma  LIST(OFF);
pragma  OPTIMIZE(TIME);
pragma  INLINE(SETMASK);
pragma  SUPPRESS(RANGE_CHECK, ON => INDEX);
```

Note:

It is recommended (but not required) that implementations issue warnings for pragmas that are not recognized and therefore ignored.

References: compilation unit 10.1, delimiter 2.2, discriminant part 3.7.1, exception handler 11.2, expression 4.4, formal part 6.1, identifier 2.3, implementation-defined pragma F, language-defined pragma B, legal 1.6, name 4.1, reserved word 2.9, statement 5, static expression 4.9, variant 3.7.3, visibility 8.3

Categories ending with "declaration" comprise: basic declaration 3.1, component declaration 3.7, entry declaration 9.5, generic parameter declaration 12.1

Categories ending with "clause" comprise: alignment clause 13.4, component clause 13.4, context clause 10.1.1, representation clause 13.1, use clause 8.4, with clause 10.1.1

Categories ending with "alternative" comprise: accept alternative 9.7.1, case statement alternative 5.4, delay alternative 9.7.1, select alternative 9.7.1, selective wait alternative 9.7.1, terminate alternative 9.7.1

2.9   Reserved Words

The identifiers listed below are called *reserved words* and are reserved for special significance in the language. For readability of this manual, the reserved words appear in lower case boldface.

abort	declare	generic	of	select
abs	delay	goto	or	separate
accept	delta		others	subtype
access	digits	if	out	
all	do	in		task
and		is	package	terminate
array			pragma	then
at	else		private	type
	elsif	limited	procedure	
	end	loop		
begin	entry		raise	use
body	exception		range	
	exit	mod	record	when
			rem	while
		new	renames	with
case	for	not	return	
constant	function	null	reverse	xor

A reserved word must not be used as a declared identifier.

Notes:

Reserved words differing only in the use of corresponding upper and lower case letters are considered as the same (see 2.3). In some attributes the identifier that appears after the apostrophe is identical to some reserved word.

References: attribute 4.1.4, declaration 3.1, identifier 2.3, lower case letter 2.1, upper case letter 2.1

2.10   Allowable Replacements of Characters

The following replacements are allowed for the vertical bar, sharp, and quotation basic characters: 1

- A vertical bar character (|) can be replaced by an exclamation mark (!) where used as a   2
  delimiter.

- The sharp characters (#) of a based literal can be replaced by colons (:) provided that the   3
  replacement is done for both occurrences.

- The quotation characters (") used as string brackets at both ends of a string literal can be   4
  replaced by percent characters (%) provided that the enclosed sequence of characters contains no quotation character, and provided that both string brackets are replaced. Any percent
  character within the sequence of characters must then be doubled and each such doubled
  percent character is interpreted as a single percent character value.

These replacements do not change the meaning of the program.   5

Notes:

It is recommended that use of the replacements for the vertical bar, sharp, and quotation   6
characters be restricted to cases where the corresponding graphical symbols are not available.
Note that the vertical bar appears as a broken bar on some equipment; replacement is not recommended in this case.

The rules given for identifiers and numeric literals are such that lower case and upper case letters   7
can be used indifferently; these lexical elements can thus be written using only characters of the
basic character set. If a string literal of the predefined type STRING contains characters that are
not in the basic character set, the same sequence of character values can be obtained by
catenating string literals that contain only characters of the basic character set with suitable
character constants declared in the predefined package ASCII. Thus the string literal "AB$CD"
could be replaced by "AB" & ASCII.DOLLAR & "CD". Similarly, the string literal "ABcd" with lower
case letters could be replaced by "AB" & ASCII.LC_C & ASCII.LC_D.

References: ascii predefined package C, based literal 2.4.2, basic character 2.1, catenation operation 4.5.3, character   8
value 3.5.2, delimiter 2.2, graphic character 2.1, graphical symbol 2.1, identifier 2.3, lexical element 2.2, lower case
letter 2.1, numeric literal 2.4, string bracket 2.6, string literal 2.6, upper case letter 2.1

appendix VI

Predefined language attributes

A. Predefined Language Attributes

This annex summarizes the definitions given elsewhere of the predefined language attributes. 1

P'ADDRESS   For a prefix P that denotes an object, a program unit, a label, or an entry: 2

Yields the address of the first of the storage units allocated to P. For a sub-program, package, task unit, or label, this value refers to the machine code associated with the corresponding body or statement. For an entry for which an address clause has been given, the value refers to the corresponding hardware interrupt. The value of this attribute is of the type ADDRESS defined in the package SYSTEM. (See 13.7.2.)

P'AFT   For a prefix P that denotes a fixed point subtype: 3

Yields the number of decimal digits needed after the point to accommodate the precision of the subtype P, unless the delta of the subtype P is greater than 0.1, in which case the attribute yields the value one. (P'AFT is the smallest positive integer N for which (10**N)*P'DELTA is greater than or equal to one.) The value of this attribute is of the type *universal_integer*. (See 3.5.10.)

P'BASE   For a prefix P that denotes a type or subtype: 4

This attribute denotes the base type of P. It is only allowed as the prefix of the name of another attribute: for example, P'BASE'FIRST. (See 3.3.3.)

P'CALLABLE   For a prefix P that is appropriate for a task type: 5

Yields the value FALSE when the execution of the task P is either completed or terminated, or when the task is abnormal; yields the value TRUE otherwise. The value of this attribute is of the predefined type BOOLEAN. (See 9.9.)

P'CONSTRAINED   For a prefix P that denotes an object of a type with discriminants:

Yields the value TRUE if a discriminant constraint applies to the object P, or if the object is a constant (including a formal parameter or generic formal parameter of mode **in**); yields the value FALSE otherwise. If P is a generic formal parameter of mode **in out**, or if P is a formal parameter of mode **in out** or **out** and the type mark given in the corresponding parameter specification denotes an unconstrained type with discriminants, then the value of this attribute is obtained from that of the corresponding actual parameter. The value of this attribute is of the predefined type BOOLEAN. (See 3.7.4.)

P'CONSTRAINED   For a prefix P that denotes a private type or subtype: 7

Yields the value FALSE if P denotes an unconstrained nonformal private type with discriminants; also yields the value FALSE if P denotes a generic formal private type and the associated actual subtype is either an unconstrained type with discriminants or an unconstrained array type; yields the value TRUE otherwise.   The value of this attribute is of the predefined type BOOLEAN. (See 7.4.2.)

P'COUNT   For a prefix P that denotes an entry of a task unit: 8

Yields the number of entry calls presently queued on the entry (if the attribute is evaluated within an accept statement for the entry P, the count does not include the calling task). The value of this attribute is of the type *universal_integer*. (See 9.9.)

P'DELTA   For a prefix P that denotes a fixed point subtype: 9

Yields the value of the delta specified in the fixed accuracy definition for the subtype P. The value of this attribute is of the type *universal_real*. (See 3.5.10.)

P'DIGITS   For a prefix P that denotes a floating point subtype: 10

Yields the number of decimal digits in the decimal mantissa of model numbers of the subtype P. (This attribute yields the number D of section 3.5.7.)   The value of this attribute is of the type *universal_integer*. (See 3.5.8.)

P'EMAX   For a prefix P that denotes a floating point subtype: 11

Yields the largest exponent value in the binary canonical form of model numbers of the subtype P. (This attribute yields the product $4*B$ of section 3.5.7.) The value of this attribute is of the type *universal_integer*. (See 3.5.8.)

P'EPSILON   For a prefix P that denotes a floating point subtype: 12

Yields the absolute value of the difference between the model number 1.0 and the next model number above, for the subtype P. The value of this attribute is of the type *universal_real*. (See 3.5.8.)

P'FIRST   For a prefix P that denotes a scalar type, or a subtype of a scalar type: 13

Yields the lower bound of P. The value of this attribute has the same type as P. (See 3.5.)

P'FIRST   For a prefix P that is appropriate for an array type, or that denotes a constrained array subtype:

Yields the lower bound of the first index range. The value of this attribute has the same type as this lower bound. (See 3.6.2 and 3.8.2.)

P'FIRST(N)   For a prefix P that is appropriate for an array type, or that denotes a constrained array subtype:

Yields the lower bound of the N-th index range. The value of this attribute has the same type as this lower bound. The argument N must be a static expression of type *universal_integer*. The value of N must be positive (nonzero) and no greater than the dimensionality of the array. (See 3.6.2 and 3.8.2.)

P'FIRST_BIT   For a prefix P that denotes a component of a record object:

Yields the offset, from the start of the first of the storage units occupied by the component, of the first bit occupied by the component. This offset is measured in bits. The value of this attribute is of the type *universal_integer*. (See 13.7.2.)

P'FORE   For a prefix P that denotes a fixed point subtype:

Yields the minimum number of characters needed for the integer part of the decimal representation of any value of the subtype P, assuming that the representation does not include an exponent, but includes a one-character prefix that is either a minus sign or a space. (This minimum number does not include superfluous zeros or underlines, and is at least two.) The value of this attribute is of the type *universal_integer*. (See 3.5.10.)

P'IMAGE   For a prefix P that denotes a discrete type or subtype:

This attribute is a function with a single parameter. The actual parameter X must be a value of the base type of P. The result type is the predefined type STRING. The result is the *image* of the value of X, that is, a sequence of characters representing the value in display form. The image of an integer value is the corresponding decimal literal; without underlines, leading zeros, exponent, or trailing spaces; but with a one character prefix that is either a minus sign or a space.

The image of an enumeration value is either the corresponding identifier in upper case or the corresponding character literal (including the two apostrophes); neither leading nor trailing spaces are included. The image of a character other than a graphic character is implementation-defined. (See 3.5.5.)

P'LARGE   For a prefix P that denotes a real subtype:

The attribute yields the largest positive model number of the subtype P. The value of this attribute is of the type *universal_real*. (See 3.5.8 and 3.5.10.)

P'LAST   For a prefix P that denotes a scalar type, or a subtype of a scalar type:

Yields the upper bound of P. The value of this attribute has the same type as P. (See 3.5.)

P'LAST   For a prefix P that is appropriate for an array type, or that denotes a constrained array subtype:

Yields the upper bound of the first index range. The value of this attribute has the same type as this upper bound. (See 3.6.2 and 3.8.2.)

LAST(N)   For a prefix P that is appropriate for an array type, or that denotes a   22
constrained array subtype:

Yields the upper bound of the N-th index range. The value of this
attribute has the same type as this upper bound. The argument N
must be a static expression of type *universal_integer*. The value of N
must be positive (nonzero) and no greater than the dimensionality of
the array. (See 3.6.2 and 3.8.2.)

'LAST_BIT   For a prefix P that denotes a component of a record object: 23

Yields the offset, from the start of the first of the storage units
occupied by the component, of the last bit occupied by the component. This offset is measured in bits. The value of this attribute is of
the type *universal_integer*. (See 13.7.2.)

'LENGTH   For a prefix P that is appropriate for an array type, or that denotes a   24
constrained array subtype:

Yields the number of values of the first index range (zero for a null
range). The value of this attribute is of the type *universal_integer*.
(See 3.6.2.)

'LENGTH(N)   For a prefix P that is appropriate for an array type, or that denotes a   25
constrained array subtype:

Yields the number of values of the N-th index range (zero for a null
range). The value of this attribute is of the type *universal_integer*.
The argument N must be a static expression of type *univer-
sal_integer*. The value of N must be positive (nonzero) and no
greater than the dimensionality of the array. (See 3.6.2 and 3.8.2.)

'MACHINE_EMAX   For a prefix P that denotes a floating point type or subtype: 26

Yields the largest value of *exponent* for the machine representation
of the base type of P. The value of this attribute is of the type *univer-
sal_integer*. (See 13.7.3.)

'MACHINE_EMIN   For a prefix P that denotes a floating point type or subtype: 27

Yields the smallest (most negative) value of *exponent* for the
machine representation of the base type of P. The value of this
attribute is of the type *universal_integer*. (See 13.7.3.)

'MACHINE_MANTISSA   For a prefix P that denotes a floating point type or subtype: 28

Yields the number of digits in the *mantissa* for the machine
representation of the base type of P (the digits are extended digits in
the range 0 to P'MACHINE_RADIX - 1). The value of this attribute is
of the type *universal_integer*. (See 13.7.3.)

'MACHINE_OVERFLOWS   For a prefix P that denotes a real type or subtype: 29

Yields the value TRUE if every predefined operation on values of the
base type of P either provides a correct result,or raises the exception
NUMERIC_ERROR in overflow situations; yields the value FALSE
otherwise. The value of this attribute is of the predefined type
BOOLEAN. (See 13.7.3.)

P'MACHINE_RADIX

For a prefix P that denotes a floating point type or subtype:

Yields the value of the *radix* used by the machine representation of the base type of P. The value of this attribute is of the type *universal_integer*. (See 13.7.3.)

P'MACHINE_ROUNDS

For a prefix P that denotes a real type or subtype:

Yields the value TRUE if every predefined arithmetic operation on values of the base type of P either returns an exact result or performs rounding; yields the value FALSE otherwise. The value of this attribute is of the predefined type BOOLEAN. (See 13.7.3.)

P'MANTISSA

For a prefix P that denotes a real subtype:

Yields the number of binary digits in the binary mantissa of model numbers of the subtype P. (This attribute yields the number B of section 3.5.7 for a floating point type, or of section 3.5.9 for a fixed point type.) The value of this attribute is of the type *universal_integer*. (See 3.5.8 and 3.5.10.)

P'POS

For a prefix P that denotes a discrete type or subtype:

This attribute is a function with a single parameter. The actual parameter X must be a value of the base type of P. The result type is the type *universal_integer*. The result is the position number of the value of the actual parameter. (See 3.5.5.)

P'POSITION

For a prefix P that denotes a component of a record object:

Yields the offset, from the start of the first storage unit occupied by the record, of the first of the storage units occupied by the component. This offset is measured in storage units. The value of this attribute is of the type *universal_integer*. (See 13.7.2.)

P'PRED

For a prefix P that denotes a discrete type or subtype:

This attribute is a function with a single parameter. The actual parameter X must be a value of the base type of P. The result type is the base type of P. The result is the value whose position number is one less than that of X. The exception CONSTRAINT_ERROR is raised if X equals P'BASE'FIRST. (See 3.5.5.)

P'RANGE

For a prefix P that is appropriate for an array type, or that denotes a constrained array subtype:

Yields the first index range of P, that is, the range P'FIRST .. P'LAST. (See 3.6.2.)

P'RANGE(N)

For a prefix P that is appropriate for an array type, or that denotes a constrained array subtype:

Yields the N-th index range of P, that is, the range P'FIRST(N) .. P'LAST(N). (See 3.6.2.)

P'SAFE_EMAX

For a prefix P that denotes a floating point type or subtype:

Yields the largest exponent value in the binary canonical form of safe numbers of the base type of P. (This attribute yields the number E of section 3.5.7.) The value of this attribute is of the type *universal_integer*. (See 3.5.8.)

P'SAFE_LARGE   For a prefix P that denotes a real type or subtype: 39

Yields the largest positive safe number of the base type of P. The value of this attribute is of the type *universal_real*. (See 3.5.8 and 3.5.10.)

P'SAFE_SMALL   For a prefix P that denotes a real type or subtype: 40

Yields the smallest positive (nonzero) safe number of the base type of P. The value of this attribute is of the type *universal_real*. (See 3.5.8 and 3.5.10.)

P'SIZE   For a prefix P that denotes an object: 41

Yields the number of bits allocated to hold the object. The value of this attribute is of the type *universal_integer*. (See 13.7.2.)

P'SIZE   For a prefix P that denotes any type or subtype: 42

Yields the minimum number of bits that is needed by the implementation to hold any possible object of the type or subtype P. The value of this attribute is of the type *universal_integer*. (See 13.7.2.)

P'SMALL   For a prefix P that denotes a real subtype: 43

Yields the smallest positive (nonzero) model number of the subtype P. The value of this attribute is of the type *universal_real*. (See 3.5.8 and 3.5.10.)

P'STORAGE_SIZE   For a prefix P that denotes an access type or subtype: 44

Yields the total number of storage units reserved for the collection associated with the base type of P. The value of this attribute is of the type *universal_integer*. (See 13.7.2.)

P'STORAGE_SIZE   For a prefix P that denotes a task type or a task object: 45

Yields the number of storage units reserved for each activation of a task of the type P or for the activation of the task object P. The value of this attribute is of the type *universal_integer*. (See 13.7.2.)

P'SUCC   For a prefix P that denotes a discrete type or subtype: 46

This attribute is a function with a single parameter. The actual parameter X must be a value of the base type of P. The result type is the base type of P. The result is the value whose position number is one greater than that of X. The exception CONSTRAINT_ERROR is raised if X equals P'BASE'LAST. (See 3.5.5.)

P'TERMINATED   For a prefix P that is appropriate for a task type: 47

Yields the value TRUE if the task P is terminated; yields the value FALSE otherwise. The value of this attribute is of the predefined type BOOLEAN. (See 9.9.)

P'VAL   For a prefix P that denotes a discrete type or subtype: 48

This attribute is a special function with a single parameter X which can be of any integer type. The result type is the base type of P. The result is the value whose position number is the *universal_integer* value corresponding to X. The exception CONSTRAINT_ERROR is raised if the *universal_integer* value corresponding to X is not in the range P'POS (P'BASE'FIRST) .. P'POS (P'BASE'LAST). (See 3.5.5.)

P'VALUE

For a prefix P that denotes a discrete type or subtype:

This attribute is a function with a single parameter. The actual parameter X must be a value of the predefined type STRING . The result type is the base type of P. Any leading and any trailing spaces of the sequence of characters that corresponds to X are ignored.

For an enumeration type, if the sequence of characters has the syntax of an enumeration literal and if this literal exists for the base type of P, the result is the corresponding enumeration value. For an integer type, if the sequence of characters has the syntax of an integer literal, with an optional single leading character that is a plus or minus sign, and if there is a corresponding value in the base type of P, the result is this value. In any other case, the exception CONSTRAINT_ERROR is raised. (See 3.5.5.)

P'WIDTH

For a prefix P that denotes a discrete subtype:

Yields the maximum image length over all values of the subtype P (the *image* is the sequence of characters returned by the attribute IMAGE). The value of this attribute is of the type *universal_integer*. (See 3.5.5.)

appendix VII

Predefined language pragmas

This annex defines the pragmas LIST, PAGE, and OPTIMIZE, and summarizes the definitions given ₁ elsewhere of the remaining language-defined pragmas.

Pragma	Meaning

CONTROLLED — Takes the simple name of an access type as the single argument. This pragma ₂ is only allowed immediately within the declarative part or package specification that contains the declaration of the access type; the declaration must occur before the pragma. This pragma is not allowed for a derived type. This pragma specifies that automatic storage reclamation must not be performed for objects designated by values of the access type, except upon leaving the innermost block statement, subprogram body, or task body that encloses the access type declaration, or after leaving the main program (see 4.8).

ELABORATE — Takes one or more simple names denoting library units as arguments. This ₃ pragma is only allowed immediately after the context clause of a compilation unit (before the subsequent library unit or secondary unit). Each argument must be the simple name of a library unit mentioned by the context clause. This pragma specifies that the corresponding library unit body must be elaborated before the given compilation unit. If the given compilation unit is a subunit, the library unit body must be elaborated before the body of the ancestor library unit of the subunit (see 10.5).

INLINE — Takes one or more names as arguments; each name is either the name of a ₄ subprogram or the name of a generic subprogram. This pragma is only allowed at the place of a declarative item in a declarative part or package specification, or after a library unit in a compilation, but before any subsequent compilation unit. This pragma specifies that the subprogram bodies should be expanded inline at each call whenever possible; in the case of a generic subprogram, the pragma applies to calls of its instantiations (see 6.3.2).

INTERFACE — Takes a language name and a subprogram name as arguments. This pragma is ₅ allowed at the place of a declarative item, and must apply in this case to a subprogram declared by an earlier declarative item of the same declarative part or package specification. This pragma is also allowed for a library unit; in this case the pragma must appear after the subprogram declaration, and before any subsequent compilation unit. This pragma specifies the other language (and thereby the calling conventions) and informs the compiler that an object module will be supplied for the corresponding subprogram (see 13.9).

LIST	Takes one of the identifiers ON or OFF as the single argument. This pragma is allowed anywhere a pragma is allowed. It specifies that listing of the compilation is to be continued or suspended until a LIST pragma with the opposite argument is given within the same compilation. The pragma itself is always listed if the compiler is producing a listing.
MEMORY_SIZE	Takes a numeric literal as the single argument. This pragma is only allowed at the start of a compilation, before the first compilation unit (if any) of the compilation. The effect of this pragma is to use the value of the specified numeric literal for the definition of the named number MEMORY_SIZE (see 13.7).
OPTIMIZE	Takes one of the identifiers TIME or SPACE as the single argument. This pragma is only allowed within a declarative part and it applies to the block or body enclosing the declarative part. It specifies whether time or space is the primary optimization criterion.
PACK	Takes the simple name of a record or array type as the single argument. The allowed positions for this pragma, and the restrictions on the named type, are governed by the same rules as for a representation clause. The pragma specifies that storage minimization should be the main criterion when selecting the representation of the given type (see 13.1).
PAGE	This pragma has no argument, and is allowed anywhere a pragma is allowed. It specifies that the program text which follows the pragma should start on a new page (if the compiler is currently producing a listing).
PRIORITY	Takes a static expression of the predefined integer subtype PRIORITY as the single argument. This pragma is only allowed within the specification of a task unit or immediately within the outermost declarative part of a main program. It specifies the priority of the task (or tasks of the task type) or the priority of the main program (see 9.8).
SHARED	Takes the simple name of a variable as the single argument. This pragma is allowed only for a variable declared by an object declaration and whose type is a scalar or access type; the variable declaration and the pragma must both occur (in this order) immediately within the same declarative part or package specification. This pragma specifies that every read or update of the variable is a synchronization point for that variable. An implementation must restrict the objects for which this pragma is allowed to objects for which each of direct reading and direct updating is implemented as an indivisible operation (see 9.11).
STORAGE_UNIT	Takes a numeric literal as the single argument. This pragma is only allowed at the start of a compilation, before the first compilation unit (if any) of the compilation. The effect of this pragma is to use the value of the specified numeric literal for the definition of the named number STORAGE_UNIT (see 13.7).
SUPPRESS	Takes as arguments the identifier of a check and optionally also the name of either an object, a type or subtype, a subprogram, a task unit, or a generic unit. This pragma is only allowed either immediately within a declarative part or immediately within a package specification. In the latter case, the only allowed form is with a name that denotes an entity (or several overloaded subprograms) declared immediately within the package specification. The permission to omit the given check extends from the place of the pragma to the end of the declarative region associated with the innermost enclosing block statement or program unit. For a pragma given in a package specification, the permission extends to the end of the scope of the named entity.

If the pragma includes a name, the permission to omit the given check is further restricted: it is given only for operations on the named object or on all objects of the base type of a named type or subtype; for calls of a named subprogram; for activations of tasks of the named task type; or for instantiations of the given generic unit (see 11.7).

SYSTEM_NAME   Takes an enumeration literal as the single argument. This pragma is only allowed at the start of a compilation, before the first compilation unit (if any) of the compilation. The effect of this pragma is to use the enumeration literal with the specified identifier for the definition of the constant SYSTEM_NAME. This pragma is only allowed if the specified identifier corresponds to one of the literals of the type NAME declared in the package SYSTEM (see 13.7).

appendix VIII

Predefined language environment

C. Predefined Language Environment

This annex outlines the specification of the package STANDARD containing all predefined identifiers in the language. The corresponding package body is implementation-defined and is not shown.

The operators that are predefined for the types declared in the package STANDARD are given in comments since they are implicitly declared. Italics are used for pseudo-names of anonymous types (such as *universal_real*) and for undefined information (such as *implementation_defined* and *any_fixed_point_type*).

```
package STANDARD is

    type BOOLEAN is (FALSE, TRUE);

    -- The predefined relational operators for this type are as follows:

    -- function "="    (LEFT, RIGHT : BOOLEAN) return BOOLEAN;
    -- function "/="   (LEFT, RIGHT : BOOLEAN) return BOOLEAN;
    -- function "<"    (LEFT, RIGHT : BOOLEAN) return BOOLEAN;
    -- function "<="   (LEFT, RIGHT : BOOLEAN) return BOOLEAN;
    -- function ">"    (LEFT, RIGHT : BOOLEAN) return BOOLEAN;
    -- function ">="   (LEFT, RIGHT : BOOLEAN) return BOOLEAN;

    -- The predefined logical operators and the predefined logical negation operator are as follows:

    -- function "and"  (LEFT, RIGHT : BOOLEAN) return BOOLEAN;
    -- function "or"   (LEFT, RIGHT : BOOLEAN) return BOOLEAN;
    -- function "xor"  (LEFT, RIGHT : BOOLEAN) return BOOLEAN;

    -- function "not"  (RIGHT : BOOLEAN) return BOOLEAN;


    -- The universal type universal_integer is predefined.

    type INTEGER is implementation_defined;

    -- The predefined operators for this type are as follows:
```

```
-- function "="    (LEFT, RIGHT : INTEGER) return BOOLEAN;
-- function "/="   (LEFT, RIGHT : INTEGER) return BOOLEAN;
-- function "<"    (LEFT, RIGHT : INTEGER) return BOOLEAN;
-- function "<="   (LEFT, RIGHT : INTEGER) return BOOLEAN;
-- function ">"    (LEFT, RIGHT : INTEGER) return BOOLEAN;
-- function ">="   (LEFT, RIGHT : INTEGER) return BOOLEAN;

-- function "+"    (RIGHT : INTEGER) return INTEGER;
-- function "-"    (RIGHT : INTEGER) return INTEGER;
-- function "abs"  (RIGHT : INTEGER) return INTEGER;

-- function "+"    (LEFT, RIGHT : INTEGER) return INTEGER;
-- function "-"    (LEFT, RIGHT : INTEGER) return INTEGER;
-- function "*"    (LEFT, RIGHT : INTEGER) return INTEGER;
-- function "/"    (LEFT, RIGHT : INTEGER) return INTEGER;
-- function "rem"  (LEFT, RIGHT : INTEGER) return INTEGER;
-- function "mod"  (LEFT, RIGHT : INTEGER) return INTEGER;

-- function "**"   (LEFT : INTEGER; RIGHT : INTEGER) return INTEGER;
```

-- An implementation may provide additional predefined integer types. It is recommended that the   7
-- names of such additional types end with INTEGER as in SHORT_INTEGER or LONG_INTEGER.
-- The specification of each operator for the type *universal_integer*, or for any additional
-- predefined integer type, is obtained by replacing INTEGER by the name of the type in the
-- specification of the corresponding operator of the type INTEGER, except for the right operand
-- of the exponentiating operator.

-- The universal type *universal_real* is predefined.   8

type FLOAT **is** *implementation_defined*;   9

-- The predefined operators for this type are as follows:

```
-- function "="    (LEFT, RIGHT : FLOAT) return BOOLEAN;
-- function "/="   (LEFT, RIGHT : FLOAT) return BOOLEAN;
-- function "<"    (LEFT, RIGHT : FLOAT) return BOOLEAN;
-- function "<="   (LEFT, RIGHT : FLOAT) return BOOLEAN;
-- function ">"    (LEFT, RIGHT : FLOAT) return BOOLEAN;
-- function ">="   (LEFT, RIGHT : FLOAT) return BOOLEAN;

-- function "+"    (RIGHT : FLOAT) return FLOAT;
-- function "-"    (RIGHT : FLOAT) return FLOAT;
-- function "abs"  (RIGHT : FLOAT) return FLOAT;

-- function "+"    (LEFT, RIGHT : FLOAT) return FLOAT;
-- function "-"    (LEFT, RIGHT : FLOAT) return FLOAT;
-- function "*"    (LEFT, RIGHT : FLOAT) return FLOAT;
-- function "/"    (LEFT, RIGHT : FLOAT) return FLOAT;

-- function "**"   (LEFT : FLOAT; RIGHT : INTEGER) return FLOAT;
```

-- An implementation may provide additional predefined floating point types. It is recom-   10
-- mended that the names of such additional types end with FLOAT as in SHORT_FLOAT or
-- LONG_FLOAT. The specification of each operator for the type *universal_real*, or for any
-- additional predefined floating point type, is obtained by replacing FLOAT by the name of the
-- type in the specification of the corresponding operator of the type FLOAT.

-- In addition, the following operators are predefined for universal types: 11

```
-- function "*"    (LEFT : universal_integer;  RIGHT : universal_real)    return universal_real;
-- function "*"    (LEFT : universal_real;     RIGHT : universal_integer) return universal_real;
-- function "/"    (LEFT : universal_real;     RIGHT : universal_integer) return universal_real;
```

-- The type *universal_fixed* is predefined. The only operators declared for this type are

-- **function** "*" (LEFT : *any_fixed_point_type*; RIGHT : *any_fixed_point_type*) **return** universal_fixe
-- **function** "/" (LEFT : *any_fixed_point_type*; RIGHT : *any_fixed_point_type*) **return** universal_fixe

-- The following characters form the standard ASCII character set. Character literals cor-
-- responding to control characters are not identifiers; they are indicated in italics in this definition.

type CHARACTER **is**

type CHARACTER **is**

    (*nul*, *soh*, *stx*, *etx*,   *eot*, *enq*, *ack*, *bel*,
    bs, *ht*, *lf*, *vt*,   *ff*, *cr*, *so*, *si*,
    dle, *dc1*, *dc2*, *dc3*,   *dc4*, *nak*, *syn*, *etb*,
    can, *em*, *sub*, *esc*,   *fs*, *gs*, *rs*, *us*,

    ' ', '!', '"', '#',   '\$', '%', '&', ''',
    '(', ')', '*', '+',   ',', '-', '.', '/',
    '0', '1', '2', '3',   '4', '5', '6', '7',
    '8', '9', ':', ';',   '<', '=', '>', '?',

    '@', 'A', 'B', 'C',   'D', 'E', 'F', 'G',
    'H', 'I', 'J', 'K',   'L', 'M', 'N', 'O',
    'P', 'Q', 'R', 'S',   'T', 'U', 'V', 'W',
    'X', 'Y', 'Z', '[',   '\\', ']', '^', '_',

    '`', 'a', 'b', 'c',   'd', 'e', 'f', 'g',
    'h', 'i', 'j', 'k',   'l', 'm', 'n', 'o',
    'p', 'q', 'r', 's',   't', 'u', 'v', 'w',
    'x', 'y', 'z', '{',   '|', '}', '~', *del*);

for CHARACTER **use** --   128 ASCII character set without holes
    (0, 1, 2, 3, 4, 5, ..., 125, 126, 127);

-- The predefined operators for the type CHARACTER are the same as for any enumeration type

package ASCII **is**

  -- Control characters:

NUL	: **constant** CHARACTER := *nul*;	SOH	: **constant** CHARACTER := *soh*
STX	: **constant** CHARACTER := *stx*;	ETX	: **constant** CHARACTER := *etx*;
EOT	: **constant** CHARACTER := *eot*;	ENQ	: **constant** CHARACTER := *enq*
ACK	: **constant** CHARACTER := *ack*;	BEL	: **constant** CHARACTER := *bel*;
BS	: **constant** CHARACTER := *bs*;	HT	: **constant** CHARACTER := *ht*;
LF	: **constant** CHARACTER := *lf*;	VT	: **constant** CHARACTER := *vt*;
FF	: **constant** CHARACTER := *ff*;	CR	: **constant** CHARACTER := *cr*;
SO	: **constant** CHARACTER := *so*;	SI	: **constant** CHARACTER := *si*;
DLE	: **constant** CHARACTER := *dle*;	DC1	: **constant** CHARACTER := *dc1*
DC2	: **constant** CHARACTER := *dc2*;	DC3	: **constant** CHARACTER := *dc3*
DC4	: **constant** CHARACTER := *dc4*;	NAK	: **constant** CHARACTER := *nak*
SYN	: **constant** CHARACTER := *syn*;	ETB	: **constant** CHARACTER := *etb*;
CAN	: **constant** CHARACTER := *can*;	EM	: **constant** CHARACTER := *em*;
SUB	: **constant** CHARACTER := *sub*;	ESC	: **constant** CHARACTER := *esc*;
FS	: **constant** CHARACTER := *fs*;	GS	: **constant** CHARACTER := *gs*;
RS	: **constant** CHARACTER := *rs*;	US	: **constant** CHARACTER := *us*;
DEL	: **constant** CHARACTER := *del*;		

-- Other characters:

EXCLAM	: **constant** CHARACTER := 'l';		QUOTATION	: **constant** CHARACTER := '"';
SHARP	: **constant** CHARACTER := '#';		DOLLAR	: **constant** CHARACTER := '$';
PERCENT	: **constant** CHARACTER := '%';		AMPERSAND	: **constant** CHARACTER := '&';
COLON	: **constant** CHARACTER := ':';		SEMICOLON	: **constant** CHARACTER := ';';
QUERY	: **constant** CHARACTER := '?';		AT_SIGN	: **constant** CHARACTER := '@';
L_BRACKET	: **constant** CHARACTER := '[';		BACK_SLASH	: **constant** CHARACTER := '\';
R_BRACKET	: **constant** CHARACTER := ']';		CIRCUMFLEX	: **constant** CHARACTER := '^';
UNDERLINE	: **constant** CHARACTER := '_';		GRAVE	: **constant** CHARACTER := '`';
L_BRACE	: **constant** CHARACTER := '{';		BAR	: **constant** CHARACTER := '	';
R_BRACE	: **constant** CHARACTER := '}';		TILDE	: **constant** CHARACTER := '~';

-- Lower case letters:

LC_A : **constant** CHARACTER := 'a';
...
LC_Z : **constant** CHARACTER := 'z';

end ASCII;

-- Predefined subtypes: 16

subtype NATURAL **is** INTEGER **range** 0 .. INTEGER'LAST;
subtype POSITIVE **is** INTEGER **range** 1 .. INTEGER'LAST;

-- Predefined string type: 17

type STRING **is array**(POSITIVE **range** <>) **of** CHARACTER;

pragma PACK(STRING);

-- The predefined operators for this type are as follows: 18

-- **function** "=" (LEFT, RIGHT : STRING) **return** BOOLEAN;
-- **function** "/=" (LEFT, RIGHT : STRING) **return** BOOLEAN;
-- **function** "<" (LEFT, RIGHT : STRING) **return** BOOLEAN;
-- **function** "<=" (LEFT, RIGHT : STRING) **return** BOOLEAN;
-- **function** ">" (LEFT, RIGHT : STRING) **return** BOOLEAN;
-- **function** ">=" (LEFT, RIGHT : STRING) **return** BOOLEAN;

-- **function** "&" (LEFT : STRING;   RIGHT : STRING)   **return** STRING;
-- **function** "&" (LEFT : CHARACTER; RIGHT : STRING)   **return** STRING;
-- **function** "&" (LEFT : STRING;   RIGHT : CHARACTER) **return** STRING;
-- **function** "&" (LEFT : CHARACTER; RIGHT : CHARACTER) **return** STRING;

type DURATION **is delta** *implementation_defined* **range** *implementation_defined*;   19

-- The predefined operators for the type DURATION are the same as for any fixed point type.

-- The predefined exceptions: 20

CONSTRAINT_ERROR : **exception**;
NUMERIC_ERROR   : **exception**;
PROGRAM_ERROR   : **exception**;
STORAGE_ERROR   : **exception**;
TASKING_ERROR   : **exception**;

end STANDARD;

Certain aspects of the predefined entities cannot be completely described in the language itself.   21
For example, although the enumeration type BOOLEAN can be written showing the two
enumeration literals FALSE and TRUE, the short-circuit control forms cannot be expressed in the
language.

Note:

The language definition predefines the following library units:

- The package CALENDAR   (see. 9.6)

- The package SYSTEM   (see 13.7)
- The package MACHINE_CODE (if provided)   (see 13.8)
- The generic procedure UNCHECKED_DEALLOCATION   (see 13.10.1)
- The generic function UNCHECKED_CONVERSION   (see 13.10.2)

- The generic package SEQUENTIAL_IO   (see 14.2.3)
- The generic package DIRECT_IO   (see 14.2.5)
- The package TEXT_IO   (see 14.3.10)
- The package IO_EXCEPTIONS   (see 14.5)
- The package LOW_LEVEL_IO   (see 14.6)

appendix IX

Representation specifications

13. Representation Clauses and Implementation-Dependent Features

·This chapter describes representation clauses, certain implementation-dependent features, and ₁
other features that are used in system programming.

13.1 Representation Clauses

Representation clauses specify how the types of the language are to be mapped onto the underly- ₁
ing machine. They can be provided to give more efficient representation or to interface with
features that are outside the domain of the language (for example, peripheral hardware).

```
representation_clause ::=                                               ₂
      type_representation_clause | address_clause

type_representation_clause ::= length_clause
   | enumeration_representation_clause | record_representation_clause
```

A type representation clause applies either to a type or to a *first named subtype* (that is, to a sub- ₃
type declared by a type declaration, the base type being therefore anonymous). Such a representation clause applies to all objects that have this type or this first named subtype. At most one
enumeration or record representation clause is allowed for a given type: an enumeration representation clause is only allowed for an enumeration type; a record representation clause, only for a
record type. (On the other hand, more than one length clause can be provided for a given type;
moreover, both a length clause and an enumeration or record representation clause can be
provided.) A length clause is the only form of representation clause allowed for a type derived from
a parent type that has (user-defined) derivable subprograms.

An address clause applies either to an object; to a subprogram, package, or task unit; or to an ₄
entry. At most one address clause is allowed for any of these entities.

A representation clause and the declaration of the entity to which the clause applies must both ₅
occur immediately within the same declarative part, package specification, or task specification;
the declaration must occur before the clause. In the absence of a representation clause for a given
declaration, a default representation of this declaration is determined by the implementation.

Such a default determination occurs no later than the end of the immediately enclosing declarative part, package specification, or task specification. For a declaration given in a declarative part, this default determination occurs before any enclosed body.

In the case of a type, certain occurrences of its name imply that the representation of the type must already have been determined. Consequently these occurrences force the default determination of any aspect of the representation not already determined by a prior type representation clause. This default determination is also forced by similar occurrences of the name of a subtype of the type, or of the name of any type or subtype that has subcomponents of the type. A forcing occurrence is any occurrence other than in a type or subtype declaration, a subprogram specification, an entity declaration, a deferred constant declaration, a pragma, or a representation clause for the type itself. In any case, an occurrence within an expression is always forcing.

A representation clause for a given entity must not appear after an occurrence of the name of the entity if this occurrence forces a default determination of representation for the entity.

Similar restrictions exist for address clauses. For an object, any occurrence of its name (after the object declaration) is a forcing occurrence. For a subprogram, package, task unit, or entry, any occurrence of a representation attribute of such an entity is a forcing occurrence.

The effect of the elaboration of a representation clause is to define the corresponding aspects of the representation.

The interpretation of some of the expressions that appear in representation clauses is implementation-dependent, for example, expressions specifying addresses. An implementation may limit its acceptance of representation clauses to those that can be handled simply by the underlying hardware. If a representation clause is accepted by an implementation, the compiler must guarantee that the net effect of the program is not changed by the presence of the clause, except for address clauses and for parts of the program that interrogate representation attributes. If a program contains a representation clause that is not accepted, the program is illegal. For each implementation, the allowed representation clauses, and the conventions used for implementation-dependent expressions, must be documented in Appendix F of the reference manual.

Whereas a representation clause is used to impose certain characteristics of the mapping of an entity onto the underlying machine, pragmas can be used to provide an implementation with criteria for its selection of such a mapping. The pragma PACK specifies that storage minimization should be the main criterion when selecting the representation of a record or array type. Its form is as follows:

    pragma PACK (*type*_simple_name);

Packing means that gaps between the storage areas allocated to consecutive components should be minimized. It need not, however, affect the mapping of each component onto storage. This mapping can itself be influenced by a pragma (or controlled by a representation clause) for the component or component type. The position of a PACK pragma, and the restrictions on the named type, are governed by the same rules as for a representation clause; in particular, the pragma must appear before any use of a representation attribute of the packed entity.

The pragma PACK is the only language-defined representation pragma. Additional representation pragmas may be provided by an implementation; these must be documented in Appendix F. (In contrast to representation clauses, a pragma that is not accepted by the implementation is ignored.)

Note:

No representation clause is allowed for a generic formal type.

References: address clause 13.5, allow 1.6, body 3.9, component 3.3, declaration 3.1, declarative part 3.9, default expression 3.2.1, deferred constant declaration 7.4, derivable subprogram 3.4, derived type 3.4, entity 3.1, entry 9.5, enumeration representation clause 13.3, expression 4.4, generic formal type 12.1.2, illegal 1.6, length clause 13.2, must 1.6, name 4.1, object 3.2, occur immediately within 8.1, package 7, package specification 7.1, parent type 3.4, pragma 2.8, record representation clause 13.4, representation attribute 13.7.2 13.7.3, subcomponent 3.3, subprogram 6, subtype 3.3, subtype declaration 3.3.2, task specification 9.1, task unit 9, type 3.3, type declaration 3.3.1

13.2   Length Clauses

A length clause specifies an amount of storage associated with a type.   1

    length_clause ::= **for** attribute **use** simple_expression;   2

The expression must be of some numeric type and is evaluated during the elaboration of the length   3
clause (unless it is a static expression). The prefix of the attribute must denote either a type or a
first named subtype. The prefix is called T in what follows. The only allowed attribute designators
in a length clause are SIZE, STORAGE_SIZE, and SMALL. The effect of the length clause depends
on the attribute designator:

(a)   Size specification: T'SIZE   4

The expression must be a static expression of some integer type. The value of the expression   5
specifies an upper bound for the number of bits to be allocated to objects of the type or first
named subtype T. The size specification must allow for enough storage space to accommodate every allowable value of these objects. A size specification for a composite type may
affect the size of the gaps between the storage areas allocated to consecutive components.
On the other hand, it need not affect the size of the storage area allocated to each component.

The size specification is only allowed if the constraints on T and on its subcomponents (if any)   6
are static. In the case of an unconstrained array type, the index subtypes must also be static.

(b)   Specification of collection size: T'STORAGE_SIZE   7

The prefix T must denote an access type. The expression must be of some integer type (but   8
need not be static); its value specifies the number of storage units to be reserved for the collection, that is, the storage space needed to contain all objects designated by values of the
access type and by values of other types derived from the access type, directly or indirectly.
This form of length clause is not allowed for a type derived from an access type.

(c)   Specification of storage for a task activation: T'STORAGE_SIZE   9

The prefix T must denote a task type. The expression must be of some integer type (but need   10
not be static); its value specifies the number of storage units to be reserved for an activation
(not the code) of a task of the type.

(d)   Specification of *small* for a fixed point type: T'SMALL   11

The prefix T must denote the first named subtype of a fixed point type. The expression must   12
be a static expression of some real type; its value must not be greater than the delta of the
first named subtype. The effect of the length clause is to use this value of *small* for the
representation of values of the fixed point base type. (The length clause thereby also affects
the amount of storage for objects that have this type.)

Notes:

A size specification is allowed for an access, task, or fixed point type, whether or not another form   13
of length clause is also given for the type.

What is considered to be part of the storage reserved for a collection or for an activation of a task is implementation-dependent. The control afforded by length clauses is therefore relative to the implementation conventions. For example, the language does not define whether the storage reserved for an activation of a task includes any storage needed for the collection associated with an access type declared within the task body. Neither does it define the method of allocation for objects denoted by values of an access type. For example, the space allocated could be on a stack; alternatively, a general dynamic allocation scheme or fixed storage could be used.

The objects allocated in a collection need not have the same size if the designated type is an unconstrained array type or an unconstrained type with discriminants. Note also that the allocator itself may require some space for internal tables and links. Hence a length clause for the collection of an access type does not always give precise control over the maximum number of allocated objects.

Examples:

```
--   assumed declarations:

type MEDIUM is range  0 .. 65000;
type SHORT  is delta  0.01  range -100.0  ..  100.0;
type DEGREE is delta  0.1   range -360.0  ..  360.0;

BYTE : constant := 8;
PAGE : constant := 2000;

--   length clauses:

for COLOR'SIZE   use 1*BYTE;  --   see 3.5.1
for MEDIUM'SIZE  use 2*BYTE;
for SHORT'SIZE   use 15;

for CAR_NAME'STORAGE_SIZE use   --   approximately 2000 cars
        2000*((CAR'SIZE/SYSTEM.STORAGE_UNIT) + 1);

for KEYBOARD_DRIVER'STORAGE_SIZE use 1*PAGE;

for DEGREE'SMALL use 360.0/2**(SYSTEM.STORAGE_UNIT - 1);
```

Notes on the examples:

In the length clause for SHORT, fifteen bits is the minimum necessary, since the type definition requires SHORT'SMALL = 2.0**(-7) and SHORT'MANTISSA = 14. The length clause for DEGREE forces the model numbers to exactly span the range of the type.

References: access type 3.8, allocator 4.8, allow 1.6, array type 3.6, attribute 4.1.4, collection 3.8, composite type 3.3, constraint 3.3, delta of a fixed point type 3.5.9, derived type 3.4, designate 3.8, elaboration 3.9, entity 3.1, evaluation 4.5, expression 4.4, first named subtype 13.1, fixed point type 3.5.9, index subtype 3.6, integer type 3.5.4, must 1.6, numeric type 3.5, object 3.2, real type 3.5.6, record type 3.7, small of a fixed point type 3.5.10, static constraint 4.9, static expression 4.9, static subtype 4.9, storage unit 13.7, subcomponent 3.3, system package 13.7, task 9, task activation 9.3, task specification 9.1, task type 9.2, type 3.3, unconstrained array type 3.6

13.3   Enumeration Representation Clauses

An enumeration representation clause specifies the internal codes for the literals of the enumeration type that is named in the clause.

```
enumeration_representation_clause ::= for type_simple_name use aggregate;
```

The aggregate used to specify this mapping is written as a one-dimensional aggregate, for which the index subtype is the enumeration type and the component type is *universal_integer*.

All literals of the enumeration type must be provided with distinct integer codes, and all choices   4
and component values given in the aggregate must be static. The integer codes specified for the
enumeration type must satisfy the predefined ordering relation of the type.

Example: 5

    type MIX_CODE **is** (ADD, SUB, MUL, LDA, STA, STZ);

    for MIX_CODE **use**
      (ADD => 1, SUB => 2, MUL => 3, LDA => 8, STA => 24, STZ => 33);

Notes:

The attributes SUCC, PRED, and POS are defined even for enumeration types with a   6
noncontiguous representation; their definition corresponds to the (logical) type declaration and is
not affected by the enumeration representation clause. In the example, because of the need to
avoid the omitted values, these functions are likely to be less efficiently implemented than they
could be in the absence of a representation clause. Similar considerations apply when such types
are used for indexing.

References: aggregate 4.3, array aggregate 4.3.2, array type 3.6, attribute of an enumeration type 3.5.5, choice   7
3.7.3, component 3.3, enumeration literal 3.5.1, enumeration type 3.5.1, function 6.5, index 3.6, index subtype 3.6,
literal 4.2, ordering relation of an enumeration type 3.5.1, representation clause 13.1, simple name 4.1, static expression 4.9, type 3.3, type declaration 3.3.1, universal_integer type 3.5.4

13.4   Record Representation Clauses

A record representation clause specifies the storage representation of records, that is, the order,   1
position, and size of record components (including discriminants, if any).

    record_representation_clause ::=   2
      for *type*_simple_name **use**
        record [alignment_clause]
          {component_clause}
        end record;

    alignment_clause ::= **at mod** *static*_simple_expression;

    component_clause ::=
      *component*_name **at** *static*_simple_expression **range** *static*_range;

The simple expression given after the reserved words **at mod** in an alignment clause, or after the   3
reserved word **at** in a component clause, must be a static expression of some integer type. If the
bounds of the range of a component clause are defined by simple expressions, then each bound of
the range must be defined by a static expression of some integer type, but the two bounds need
not have the same integer type.

An alignment clause forces each record of the given type to be allocated at a starting address that   4
is a multiple of the value of the given expression (that is, the address modulo the expression must
be zero). An implementation may place restrictions on the allowable alignments.

A component clause specifies the *storage place* of a component, relative to the start of the record.   5
The integer defined by the static expression of a component clause is a relative address expressed
in storage units. The range defines the bit positions of the storage place, relative to the storage
unit. The first storage unit of a record is numbered zero. The first bit of a storage unit is numbered
zero. The ordering of bits in a storage unit is machine-dependent and may extend to adjacent
storage units. (For a specific machine, the size in bits of a storage unit is given by the

configuration-dependent named number SYSTEM.STORAGE_UNIT.) Whether a component is allowed to overlap a storage boundary, and if so, how, is implementation-defined.

At most one component clause is allowed for each component of the record type, including for each discriminant (component clauses may be given for some, all, or none of the components). If no component clause is given for a component, then the choice of the storage place for the component is left to the compiler. If component clauses are given for all components, the record representation clause completely specifies the representation of the record type and must be obeyed exactly by the compiler.

Storage places within a record variant must not overlap, but overlap of the storage for distinct variants is allowed. Each component clause must allow for enough storage space to accommodate every allowable value of the component. A component clause is only allowed for a component if any constraint on this component or on any of its subcomponents is static.

An implementation may generate names that denote implementation-dependent components (for example, one containing the offset of another component). Such implementation-dependent names can be used in record representation clauses (these names need not be simple names; for example, they could be implementation-dependent attributes).

Example:

```
WORD : constant := 4;  --  storage unit is byte, 4 bytes per word

type STATE        is (A, M, W, P);
type MODE         is (FIX, DEC, EXP, SIGNIF);

type BYTE_MASK    is array (0 .. 7) of BOOLEAN;
type STATE_MASK   is array (STATE) of BOOLEAN;
type MODE_MASK    is array (MODE) of BOOLEAN;

type PROGRAM_STATUS_WORD is
   record
      SYSTEM_MASK       : BYTE_MASK;
      PROTECTION_KEY    : INTEGER range 0 .. 3;
      MACHINE_STATE     : STATE_MASK;
      INTERRUPT_CAUSE   : INTERRUPTION_CODE;
      ILC               : INTEGER range 0 .. 3;
      CC                : INTEGER range 0 .. 3;
      PROGRAM_MASK      : MODE_MASK;
      INST_ADDRESS      : ADDRESS;
   end record;

for PROGRAM_STATUS_WORD use
   record at mod 8;
      SYSTEM_MASK      at 0*WORD  range 0   .. 7;
      PROTECTION_KEY   at 0*WORD  range 10  .. 11;  --  bits 8, 9 unused
      MACHINE_STATE    at 0*WORD  range 12  .. 15;
      INTERRUPT_CAUSE  at 0*WORD  range 16  .. 31;
      ILC              at 1*WORD  range 0   .. 1;   --  second word
      CC               at 1*WORD  range 2   .. 3;
      PROGRAM_MASK     at 1*WORD  range 4   .. 7;
      INST_ADDRESS     at 1*WORD  range 8   .. 31;
   end record;

for PROGRAM_STATUS_WORD'SIZE use 8*SYSTEM.STORAGE_UNIT;
```

Note on the example:

The record representation clause defines the record layout. The length clause guarantees that exactly eight storage units are used.

References: allow 1.6, attribute 4.1.4, constant 3.2.1, constraint 3.3, discriminant 3.7.1, integer type 3.5.4, must

1.6, named number 3.2, range 3.5, record component 3.7, record type 3.7, simple expression 4.4, simple name 4.1, static constraint 4.9, static expression 4.9, storage unit 13.7, subcomponent 3.3, system package 13.7, variant 3.7.3

13.5   Address Clauses

An address clause specifies a required address in storage for an entity.   1

    address_clause ::= **for** simple_name **use at** simple_expression;   2

The expression given after the reserved word **at** must be of the type ADDRESS defined in the   3
package SYSTEM (see 13.7); this package must be named by a with clause that applies to the
compilation unit in which the address clause occurs. The conventions that define the interpretation
of a value of the type ADDRESS as an address, as an interrupt level, or whatever it may be, are
implementation-dependent. The allowed nature of the simple name and the meaning of the corresponding address are as follows:

(a)   Name of an object: the address is that required for the object (variable or constant).   4

(b)   Name of a subprogram, package, or task unit: the address is that required for the machine   5
    code associated with the body of the program unit.

(c)   Name of a single entry: the address specifies a hardware interrupt to which the single entry is   6
    to be linked.

If the simple name is that of a single task, the address clause is understood to refer to the task unit   7
and not to the task object. In all cases, the address clause is only legal if exactly one declaration
with this identifier occurs earlier, immediately within the same declarative part, package specification, or task specification. A name declared by a renaming declaration is not allowed as the simple
name.

Address clauses should not be used to achieve overlays of objects or overlays of program units.   8
Nor should a given interrupt be linked to more than one entry. Any program using address clauses
to achieve such effects is erroneous.

Example: 9

    for CONTROL **use at** 16#0020#;   --   assuming that SYSTEM.ADDRESS is an integer typ

Notes:

The above rules imply that if two subprograms overload each other and are visible at a given point,   10
an address clause for any of them is not legal at this point. Similarly if a task specification declares
entries that overload each other, they cannot be interrupt entries. The syntax does not allow an
address clause for a library unit. An implementation may provide pragmas for the specification of
program overlays.

References: address predefined type 13.7, apply 10.1.1, compilation unit 10.1, constant 3.2.1, entity 3.1, entry 9.5,   11
erroneous 1.6, expression 4.4, library unit 10.1, name 4.1, object 3.2, package 7, pragma 2.8, program unit 6,
reserved word 2.9, simple expression 4.4, simple name 4.1, subprogram 6, subprogram body 6.3, system package
13.7, task body 9.1, task object 9.2, task unit 9, type 3.3, variable 3.2.1, with clause 10.1.1

13.5.1   Interrupts

An address clause given for an entry associates the entry with some device that may cause an
interrupt;   such an entry is referred to in this section as an *interrupt entry*.   If control information is

supplied upon an interrupt, it is passed to an associated interrupt entry as one or more parameters of mode **in**; only parameters of this mode are allowed.

An interrupt acts as an entry call issued by a hardware task whose priority is higher than the priority of the main program, and also higher than the priority of any user-defined task (that is, any task whose type is declared by a task unit in the program). The entry call may be an ordinary entry call, a timed entry call, or a conditional entry call, depending on the kind of interrupt and on the implementation.

If a select statement contains both a terminate alternative and an accept alternative for an interrupt entry, then an implementation may impose further requirements for the selection of the terminate alternative in addition to those given in section 9.4.

Example:

```
task INTERRUPT_HANDLER is
   entry DONE;
   for DONE use at 16#40#;  --  assuming that SYSTEM.ADDRESS is an integer type
end INTERRUPT_HANDLER;
```

Notes:

Interrupt entry calls need only have the semantics described above; they may be implemented by having the hardware directly execute the appropriate accept statements.

Queued interrupts correspond to ordinary entry calls. Interrupts that are lost if not immediately processed correspond to conditional entry calls. It is a consequence of the priority rules that an accept statement executed in response to an interrupt takes precedence over ordinary, user-defined tasks, and can be executed without first invoking a scheduling action.

One of the possible effects of an address clause for an interrupt entry is to specify the priority of the interrupt (directly or indirectly). Direct calls to an interrupt entry are allowed.

References: accept alternative 9.7.1, accept statement 9.5, address predefined type 13.7, allow 1.6, conditional entry call 9.7.2, entry 9.5, entry call 9.5, mode 6.1, parameter of a subprogram 6.2, priority of a task 9.8, select alternative 9.7.1, select statement 9.7, system package 13.7, task 9, terminate alternative 9.7.1, timed entry call 9.7.3

13.6 Change of Representation

At most one representation clause is allowed for a given type and a given aspect of its representation. Hence, if an alternative representation is needed, it is necessary to declare a second type, derived from the first, and to specify a different representation for the second type.

Example:

```
--  PACKED_DESCRIPTOR and DESCRIPTOR are two different types
--  with identical characteristics, apart from their representation

type DESCRIPTOR is
record
   --  components of a descriptor
end record;

type PACKED_DESCRIPTOR is new DESCRIPTOR;

for PACKED_DESCRIPTOR use
   record
      --  component clauses for some or for all components
   end record;
```

Change of representation can now be accomplished by assignment with explicit type conversions: 3

```
D   : DESCRIPTOR;
P   : PACKED_DESCRIPTOR;

P   := PACKED_DESCRIPTOR(D);   --   pack D
D   := DESCRIPTOR(P);          --   unpack P
```

References: assignment 5.2, derived type 3.4, type 3.3, type conversion 4.6, type declaration 3.1, representation   4
clause 13.1

13.7 The Package System

For each implementation there is a predefined library package called SYSTEM which includes the   1
definitions of certain configuration-dependent characteristics. The specification of the package
SYSTEM is implementation-dependent and must be given in Appendix F. The visible part of this
package must contain at least the following declarations.

```
package SYSTEM is
   type ADDRESS   is implementation_defined;
   type NAME      is implementation_defined_enumeration_type;

   SYSTEM_NAME    : constant NAME := implementation_defined;

   STORAGE_UNIT   : constant := implementation_defined;
   MEMORY_SIZE    : constant := implementation_defined;

   --   System-Dependent Named Numbers:

   MIN_INT        : constant := implementation_defined;
   MAX_INT        : constant := implementation_defined;
   MAX_DIGITS     : constant := implementation_defined;
   MAX_MANTISSA   : constant := implementation_defined;
   FINE_DELTA     : constant := implementation_defined;
   TICK           : constant := implementation_defined;

   --   Other System-Dependent Declarations

   subtype PRIORITY is INTEGER range implementation_defined;

   ...
end SYSTEM;
```
   2

The type ADDRESS is the type of the addresses provided in address clauses; it is also the type of   3
the result delivered by the attribute ADDRESS. Values of the enumeration type NAME are the
names of alternative machine configurations handled by the implementation; one of these is the
constant SYSTEM_NAME. The named number STORAGE_UNIT is the number of bits per storage
unit; the named number MEMORY_SIZE is the number of available storage units in the
configuration; these named numbers are of the type *universal_integer*.

An alternative form of the package SYSTEM, with given values for any of SYSTEM_NAME,   4
STORAGE_UNIT, and MEMORY_SIZE, can be obtained by means of the corresponding pragmas.
These pragmas are only allowed at the start of a compilation, before the first compilation unit (if
any) of the compilation.

   pragma SYSTEM_NAME (enumeration_literal);   5

The effect of the above pragma is to use the enumeration literal with the specified identifier for the   6
definition of the constant SYSTEM_NAME. This pragma is only allowed if the specified identifier
corresponds to one of the literals of the type NAME.

pragma STORAGE_UNIT (numeric_literal);

The effect of the above pragma is to use the value of the specified numeric literal for the definition of the named number STORAGE_UNIT.

pragma MEMORY_SIZE (numeric_literal);

The effect of the above pragma is to use the value of the specified numeric literal for the definition of the named number MEMORY_SIZE.

The compilation of any of these pragmas causes an implicit recompilation of the package SYSTEM. Consequently any compilation unit that names SYSTEM in its context clause becomes obsolete after this implicit recompilation. An implementation may impose further limitations on the use of these pragmas. For example, an implementation may allow them only at the start of the first compilation, when creating a new program library.

Note:

It is a consequence of the visibility rules that a declaration given in the package SYSTEM is not visible in a compilation unit unless this package is mentioned by a with clause that applies (directly or indirectly) to the compilation unit.

References: address clause 13.5, apply 10.1.1, attribute 4.1.4, compilation unit 10.1, declaration 3.1, enumeration literal 3.5.1, enumeration type 3.5.1, identifier 2.3, library unit 10.1, must 1.6, named number 3.2, number declaration 3.2.2, numeric literal 2.4, package 7, package specification 7.1, pragma 2.8, program library 10.1, type 3.3, visibility 8.3, visible part 7.2, with clause 10.1.1

13.7.1 System-Dependent Named Numbers

Within the package SYSTEM, the following named numbers are declared. The numbers FINE_DELTA and TICK are of the type *universal_real*; the others are of the type *universal_integer*.

MIN_INT   The smallest (most negative) value of all predefined integer types.

MAX_INT   The largest (most positive) value of all predefined integer types.

MAX_DIGITS   The largest value allowed for the number of significant decimal digits in a floating point constraint.

MAX_MANTISSA   The largest possible number of binary digits in the mantissa of model numbers of a fixed point subtype.

FINE_DELTA   The smallest delta allowed in a fixed point constraint that has the range constraint -1.0 .. 1.0.

TICK   The basic clock period, in seconds.

References: allow 1.6, delta of a fixed point constraint 3.5.9, fixed point constraint 3.5.9, floating point constraint 3.5.7, integer type 3.5.4, model number 3.5.6, named number 3.2, package 7, range constraint 3.5, system package 13.7, type 3.3, universal_integer type 3.5.4, universal_real type 3.5.6

13.7.2 Representation Attributes

The values of certain implementation-dependent characteristics can be obtained by interrogating appropriate *representation attributes*. These attributes are described below.

For any object, program unit, label, or entry X:

X'ADDRESS   Yields the address of the first of the storage units allocated to X. For a subprogram, package, task unit or label, this value refers to the machine code associated with the corresponding body or statement. For an entry for which an address clause has been given, the value refers to the corresponding hardware interrupt. The value of this attribute is of the type ADDRESS defined in the package SYSTEM.

For any type or subtype X, or for any object X:

X'SIZE   Applied to an object, yields the number of bits allocated to hold the object. Applied to a type or subtype, yields the minimum number of bits that is needed by the implementation to hold any possible object of this type or subtype. The value of this attribute is of the type *universal_integer*.

For the above two representation attributes, if the prefix is the name of a function, the attribute is understood to be an attribute of the function (not of the result of calling the function). Similarly, if the type of the prefix is an access type, the attribute is understood to be an attribute of the prefix (not of the designated object: attributes of the latter can be written with a prefix ending with the reserved word **all**).

For any component C of a record object R:

R.C'POSITION   Yields the offset, from the start of the first storage unit occupied by the record, of the first of the storage units occupied by C. This offset is measured in storage units. The value of this attribute is of the type *universal_integer*.

R.C'FIRST_BIT Yields the offset, from the start of the first of the storage units occupied by C, of the first bit occupied by C. This offset is measured in bits. The value of this attribute is of the type *universal_integer*.

R.C'LAST_BIT   Yields the offset, from the start of the first of the storage units occupied by C, of the last bit occupied by C. This offset is measured in bits. The value of this attribute is of the type *universal_integer*.

For any access type or subtype T:

T'STORAGE_SIZE Yields the total number of storage units reserved for the collection associated with the base type of T. The value of this attribute is of the type *universal_integer*.

For any task type or task object T:

T'STORAGE_SIZE Yields the number of storage units reserved for each activation of a task of the type T or for the activation of the task object T. The value of this attribute is of the type *universal_integer*.

Notes:

For a task object X, the attribute X'SIZE gives the number of bits used to hold the object X, whereas X'STORAGE_SIZE gives the number of storage units allocated for the activation of the task designated by X. For a formal parameter X, if parameter passing is achieved by copy, then the attribute X'ADDRESS yields the address of the local copy; if parameter passing is by reference then the address is that of the actual parameter.

References: access subtype 3.8, access type 3.8, activation 9.3, actual parameter 6.2, address clause 13.5, address predefined type 13.7, attribute 4.1.4, base type 3.3, collection 3.8, component 3.3, entry 9.5, formal parameter 6.1 6.2, label 5.1, object 3.2, package 7, package body 7.1, parameter passing 6.2, program unit 6, record object 3.7, statement 5, storage unit 13.7, subprogram 6, subprogram body 6.3, subtype 3.3, system predefined package 13.7, task 9, task body 9.1, task object 9.2, task type 9.2, task unit 9, type 3.3, universal_integer type 3.5.4

13.7.3 Representation Attributes of Real Types

For every real type or subtype T, the following machine-dependent attributes are defined, which are not related to the model numbers. Programs using these attributes may thereby exploit properties that go beyond the minimal properties associated with the numeric type (see section 4.5.7 for the rules defining the accuracy of operations with real operands). Precautions must therefore be taken when using these machine-dependent attributes if portability is to be ensured.

For both floating point and fixed point types:

T'MACHINE_ROUNDS   Yields the value TRUE if every predefined arithmetic operation on values of the base type of T either returns an exact result or performs rounding; yields the value FALSE otherwise. The value of this attribute is of the predefined type BOOLEAN.

T'MACHINE_OVERFLOWS   Yields the value TRUE if every predefined operation on values of the base type of T either provides a correct result, or raises the exception NUMERIC_ERROR in overflow situations (see 4.5.7); yields the value FALSE otherwise. The value of this attribute is of the predefined type BOOLEAN.

For floating point types, the following attributes provide characteristics of the underlying machine representation, in terms of the canonical form defined in section 3.5.7:

T'MACHINE_RADIX   Yields the value of the *radix* used by the machine representation of the base type of T. The value of this attribute is of the type *universal_integer*.

T'MACHINE_MANTISSA   Yields the number of digits in the *mantissa* for the machine representation of the base type of T (the digits are extended digits in the range 0 to T'MACHINE_RADIX -1). The value of this attribute is of the type *universal_integer*.

T'MACHINE_EMAX   Yields the largest value of *exponent* for the machine representation of the base type of T. The value of this attribute is of the type *universal_integer*.

T'MACHINE_EMIN   Yields the smallest (most negative) value of *exponent* for the machine representation of the base type of T. The value of this attribute is of the type *universal_integer*.

For many machines the largest machine representable number of type F is almost

(F'MACHINE_RADIX)**(F'MACHINE_EMAX),

and the smallest positive representable number is

F'MACHINE_RADIX ** (F'MACHINE_EMIN - 1)

References: arithmetic operator 4.5, attribute 4.1.4; base type 3.3, boolean predefined type 3.5.3, false boolean   12
value 3.5.3, fixed point type 3.5.9, floating point type 3.5.7, model number 3.5.6, numeric type 3.5, numeric_error
exception 11.1, predefined operation 3.3.3, radix 3.5.7, real type 3.5.6, subtype 3.3, true boolean value 3.5.3, type
3.3, universal_integer type 3.5.4

13.8 Machine Code Insertions

A machine code insertion can be achieved by a call to a procedure whose sequence of statements   1
contains code statements.

    code_statement ::= type_mark'*record*_aggregate;   2

A code statement is only allowed in the sequence of statements of a procedure body. If a   3
procedure body contains code statements, then within this procedure body the only allowed form
of statement is a code statement (labeled or not), the only allowed declarative items are use
clauses, and no exception handler is allowed (comments and pragmas are allowed as usual).

Each machine instruction appears as a record aggregate of a record type that defines the cor-   4
responding instruction. The base type of the type mark of a code statement must be declared
within the predefined library package called MACHINE_CODE; this package must be named by a
with clause that applies to the compilation unit in which the code statement occurs. An implementation is not required to provide such a package.

An implementation is allowed to impose further restrictions on the record aggregates allowed in   5
code statements. For example, it may require that expressions contained in such aggregates be
static expressions.

An implementation may provide machine-dependent pragmas specifying register conventions and   6
calling conventions. Such pragmas must be documented in Appendix F.

Example: 7

    M : MASK;
    procedure SET_MASK; pragma INLINE(SET_MASK);

    procedure SET_MASK is
      use MACHINE_CODE;
    begin
      SI_FORMAT'(CODE => SSM, B => M'BASE_REG, D => M'DISP);
      -- M'BASE_REG and M'DISP are implementation-specific predefined attributes
    end;

References: allow 1.6, apply 10.1.1, comment 2.7, compilation unit 10.1, declarative item 3.9, exception handler   8
11.2, inline pragma 6.3.2, labeled statement 5.1, library unit 10.1, package 7, pragma 2.8, procedure 6 6.1, procedure
body 6.3, record aggregate 4.3.1, record type 3.7, sequence of statements 5.1, statement 5, static expression 4.9, use
clause 8.4, with clause 10.1.1

13.9 Interface to Other Languages

A subprogram written in another language can be called from an Ada program provided that all   1
communication is achieved via parameters and function results. A pragma of the form

    pragma INTERFACE (*language*_name, *subprogram*_name);   2

must be given for each such subprogram; a subprogram name is allowed to stand for several   3
overloaded subprograms. This pragma is allowed at the place of a declarative item, and must apply

in this case to a subprogram declared by an earlier declarative item of the same declarative part or package specification. The pragma is also allowed for a library unit; in this case the pragma must appear after the subprogram declaration, and before any subsequent compilation unit. The pragma specifies the other language (and thereby the calling conventions) and informs the compiler that an object module will be supplied for the corresponding subprogram. A body is not allowed for such a subprogram (not even in the form of a body stub) since the instructions of the subprogram are written in another language.

This capability need not be provided by all implementations.   An implementation may place restrictions on the allowable forms and places of parameters and calls.

Example:

```
package FORT_LIB is
   function SQRT (X : FLOAT) return FLOAT;
   function EXP   (X : FLOAT) return FLOAT;
private
   pragma INTERFACE(FORTRAN, SQRT);
   pragma INTERFACE(FORTRAN, EXP);
end FORT_LIB;
```

Notes:

The conventions used by other language processors that call Ada programs are not part of the Ada language definition. Such conventions must be defined by these other language processors.

The pragma INTERFACE is not defined for generic subprograms.

References: allow 1.6, body stub 10.2, compilation unit 10.1, declaration 3.1, declarative item 3.9, declarative part 3.9, function result 6.5, library unit 10.1, must 1.6, name 4.1, overloaded subprogram 6.6, package specification 7.1, parameter of a subprogram 6.2, pragma 2.8, subprogram 6, subprogram body 6.3, subprogram call 6.4, subprogram declaration 6.1

13.10 Unchecked Programming

The   predefined   generic   library   subprograms   UNCHECKED_DEALLOCATION   and UNCHECKED_CONVERSION are used for unchecked storage deallocation and for unchecked type conversions.

```
generic
   type OBJECT  is limited private;
   type NAME    is access OBJECT;
procedure UNCHECKED_DEALLOCATION(X : in out NAME);

generic
   type SOURCE is limited private;
   type TARGET is limited private;
function UNCHECKED_CONVERSION(S : SOURCE) return TARGET;
```

References: generic subprogram 12.1, library unit 10.1, type 3.3

13.10.1 Unchecked Storage Deallocation

Unchecked storage deallocation of an object designated by a value of an access type is achieved by a call of a procedure that is obtained by instantiation of the generic procedure UNCHECKED_DEALLOCATION. For example:

procedure FREE **is new** UNCHECKED_DEALLOCATION (*object_type_*name, *access_type_*name);

Such a FREE procedure has the following effect: 2

(a)   after executing FREE (X), the value of X is **null**;   3

(b)   FREE (X), when X is already equal to **null**, has no effect;   4

(c)   FREE (X), when X is not equal to **null**, is an indication that the object designated by X is no   5
      longer required, and that the storage it occupies is to be reclaimed.

If X and Y designate the same object, then accessing this object through Y is erroneous if this   6
access is performed (or attempted) after the call FREE (X); the effect of each such access is not
defined by the language.

Notes: 7

It is a consequence of the visibility rules that the generic procedure UNCHECKED_DEALLOCATION   7
is not visible in a compilation unit unless this generic procedure is mentioned by a with clause that
applies to the compilation unit.

If X designates a task object, the call FREE (X) has no effect on the task designated by the value of   8
this task object. The same holds for any subcomponent of the object designated by X, if this subcomponent is a task object.

References: access type 3.8, apply 10.1.1, compilation unit 10.1, designate 3.8 9.1, erroneous 1.6, generic   9
instantiation 12.3, generic procedure 12.1, generic unit 12, library unit 10.1, null access value 3.8, object 3.2,
procedure 6, procedure call 6.4, subcomponent 3.3, task 9, task object 9.2, visibility 8.3, with clause 10.1.1

13.10.2   Unchecked Type Conversions

An unchecked type conversion can be achieved by a call of a function that is obtained by instantia-   1
tion of the generic function UNCHECKED_CONVERSION.

The effect of an unchecked conversion is to return the (uninterpreted) parameter value as a value   2
of the target type, that is, the bit pattern defining the source value is returned unchanged as the bit
pattern defining a value of the target type. An implementation may place restrictions on unchecked
conversions, for example, restrictions depending on the respective sizes of objects of the source
and target type. Such restrictions must be documented in appendix F.

Whenever unchecked conversions are used, it is the programmer's responsibility to ensure that   3
these conversions maintain the properties that are guaranteed by the language for objects of the
target type.   Programs that violate these properties by means of unchecked conversions are
erroneous.

Note:

It is a consequence of the visibility rules that the generic function UNCHECKED_CONVERSION is   4
not visible in a compilation unit unless this generic function is mentioned by a with clause that
applies to the compilation unit.

References: apply 10.1.1, compilation unit 10.1, erroneous 1.6, generic function 12.1, instantiation 12.3, parameter   5
of a subprogram 6.2, type 3.3, with clause 10.1.1

appendix X

Input-output

14. Input-Output

Input-output is provided in the language by means of predefined packages. The generic packages SEQUENTIAL_IO and DIRECT_IO define input-output operations applicable to files containing elements of a given type. Additional operations for text input-output are supplied in the package TEXT_IO. The package IO_EXCEPTIONS defines the exceptions needed by the above three packages. Finally, a package LOW_LEVEL_IO is provided for direct control of peripheral devices.

References: direct_io package 14.2 14.2.4, io_exceptions package 14.5, low_level_io package 14.6, sequential_io package 14.2 14.2.2, text_io package 14.3

14.1 External Files and File Objects

Values input from the external environment of the program, or output to the environment, are considered to occupy *external files*. An external file can be anything external to the program that can produce a value to be read or receive a value to be written. An external file is identified by a string (the *name*). A second string (the *form*) gives further system-dependent characteristics that may be associated with the file, such as the physical organization or access rights. The conventions governing the interpretation of such strings must be documented in Appendix F.

Input and output operations are expressed as operations on objects of some *file type*, rather than directly in terms of the external files. In the remainder of this chapter, the term *file* is always used to refer to a file object; the term *external file* is used otherwise. The values transferred for a given file must all be of one type.

Input-output for sequential files of values of a single element type is defined by means of the generic package SEQUENTIAL_IO. The skeleton of this package is given below.

```
with IO_EXCEPTIONS;
generic
   type ELEMENT_TYPE is private;
package SEQUENTIAL_IO is
   type FILE_TYPE is limited private;

   type FILE_MODE is (IN_FILE, OUT_FILE);
   ...
   procedure OPEN (FILE : in out FILE_TYPE; ...);
   ...
   procedure READ  (FILE : in FILE_TYPE; ITEM : out ELEMENT_TYPE);
   procedure WRITE (FILE : in FILE_TYPE; ITEM : in ELEMENT_TYPE);
   ...
end SEQUENTIAL_IO;
```

n order to define sequential input-output for a given element type, an instantiation of this generic
unit, with the given type as actual parameter, must be declared. The resulting package contains
the declaration of a file type (called FILE_TYPE) for files of such elements, as well as the operations applicable to these files, such as the OPEN, READ, and WRITE procedures.

Input-output for direct access files is likewise defined by a generic package called DIRECT_IO.
Input-output in human-readable form is defined by the (nongeneric) package TEXT_IO.

Before input or output operations can be performed on a file, the file must first be associated with
an external file. While such an association is in effect, the file is said to be *open*, and otherwise the
file is said to be *closed*.

The language does not define what happens to external files after the completion of the main
program (in particular, if corresponding files have not been closed). The effect of input-output for
access types is implementation-dependent.

An open file has a *current mode*, which is a value of one of the enumeration types

```
type FILE_MODE is (IN_FILE, INOUT_FILE, OUT_FILE);   --  for DIRECT_IO
type FILE_MODE is (IN_FILE, OUT_FILE);               --  for SEQUENTIAL_IO and TEXT_IO
```

These values correspond respectively to the cases where only reading, both reading and writing, or
only writing are to be performed. The mode of a file can be changed.

Several file management operations are common to the three input-output packages. These
operations are described in section 14.2.1 for sequential and direct files. Any additional effects
concerning text input-output are described in section 14.3.1.

The exceptions that can be raised by a call of an input-output subprogram are all defined in the
package IO_EXCEPTIONS; the situations in which they can be raised are described, either
following the description of the subprogram (and in section 14.4), or in Appendix F in the case of
error situations that are implementation-dependent.

Notes:

Each instantiation of the generic packages SEQUENTIAL_IO and DIRECT_IO declares a different
type FILE_TYPE; in the case of TEXT_IO, the type FILE_TYPE is unique.

A bidirectional device can often be modeled as two sequential files associated with the device,
one of mode IN_FILE, and one of mode OUT_FILE. An implementation may restrict the number of
files that may be associated with a given external file. The effect of sharing an external file in this
way by several file objects is implementation-dependent.

References: create procedure 14.2.1, current index 14.2, current size 14.2, delete procedure 14.2.1, direct access
14.2, direct file procedure 14.2, direct_io package 14.1 14.2, enumeration type 3.5.1, exception 11, file mode 14.2.3,
generic instantiation 12.3, index 14.2, input file 14.2.2, io_exceptions package 14.5, open file 14.1, open procedure
14.2.1, output file 14.2.2, read procedure 14.2.4, sequential access 14.2, sequential file 14.2, sequential input-output
14.2.2, sequential_io package 14.2 14.2.2, string 3.6.3, text_io package 14.3, write procedure 14.2.4

14.2 Sequential and Direct Files

Two kinds of access to external files are defined: *sequential access* and *direct access*. The corresponding file types and the associated operations are provided by the generic packages
SEQUENTIAL_IO and DIRECT_IO. A file object to be used for sequential access is called a
sequential file, and one to be used for direct access is called a *direct file*.

For sequential access, the file is viewed as a sequence of values that are transferred in the order of
their appearance (as produced by the program or by the environment). When the file is opened,
transfer starts from the beginning of the file.

For direct access, the file is viewed as a set of elements occupying consecutive positions in linear order; a value can be transferred to or from an element of the file at any selected position. The position of an element is specified by its *index*, which is a number, greater than zero, of the implementation-defined integer type COUNT. The first element, if any, has index one; the index of the last element, if any, is called the *current size*; the current size is zero if there are no elements. The current size is a property of the external file.

An open direct file has a *current index*, which is the index that will be used by the next read or write operation. When a direct file is opened, the current index is set to one. The current index of a direct file is a property of a file object, not of an external file.

All three file modes are allowed for direct files. The only allowed modes for sequential files are the modes IN_FILE and OUT_FILE.

References: count type 14.3, file mode 14.1, in_file 14.1, out_file 14.1

14.2.1   File Management

The procedures and functions described in this section provide for the control of external files; their declarations are repeated in each of the three packages for sequential, direct, and text input-output. For text input-output, the procedures CREATE, OPEN, and RESET have additional effects described in section 14.3.1.

```
procedure CREATE(FILE : in out FILE_TYPE;
                 MODE : in FILE_MODE := default_mode;
                 NAME : in STRING := "";
                 FORM : in STRING := "");
```

Establishes a new external file, with the given name and form, and associates this external file with the given file. The given file is left open. The current mode of the given file is set to the given access mode. The default access mode is the mode OUT_FILE for sequential and text input-output; it is the mode INOUT_FILE for direct input-output. For direct access, the size of the created file is implementation-dependent. A null string for NAME specifies an external file that is not accessible after the completion of the main program (a temporary file). A null string for FORM specifies the use of the default options of the implementation for the external file.

The exception STATUS_ERROR is raised if the given file is already open. The exception NAME_ERROR is raised if the string given as NAME does not allow the identification of an external file. The exception USE_ERROR is raised if, for the specified mode, the environment does not support creation of an external file with the given name (in the absence of NAME_ERROR) and form.

```
procedure OPEN( FILE : in out FILE_TYPE;
                MODE : in FILE_MODE;
                NAME : in STRING;
                FORM : in STRING := "");
```

Associates the given file with an existing external file having the given name and form, and sets the current mode of the given file to the given mode. The given file is left open.

The exception STATUS_ERROR is raised if the given file is already open. The exception NAME_ERROR is raised if the string given as NAME does not allow the identification of an external file; in particular, this exception is raised if no external file with the given name exists. The exception USE_ERROR is raised if, for the specified mode, the environment does not support opening for an external file with the given name (in the absence of NAME_ERROR) and form.

procedure CLOSE(FILE : **in out** FILE_TYPE);   8

> Severs the association between the given file and its associated external file. The   9
> given file is left closed.

> The exception STATUS_ERROR is raised if the given file is not open.   10

procedure DELETE(FILE : **in out** FILE_TYPE);   11

> Deletes the external file associated with the given file. The given file is closed, and   12
> the external file ceases to exist.

> The exception STATUS_ERROR is raised if the given file is not open. The exception   13
> USE_ERROR is raised if (as fully defined in Appendix F) deletion of the external file
> is not supported by the environment.

procedure RESET(FILE : **in out** FILE_TYPE; MODE : **in** FILE_MODE);   14
procedure RESET(FILE : **in out** FILE_TYPE);

> Resets the given file so that reading from or writing to its elements can be   15
> restarted from the beginning of the file; in particular, for direct access this means
> that the current index is set to one. If a MODE parameter is supplied, the current
> mode of the given file is set to the given mode.

> The exception STATUS_ERROR is raised if the file is not open. The exception   16
> USE_ERROR is raised if the environment does not support resetting for the external
> file and, also, if the environment does not support resetting to the specified mode
> for the external file.

function MODE(FILE : **in** FILE_TYPE) **return** FILE_MODE;   17

> Returns the current mode of the given file.   18

> The exception STATUS_ERROR is raised if the file is not open.   19

function NAME(FILE : **in** FILE_TYPE) **return** STRING;   20

> Returns a string which uniquely identifies the external file currently associated with   21
> the given file (and may thus be used in an OPEN operation). If an environment
> allows alternative specifications of the name (for example, abbreviations), the str-
> ing returned by the function should correspond to a full specification of the name.

> The exception STATUS_ERROR is raised if the given file is not open.   22

function FORM(FILE : **in** FILE_TYPE) **return** STRING;   23

> Returns the form string for the external file currently associated with the given file.   24
> If an environment allows alternative specifications of the form (for example,
> abbreviations using default options), the string returned by the function should cor-
> respond to a full specification (that is, it should indicate explicitly all options
> selected, including default options).

> The exception STATUS_ERROR is raised if the given file is not open.   25

function IS_OPEN(FILE : **in** FILE_TYPE) **return** BOOLEAN;

> Returns TRUE if the file is open (that is, if it is associated with an external file), otherwise returns FALSE.

References: current mode 14.1, current size 14.1, closed file 14.1, direct access 14.2, external file 14.1, file 14.1, file_mode type 14.1, file_type type 14.1, form string 14.1, inout_file 14.2.4, mode 14.1, name string 14.1, name_error exception 14.4, open file 14.1, out_file 14.1, status_error exception 14.4, use_error exception 14.4

14.2.2 Sequential Input-Output

The operations available for sequential input and output are described in this section. The exception STATUS_ERROR is raised if any of these operations is attempted for a file that is not open.

procedure READ(FILE : **in** FILE_TYPE; ITEM : **out** ELEMENT_TYPE);

> Operates on a file of mode IN_FILE. Reads an element from the given file, and returns the value of this element in the ITEM parameter.

> The exception MODE_ERROR is raised if the mode is not IN_FILE. The exception END_ERROR is raised if no more elements can be read from the given file. The exception DATA_ERROR is raised if the element read cannot be interpreted as a value of the type ELEMENT_TYPE; however, an implementation is allowed to omit this check if performing the check is too complex.

procedure WRITE(FILE : **in** FILE_TYPE; ITEM : **in** ELEMENT_TYPE);

> Operates on a file of mode OUT_FILE. Writes the value of ITEM to the given file.

> The exception MODE_ERROR is raised if the mode is not OUT_FILE. The exception USE_ERROR is raised if the capacity of the external file is exceeded.

function END_OF_FILE(FILE : **in** FILE_TYPE) **return** BOOLEAN;

> Operates on a file of mode IN_FILE. Returns TRUE if no more elements can be read from the given file; otherwise returns FALSE.

> The exception MODE_ERROR is raised if the mode is not IN_FILE.

References: data_error exception 14.4, element 14.1, element_type 14.1, end_error exception 14.4, external file 14.1, file 14.1, file mode 14.1, file_type 14.1, in_file 14.1, mode_error exception 14.4, out_file 14.1, status_error exception 14.4, use_error exception 14.4

14.2.3 Specification of the Package Sequential_IO

```
with IO_EXCEPTIONS;
generic
   type ELEMENT_TYPE is private;
package SEQUENTIAL_IO is

   type FILE_TYPE   is limited private;

   type FILE_MODE is (IN_FILE, OUT_FILE);


   -- File management

   procedure CREATE (FILE    : in out FILE_TYPE;
                     MODE : in FILE_MODE := OUT_FILE;
                     NAME : in STRING := "";
                     FORM : in STRING := "");

   procedure OPEN    (FILE    : in out FILE_TYPE;
                     MODE : in FILE_MODE;
                     NAME : in STRING;
                     FORM : in STRING := "");

   procedure CLOSE  (FILE : in out FILE_TYPE);
   procedure DELETE (FILE : in out FILE_TYPE);
   procedure RESET  (FILE : in out FILE_TYPE; MODE : in FILE_MODE);
   procedure RESET  (FILE : in out FILE_TYPE);

   function MODE    (FILE : in FILE_TYPE) return FILE_MODE;
   function NAME    (FILE : in FILE_TYPE) return STRING;
   function FORM    (FILE : in FILE_TYPE) return STRING;

   function IS_OPEN (FILE : in FILE_TYPE) return BOOLEAN;

   -- Input and output operations

   procedure READ    (FILE : in FILE_TYPE; ITEM : out ELEMENT_TYPE);
   procedure WRITE  (FILE : in FILE_TYPE; ITEM : in ELEMENT_TYPE);

   function END_OF_FILE(FILE : in FILE_TYPE) return BOOLEAN;

   -- Exceptions

   STATUS_ERROR : exception renames IO_EXCEPTIONS.STATUS_ERROR;
   MODE_ERROR   : exception renames IO_EXCEPTIONS.MODE_ERROR;
   NAME_ERROR   : exception renames IO_EXCEPTIONS.NAME_ERROR;
   USE_ERROR    : exception renames IO_EXCEPTIONS.USE_ERROR;
   DEVICE_ERROR : exception renames IO_EXCEPTIONS.DEVICE_ERROR;
   END_ERROR    : exception renames IO_EXCEPTIONS.END_ERROR;
   DATA_ERROR   : exception renames IO_EXCEPTIONS.DATA_ERROR;

private
   -- implementation-dependent
end SEQUENTIAL_IO;
```

References: close procedure 14.2.1, create procedure 14.2.1, data_error exception 14.4, delete procedure 14.2.1, device_error exception 14.4, end_error exception 14.4, end_of_file function 14.2.2, file_mode 14.1, file_type 14.1, form function 14.2.1, in_file 14.1, io_exceptions 14.4, is_open function 14.2.1, mode function 14.2.1, mode_error exception 14.4, name function 14.2.1, name_error exception 14.4, open procedure 14.2.1, out_file 14.1, read procedure 14.2.2, reset procedure 14.2.1, sequential_io package 14.2 14.2.2, status_error exception 14.4, use_error exception 14.4, write procedure 14.2.2,

14.2.4 Direct Input-Output

The operations available for direct input and output are described in this section. The exception STATUS_ERROR is raised if any of these operations is attempted for a file that is not open.

procedure READ(FILE : **in** FILE_TYPE; ITEM : **out** ELEMENT_TYPE;
                                  FROM : **in**   POSITIVE_COUNT);
procedure READ(FILE : **in** FILE_TYPE; ITEM : **out** ELEMENT_TYPE);

> Operates on a file of mode IN_FILE or INOUT_FILE. In the case of the first form, sets the current index of the given file to the index value given by the parameter FROM. Then (for both forms) returns, in the parameter ITEM, the value of the element whose position in the given file is specified by the current index of the file; finally, increases the current index by one.

> The exception MODE_ERROR is raised if the mode of the given file is OUT_FILE. The exception END_ERROR is raised if the index to be used exceeds the size of the external file. The exception DATA_ERROR is raised if the element read cannot be interpreted as a value of the type ELEMENT_TYPE; however, an implementation is allowed to omit this check if performing the check is too complex.

procedure WRITE(FILE : **in** FILE_TYPE; ITEM : **in** ELEMENT_TYPE;
                                   TO   : **in** POSITIVE_COUNT);
procedure WRITE(FILE : **in** FILE_TYPE; ITEM : **in** ELEMENT_TYPE);

> Operates on a file of mode INOUT_FILE or OUT_FILE. In the case of the first form, sets the index of the given file to the index value given by the parameter TO. Then (for both forms) gives the value of the parameter ITEM to the element whose position in the given file is specified by the current index of the file; finally, increases the current index by one.

> The exception MODE_ERROR is raised if the mode of the given file is IN_FILE. The exception USE_ERROR is raised if the capacity of the external file is exceeded.

procedure SET_INDEX(FILE : **in** FILE_TYPE; TO : **in** POSITIVE_COUNT);

> Operates on a file of any mode. Sets the current index of the given file to the given index value (which may exceed the current size of the file).

function INDEX(FILE : **in** FILE_TYPE) **return** POSITIVE_COUNT;

> Operates on a file of any mode. Returns the current index of the given file.

function SIZE(FILE : **in** FILE_TYPE) **return** COUNT;

> Operates on a file of any mode. Returns the current size of the external file that is associated with the given file.

function END_OF_FILE(FILE : in FILE_TYPE)   return BOOLEAN;   14

> Operates on a file of mode IN_FILE or INOUT_FILE. Returns TRUE if the current   15
> index exceeds the size of the external file; otherwise returns FALSE.

> The exception MODE_ERROR is raised if the mode of the given file is OUT_FILE.   16

References: count type 14.2, current index 14.2, current size 14.2, data_error exception 14.4, element 14.1,   17
element_type 14.1, end_error exception 14.4, external file 14.1, file 14.1, file mode 14.1, file_type 14.1, in_file 14.1,
index 14.2, inout_file 14.1, mode_error exception 14.4, open file 14.1, positive_count 14.3, status_error exception
14.4, use_error exception 14.4

14.2.5 Specification of the Package Direct_IO

```
with IO_EXCEPTIONS;
generic
   type ELEMENT_TYPE is private;
package DIRECT_IO is

   type FILE_TYPE   is limited private;

   type      FILE_MODE is (IN_FILE, INOUT_FILE, OUT_FILE);
   type      COUNT     is range 0 .. implementation_defined;
   subtype POSITIVE_COUNT is COUNT range 1 .. COUNT'LAST;


   -- File management

   procedure CREATE ( FILE   : in out FILE_TYPE;
                      MODE : in FILE_MODE := INOUT_FILE;
                      NAME : in STRING := "";
                      FORM : in STRING := "");

   procedure OPEN    ( FILE   : in out FILE_TYPE;
                       MODE : in FILE_MODE;
                       NAME : in STRING;
                       FORM : in STRING := "");

   procedure CLOSE  (FILE : in out FILE_TYPE);
   procedure DELETE (FILE : in out FILE_TYPE);
   procedure RESET  (FILE : in out FILE_TYPE; MODE : in FILE_MODE);
   procedure RESET  (FILE : in out FILE_TYPE);

   function MODE    (FILE : in FILE_TYPE) return FILE_MODE;
   function NAME    (FILE : in FILE_TYPE) return STRING;
   function FORM    (FILE : in FILE_TYPE) return STRING;

   function IS_OPEN (FILE : in FILE_TYPE) return BOOLEAN;

   -- Input and output operations

   procedure READ (FILE : in FILE_TYPE; ITEM : out ELEMENT_TYPE; FROM : POSITIVE_COUNT);
   procedure READ (FILE : in FILE_TYPE; ITEM : out ELEMENT_TYPE);

   procedure WRITE (FILE : in FILE_TYPE; ITEM : in  ELEMENT_TYPE; TO : POSITIVE_COUNT);
   procedure WRITE (FILE : in FILE_TYPE; ITEM : in ELEMENT_TYPE);

   procedure SET_INDEX(FILE : in FILE_TYPE; TO : in POSITIVE_COUNT);

   function INDEX(FILE : in FILE_TYPE) return POSITIVE_COUNT;
   function SIZE  (FILE : in FILE_TYPE) return COUNT;

   function END_OF_FILE (FILE : in FILE_TYPE) return BOOLEAN;
```

-- Exceptions

```
STATUS_ERROR   : exception renames IO_EXCEPTIONS.STATUS_ERROR;
MODE_ERROR     : exception renames IO_EXCEPTIONS.MODE_ERROR;
NAME_ERROR     : exception renames IO_EXCEPTIONS.NAME_ERROR;
USE_ERROR      : exception renames IO_EXCEPTIONS.USE_ERROR;
DEVICE_ERROR   : exception renames IO_EXCEPTIONS.DEVICE_ERROR;
END_ERROR      : exception renames IO_EXCEPTIONS.END_ERROR;
DATA_ERROR     : exception renames IO_EXCEPTIONS.DATA_ERROR;
```

private
    -- implementation-dependent
end DIRECT_IO;

References close procedure 14.2.1, count type 14.2, create procedure 14.2.1, data_error exception 14.4, default_mode 14.2.5, delete procedure 14.2.1, device_error exception 14.4, element_type 14.2.4, end_error exception 14.4, end_of_file function 14.2.4, file_mode 14.2.5, file_type 14.2.4, form function 14.2.1, in_file 14.2.4, index function 14.2.4, inout_file 14.2.4 14.2.1, io_exceptions package 14.4, is_open function 14.2.1, mode function 14.2.1, mode_error exception 14.4, name function 14.2.1, name_error exception 14.4, open procedure 14.2.1, out_file 14.2.1, read procedure 14.2.4, set_index procedure 14.2.4, size function 14.2.4, status_error exception 14.4, use_error exception 14.4, write procedure 14.2.4 14.2.1

14.3 Text Input-Output

This section describes the package TEXT_IO, which provides facilities for input and output in human-readable form. Each file is read or written sequentially, as a sequence of characters grouped into lines, and as a sequence of lines grouped into pages. The specification of the package is given below in section 14.3.10.

The facilities for file management given above, in sections 14.2.1 and 14.2.2, are available for text input-output. In place of READ and WRITE, however, there are procedures GET and PUT that input values of suitable types from text files, and output values to them. These values are provided to the PUT procedures, and returned by the GET procedures, in a parameter ITEM. Several overloaded procedures of these names exist, for different types of ITEM. These GET procedures analyze the input sequences of characters as lexical elements (see Chapter 2) and return the corresponding values; the PUT procedures output the given values as appropriate lexical elements. Procedures GET and PUT are also available that input and output individual characters treated as character values rather than as lexical elements.

In addition to the procedures GET and PUT for numeric and enumeration types of ITEM that operate on text files, analogous procedures are provided that read from and write to a parameter of type STRING. These procedures perform the same analysis and composition of character sequences as their counterparts which have a file parameter.

For all GET and PUT procedures that operate on text files, and for many other subprograms, there are forms with and without a file parameter. Each such GET procedure operates on an input file and each such PUT procedure operates on an output file. If no file is specified, a default input file or a default output file is used.

At the beginning of program execution the default input and output files are the so-called standard input file and standard output file. These files are open, have respectively the current modes IN_FILE and OUT_FILE, and are associated with two implementation-defined external files. Procedures are provided to change the current default input file and the current default output file.

From a logical point of view, a text file is a sequence of pages, a page is a sequence of lines, and a line is a sequence of characters; the end of a line is marked by a *line terminator*; the end of a page is marked by the combination of a line terminator immediately followed by a *page terminator*; and the end of a file is marked by the combination of a line terminator immediately followed by a page terminator and then a *file terminator*. Terminators are generated during output; either by calls of procedures provided expressly for that purpose; or implicitly as part of other operations, for example, when a bounded line length, a bounded page length, or both, have been specified for a file.

The actual nature of terminators is not defined by the language and hence depends on the implementation. Although terminators are recognized or generated by certain of the procedures that follow, they are not necessarily implemented as characters or as sequences of characters. Whether they are characters (and if so which ones) in any particular implementation need not concern a user who neither explicitly outputs nor explicitly inputs control characters. The effect of input or output of control characters (other than horizontal tabulation) is not defined by the language.

The characters of a line are numbered, starting from one; the number of a character is called its *column number*. For a line terminator, a column number is also defined: it is one more than the number of characters in the line. The lines of a page, and the pages of a file, are similarly numbered. The *current column number* is the column number of the next character or line terminator to be transferred. The *current line number* is the number of the current line. The *current page number* is the number of the current page. These numbers are values of the subtype POSITIVE_COUNT of the type COUNT (by convention, the value zero of the type COUNT is used to indicate special conditions).

```
type COUNT is range 0 .. implementation_defined;
subtype POSITIVE_COUNT is COUNT range 1 .. COUNT'LAST;
```

For an output file, a *maximum line length* can be specified and a *maximum page length* can be specified. If a value to be output cannot fit on the current line, for a specified maximum line length, then a new line is automatically started before the value is output; if, further, this new line cannot fit on the current page, for a specified maximum page length, then a new page is automatically started before the value is output. Functions are provided to determine the maximum line length and the maximum page length. When a file is opened with mode OUT_FILE, both values are zero: by convention, this means that the line lengths and page lengths are unbounded. (Consequently, output consists of a single line if the subprograms for explicit control of line and page structure are not used.) The constant UNBOUNDED is provided for this purpose.

References: count type 14.3.10, default current input file 14.3.2, default current output file 14.3.2, external file 14.1, file 14.1, get procedure 14.3.5, in_file 14.1, out_file 14.1, put procedure 14.3.5, read 14.2.2, sequential access 14.1, standard input file 14.3.2, standard output file 14.3.2

14.3.1 File Management

The only allowed file modes for text files are the modes IN_FILE and OUT_FILE. The subprograms given in section 14.2.1 for the control of external files, and the function END_OF_FILE given in section 14.2.2 for sequential input-output, are also available for text files. There is also a version of END_OF_FILE that refers to the current default input file. For text files, the procedures have the following additional effects:

- For the procedures CREATE and OPEN: After opening a file with mode OUT_FILE, the page length and line length are unbounded (both have the conventional value zero). After opening a file with mode IN_FILE or OUT_FILE, the current column, current line, and current page numbers are set to one.

- For the procedure CLOSE: If the file has the current mode OUT_FILE, has the effect of calling NEW_PAGE, unless the current page is already terminated; then outputs a file terminator.

- For the procedure RESET: If the file has the current mode OUT_FILE, has the effect of calling NEW_PAGE, unless the current page is already terminated; then outputs a file terminator. If the new file mode is OUT_FILE, the page and line lengths are unbounded. For all modes, the current column, line, and page numbers are set to one.

The exception MODE_ERROR is raised by the procedure RESET upon an attempt to change the mode of a file that is either the current default input file, or the current default output file.

References: create procedure 14.2.1, current column number 14.3, current default input file 14.3, current line number 14.3, current page number 14.3, end_of_file 14.3, external file 14.1, file 14.1, file mode 14.1, file terminator 14.3, in_file 14.1, line length 14.3, mode_error exception 14.4, open procedure 14.2.1, out_file 14.1, page length 14.3, reset procedure 14.2.1

14.3.2   Default Input and Output Files

The following subprograms provide for the control of the particular default files that are used when a file parameter is omitted from a GET, PUT or other operation of text input-output described below.

> **procedure** SET_INPUT(FILE : **in** FILE_TYPE);
>
>> Operates on a file of mode IN_FILE. Sets the current default input file to FILE.
>>
>> The exception STATUS_ERROR is raised if the given file is not open. The exception MODE_ERROR is raised if the mode of the given file is not IN_FILE.

> **procedure** SET_OUTPUT(FILE : **in** FILE_TYPE);
>
>> Operates on a file of mode OUT_FILE. Sets the current default output file to FILE.
>>
>> The exception STATUS_ERROR is raised if the given file is not open. The exception MODE_ERROR is raised if the mode of the given file is not OUT_FILE.

> **function** STANDARD_INPUT **return** FILE_TYPE;
>
>> Returns the standard input file (see 14.3).

> **function** STANDARD_OUTPUT **return** FILE_TYPE;
>
>> Returns the standard output file (see 14.3).

> **function** CURRENT_INPUT **return** FILE_TYPE;
>
>> Returns the current default input file.

> **function** CURRENT_OUTPUT **return** FILE_TYPE;
>
>> Returns the current default output file.

Note:

The standard input and the standard output files cannot be opened, closed, reset, or deleted, because the parameter FILE of the corresponding procedures has the mode **in out**.

References: current default file 14.3, default file 14.3, file_type 14.1, get procedure 14.3.5, mode_error exception 14.4, put procedure 14.3.5, status_error exception 14.4

14.3.3 Specification of Line and Page Lengths

The subprograms described in this section are concerned with the line and page structure of a file   1
of mode OUT_FILE. They operate either on the file given as the first parameter, or, in the absence
of such a file parameter, on the current default output file. They provide for output of text with a
specified maximum line length or page length. In these cases, line and page terminators are output implicitly and automatically when needed. When line and page lengths are unbounded (that is,
when they have the conventional value zero), as in the case of a newly opened file, new lines and
new pages are only started when explicitly called for.

In all cases, the exception STATUS_ERROR is raised if the file to be used is not open; the exception   2
MODE_ERROR is raised if the mode of the file is not OUT_FILE.

```
procedure  SET_LINE_LENGTH(FILE  : in FILE_TYPE; TO : in COUNT);
procedure  SET_LINE_LENGTH(TO    : in COUNT);
```
                                                                                                    3

   Sets the maximum line length of the specified output file to the number of   4
   characters specified by TO. The value zero for TO specifies an unbounded line
   length.

   The exception USE_ERROR is raised if the specified line length is inappropriate for   5
   the associated external file.

```
procedure  SET_PAGE_LENGTH (FILE  : in FILE_TYPE; TO : in COUNT);
procedure  SET_PAGE_LENGTH (TO    : in COUNT);
```
                                                                                                    6

   Sets the maximum page length of the specified output file to the number of lines   7
   specified by TO. The value zero for TO specifies an unbounded page length.

   The exception USE_ERROR is raised if the specified page length is inappropriate for   8
   the associated external file.

```
function  LINE_LENGTH(FILE : in FILE_TYPE) return COUNT;
function  LINE_LENGTH return COUNT;
```
                                                                                                    9

   Returns the maximum line length currently set for the specified output file, or zero   10
   if the line length is unbounded.

```
function  PAGE_LENGTH(FILE : in FILE_TYPE) return COUNT;
function  PAGE_LENGTH return COUNT;
```
                                                                                                    11

   Returns the maximum page length currently set for the specified output file, or zero   12
   if the page length is unbounded.

References: count type 14.3, current default output file 14.3, external file 14.1, file 14.1, file_type 14.1, line 14.3,   13
ne length 14.3, line terminator 14.3, maximum line length 14.3, maximum page length 14.3, mode_error exception
4.4, open file 14.1, out_file 14.1, page 14.3, page length 14.3, page terminator 14.3, status_error exception 14.4,
nbounded page length 14.3, use_error exception 14.4

4.3.4 Operations on Columns, Lines, and Pages

ne subprograms described in this section provide for explicit control of line and page structure;
ey operate either on the file given as the first parameter, or, in the absence of such a file

parameter, on the appropriate (input or output) current default file. The exception STATUS_ERROR is raised by any of these subprograms if the file to be used is not open.

procedure NEW_LINE(FILE : **in** FILE_TYPE; SPACING : **in** POSITIVE_COUNT := 1);
procedure NEW_LINE(SPACING : **in** POSITIVE_COUNT := 1);

> Operates on a file of mode OUT_FILE.
>
> For a SPACING of one: Outputs a line terminator and sets the current column number to one. Then increments the current line number by one, except in the case that the current line number is already greater than or equal to the maximum page length, for a bounded page length; in that case a page terminator is output, the current page number is incremented by one, and the current line number is set to one.
>
> For a SPACING greater than one, the above actions are performed SPACING times.
>
> The exception MODE_ERROR is raised if the mode is not OUT_FILE.

procedure SKIP_LINE(FILE   : **in** FILE_TYPE; SPACING : **in** POSITIVE_COUNT := 1);
procedure SKIP_LINE(SPACING : **in** POSITIVE_COUNT := 1);

> Operates on a file of mode IN_FILE.
>
> For a SPACING of one: Reads and discards all characters until a line terminator has been read, and then sets the current column number to one. If the line terminator is not immediately followed by a page terminator, the current line number is incremented by one. Otherwise, if the line terminator is immediately followed by a page terminator, then the page terminator is skipped, the current page number is incremented by one, and the current line number is set to one.
>
> For a SPACING greater than one, the above actions are performed SPACING times.
>
> The exception MODE_ERROR is raised if the mode is not IN_FILE. The exception END_ERROR is raised if an attempt is made to read a file terminator.

function END_OF_LINE(FILE : **in** FILE_TYPE) **return** BOOLEAN;
function END_OF_LINE **return** BOOLEAN;

> Operates on a file of mode IN_FILE. Returns TRUE if a line terminator or a file terminator is next; otherwise returns FALSE.
>
> The exception MODE_ERROR is raised if the mode is not IN_FILE.

procedure NEW_PAGE(FILE : **in** FILE_TYPE);
procedure NEW_PAGE;

> Operates on a file of mode OUT_FILE. Outputs a line terminator if the current line is not terminated, or if the current page is empty (that is, if the current column and line numbers are both equal to one). Then outputs a page terminator, which terminates the current page. Adds one to the current page number and sets the current column and line numbers to one.
>
> The exception MODE_ERROR is raised if the mode is not OUT_FILE.

procedure SKIP_PAGE(FILE : **in** FILE_TYPE);   17
procedure SKIP_PAGE;

> Operates on a file of mode IN_FILE. Reads and discards all characters and line   18
> terminators until a page terminator has been read. Then adds one to the current
> page number, and sets the current column and line numbers to one.

> The exception MODE_ERROR is raised if the mode is not IN_FILE. The exception   19
> END_ERROR is raised if an attempt is made to read a file terminator.

function END_OF_PAGE(FILE : **in** FILE_TYPE) **return** BOOLEAN;   20
function END_OF_PAGE **return** BOOLEAN;

> Operates on a file of mode IN_FILE. Returns TRUE if the combination of a line   21
> terminator and a page terminator is next, or if a file terminator is next; otherwise
> returns FALSE.

> The exception MODE_ERROR is raised if the mode is not IN_FILE.   22

function END_OF_FILE(FILE : **in** FILE_TYPE) **return** BOOLEAN;   23
function END_OF_FILE **return** BOOLEAN;

> Operates on a file of mode IN_FILE. Returns TRUE if a file terminator is next, or if   24
> the combination of a line, a page, and a file terminator is next; otherwise returns
> FALSE.

> The exception MODE_ERROR is raised if the mode is not IN_FILE.   25

The following subprograms provide for the control of the current position of reading or writing in a   26
file. In all cases, the default file is the current output file.

procedure SET_COL(FILE : **in** FILE_TYPE; TO : **in** POSITIVE_COUNT);   27
procedure SET_COL(TO   : **in** POSITIVE_COUNT);

> If the file mode is OUT_FILE :   28

>> If the value specified by TO is greater than the current column number,   29
>> outputs spaces, adding one to the current column number after each
>> space, until the current column number equals the specified value. If the
>> value specified by TO is equal to the current column number, there is no
>> effect. If the value specified by TO is less than the current column number,
>> has the effect of calling NEW_LINE (with a spacing of one), then outputs
>> (TO - 1) spaces, and sets the current column number to the specified value.

>> The exception LAYOUT_ERROR is raised if the value specified by TO   30
>> exceeds LINE_LENGTH when the line length is bounded (that is, when it
>> does not have the conventional value zero).

> If the file mode is IN_FILE :   31

>> Reads (and discards) individual characters, line terminators, and page ter-   32
>> minators, until the next character to be read has a column number that
>> equals the value specified by TO; there is no effect if the current column
>> number already equals this value. Each transfer of a character or ter-
>> minator maintains the current column, line, and page numbers in the same
>> way as a GET procedure (see 14.3.5). (Short lines will be skipped until a
>> line is reached that has a character at the specified column position.)

The exception END_ERROR is raised if an attempt is made to read a file terminator.

procedure SET_LINE(FILE   : **in** FILE_TYPE; TO : **in** POSITIVE_COUNT); .
procedure SET_LINE(TO   : **in** POSITIVE_COUNT);

If the file mode is OUT_FILE :

If the value specified by TO is greater than the current line number, has the effect of repeatedly calling NEW_LINE (with a spacing of one), until the current line number equals the specified value. If the value specified by TO is equal to the current line number, there is no effect. If the value specified by TO is less than the current line number, has the effect of calling NEW_PAGE followed by a call of NEW_LINE with a spacing equal to (TO - 1).

The exception LAYOUT_ERROR is raised if the value specified by TO exceeds PAGE_LENGTH when the page length is bounded (that is, when it does not have the conventional value zero).

If the mode is IN_FILE :

Has the effect of repeatedly calling SKIP_LINE (with a spacing of one), until the current line number equals the value specified by TO ; there is no effect if the current line number already equals this value. (Short pages will be skipped until a page is reached that has a line at the specified line position.)

The exception END_ERROR is raised if an attempt is made to read a file terminator.

function COL(FILE : **in** FILE_TYPE) **return** POSITIVE_COUNT;
function COL **return** POSITIVE_COUNT;

Returns the current column number.

The exception LAYOUT_ERROR is raised if this number exceeds COUNT'LAST.

function LINE(FILE   : **in** FILE_TYPE)   **return** POSITIVE_COUNT;
function LINE **return** POSITIVE_COUNT;

Returns the current line number.

The exception LAYOUT_ERROR is raised if this number exceeds COUNT'LAST.

function PAGE(FILE : **in** FILE_TYPE) **return** POSITIVE_COUNT;
function PAGE **return** POSITIVE_COUNT;

Returns the current page number.

The exception LAYOUT_ERROR is raised if this number exceeds COUNT'LAST.

The column number, line number, or page number are allowed to exceed COUNT'LAST (as a consequence of the input or output of sufficiently many characters, lines, or pages). These events do not cause any exception to be raised. However, a call of COL, LINE, or PAGE raises the exception LAYOUT_ERROR if the corresponding number exceeds COUNT'LAST.

Note:

A page terminator is always skipped whenever the preceding line terminator is skipped. An 51
implementation may represent the combination of these terminators by a single character,
provided that it is properly recognized at input.

References: current column number 14.3, current default file 14.3, current line number 14.3, current page number 52
14.3, end_error exception 14.4, file 14.1, file terminator 14.3, get procedure 14.3.5, in_file 14.1, layout_error exception 14.4, line 14.3, line number 14.3, line terminator 14.3, maximum page length 14.3, mode_error exception 14.4,
open file 14.1, page 14.3, page length 14.3, page terminator 14.3, positive count 14.3, status_error exception 14.4

14.3.5 Get and Put Procedures

The procedures GET and PUT for items of the types CHARACTER, STRING, numeric types, and 1
enumeration types are described in subsequent sections. Features of these procedures that are
common to most of these types are described in this section. The GET and PUT procedures for
items of type CHARACTER and STRING deal with individual character values; the GET and PUT
procedures for numeric and enumeration types treat the items as lexical elements.

All procedures GET and PUT have forms with a file parameter, written first. Where this parameter 2
is omitted, the appropriate (input or output) current default file is understood to be specified. Each
procedure GET operates on a file of mode IN_FILE. Each procedure PUT operates on a file of
mode OUT_FILE.

All procedures GET and PUT maintain the current column, line, and page numbers of the specified 3
file: the effect of each of these procedures upon these numbers is the resultant of the effects of
individual transfers of characters and of individual output or skipping of terminators. Each transfer
of a character adds one to the current column number. Each output of a line terminator sets the
current column number to one and adds one to the current line number. Each output of a page
terminator sets the current column and line numbers to one and adds one to the current page
number. For input, each skipping of a line terminator sets the current column number to one and
adds one to the current line number; each skipping of a page terminator sets the current column
and line numbers to one and adds one to the current page number. Similar considerations apply to
the procedures GET_LINE, PUT_LINE, and SET_COL.

Several GET and PUT procedures, for numeric and enumeration types, have *format* parameters 4
which specify field lengths; these parameters are of the nonnegative subtype FIELD of the type
INTEGER.

Input-output of enumeration values uses the syntax of the corresponding lexical elements. Any 5
GET procedure for an enumeration type begins by skipping any leading blanks, or line or page terminators; a *blank* being defined as a space or a horizontal tabulation character. Next, characters
are input only so long as the sequence input is an initial sequence of an identifier or of a character
literal (in particular, input ceases when a line terminator is encountered). The character or line terminator that causes input to cease remains available for subsequent input.

For a numeric type, the GET procedures have a format parameter called WIDTH. If the value given 6
for this parameter is zero, the GET procedure proceeds in the same manner as for enumeration
types, but using the syntax of numeric literals instead of that of enumeration literals. If a nonzero
value is given, then exactly WIDTH characters are input, or the characters up to a line terminator,
whichever comes first; any skipped leading blanks are included in the count. The syntax used for
numeric literals is an extended syntax that allows a leading sign (but no intervening blanks, or line
or page terminators).

Any PUT procedure, for an item of a numeric or an enumeration type, outputs the value of the item 7
as a numeric literal, identifier, or character literal, as appropriate. This is preceded by leading
spaces if required by the format parameters WIDTH or FORE (as described in later sections), and
then a minus sign for a negative value; for an enumeration type, the spaces follow instead of
leading. The format given for a PUT procedure is overridden if it is insufficiently wide.

Two further cases arise for PUT procedures for numeric and enumeration types, if the line length of the specified output file is bounded (that is, if it does not have the conventional value zero). If the number of characters to be output does not exceed the maximum line length, but is such that they cannot fit on the current line, starting from the current column, then (in effect) NEW_LINE is called (with a spacing of one) before output of the item. Otherwise, if the number of characters exceeds the maximum line length, then the exception LAYOUT_ERROR is raised and no characters are output.

The exception STATUS_ERROR is raised by any of the procedures GET, GET_LINE, PUT, and PUT_LINE if the file to be used is not open. The exception MODE_ERROR is raised by the procedures GET and GET_LINE if the mode of the file to be used is not IN_FILE; and by the procedures PUT and PUT_LINE, if the mode is not OUT_FILE.

The exception END_ERROR is raised by a GET procedure if an attempt is made to skip a file terminator. The exception DATA_ERROR is raised by a GET procedure if the sequence finally input is not a lexical element corresponding to the type, in particular if no characters were input; for this test, leading blanks are ignored; for an item of a numeric type, when a sign is input, this rule applies to the succeeding numeric literal. The exception LAYOUT_ERROR is raised by a PUT procedure that outputs to a parameter of type STRING, if the length of the actual string is insufficient for the output of the item.

amples:

In the examples, here and in sections 14.3.7 and 14.3.8, the string quotes and the lower case letter b are not transferred: they are shown only to reveal the layout and spaces.

```
N : INTEGER;
...
GET(N);
```

-- Characters at input	Sequence input	Value of N
-- bb-12535b	-12535	-12535
-- bb12_535E1b	12_535E1	125350
-- bb12_535E;	12_535E	(none) DATA_ERROR raised

Example of overridden width parameter:

```
PUT(ITEM => -23, WIDTH => 2);   --  "-23"
```

References: blank 14.3.9, column number 14.3, current default file 14.3, data_error exception 14.4, end_error exception 14.4, file 14.1, fore 14.3.8, get procedure 14.3.6 14.3.7 14.3.8 14.3.9, in_file 14.1, layout_error exception 14.4, line number 14.1, line terminator 14.1, maximum line length 14.3, mode 14.1, mode_error exception 14.4, new_file procedure 14.3.4, out_file 14.1, page number 14.1, page terminator 14.1, put procedure 14.3.6 14.3.7 14.3.8 14.3.9, skipping 14.3.7 14.3.8 14.3.9, status_error exception 14.4, width 14.3.5 14.3.7 14.3.9

14.3.6 Input-Output of Characters and Strings

For an item of type CHARACTER the following procedures are provided:

```
procedure GET(FILE  : in FILE_TYPE; ITEM : out CHARACTER);
procedure GET(ITEM  : out CHARACTER);
```

After skipping any line terminators and any page terminators, reads the next character from the specified input file and returns the value of this character in the **out** parameter ITEM.

The exception END_ERROR is raised if an attempt is made to skip a file terminator.

procedure PUT(FILE   : **in** FILE_TYPE; ITEM : **in** CHARACTER);   5
procedure PUT(ITEM   : **in** CHARACTER);

> If the line length of the specified output file is bounded (that is, does not have the   6
> conventional value zero), and the current column number exceeds it, has the effect
> of calling NEW_LINE with a spacing of one. Then, or otherwise, outputs the given
> character to the file.

For an item of type STRING the following procedures are provided: 7

procedure GET(FILE   : **in** FILE_TYPE; ITEM : **out** STRING);   8
procedure GET(ITEM   : **out** STRING);

> Determines the length of the given string and attempts that number of GET   9
> operations for successive characters of the string (in particular, no operation is per-
> formed if the string is null).

procedure PUT(FILE   : **in** FILE_TYPE; ITEM : **in** STRING);   10
procedure PUT(ITEM   : **in** STRING);

> Determines the length of the given string and attempts that number of PUT   11
> operations for successive characters of the string (in particular, no operation is per-
> formed if the string is null).

procedure GET_LINE(FILE : **in** FILE_TYPE; ITEM : **out** STRING; LAST : **out** NATURAL);   12
procedure GET_LINE(ITEM : **out** STRING; LAST : **out** NATURAL);

> Replaces successive characters of the specified string by successive characters   13
> read from the specified input file. Reading stops if the end of the line is met, in
> which case the procedure SKIP_LINE is then called (in effect) with a spacing of
> one; reading also stops if the end of the string is met. Characters not replaced are
> left undefined.

> If characters are read, returns in LAST the index value such that ITEM (LAST) is the   14
> last character replaced (the index of the first character replaced is ITEM'FIRST). If
> no characters are read, returns in LAST an index value that is one less than
> ITEM'FIRST.

> The exception END_ERROR is raised if an attempt is made to skip a file terminator.   15

procedure PUT_LINE(FILE : **in** FILE_TYPE; ITEM : **in** STRING);
procedure PUT_LINE(ITEM : **in** STRING);

> Calls the procedure PUT for the given string, and then the procedure NEW_LINE   17
> with a spacing of one.

Notes:

In a literal string parameter of PUT, the enclosing string bracket characters are not output. Each   18
doubled string bracket character in the enclosed string is output as a single string bracket
character, as a consequence of the rule for string literals (see 2.6).

A string read by GET or written by PUT can extend over several lines.   19

References: current column number 14.3, end_error exception 14.4, file 14.1, file terminator 14.3, get procedure   20
14.3.5, line 14.3, line length 14.3, new_line procedure 14.3.4, put procedure 14.3.4, skipping
14.3.5

14.3.7   Input-Output for Integer Types

The following procedures are defined in the generic package INTEGER_IO. This must be instantiated for the appropriate integer type (indicated by NUM in the specification).

Values are output as decimal or based literals, without underline characters or exponent, and preceded by a minus sign if negative. The format (which includes any leading spaces and minus sign) can be specified by an optional field width parameter. Values of widths of fields in output formats are of the nonnegative integer subtype FIELD. Values of bases are of the integer subtype NUMBER_BASE.

```
subtype NUMBER_BASE is INTEGER range 2 .. 16;
```

The default field width and base to be used by output procedures are defined by the following variables that are declared in the generic package INTEGER_IO :

```
DEFAULT_WIDTH   : FIELD := NUM'WIDTH;
DEFAULT_BASE    : NUMBER_BASE := 10;
```

The following procedures are provided:

```
procedure GET(FILE  : in FILE_TYPE; ITEM : out NUM; WIDTH : in FIELD := 0);
procedure GET(ITEM  : out NUM; WIDTH : in FIELD := 0);
```

If the value of the parameter WIDTH is zero, skips any leading blanks, line terminators, or page terminators, then reads a plus or a minus sign if present, then reads according to the syntax of an integer literal (which may be a based literal). If a nonzero value of WIDTH is supplied, then exactly WIDTH characters are input, or the characters (possibly none) up to a line terminator, whichever comes first; any skipped leading blanks are included in the count.

Returns, in the parameter ITEM, the value of type NUM that corresponds to the sequence input.

The exception DATA_ERROR is raised if the sequence input does not have the required syntax or if the value obtained is not of the subtype NUM.

```
procedure PUT(FILE   : in FILE_TYPE;
              ITEM    : in NUM;
              WIDTH   : in FIELD := DEFAULT_WIDTH;
              BASE    : in NUMBER_BASE := DEFAULT_BASE);

procedure PUT(ITEM   : in NUM;
              WIDTH   : in FIELD := DEFAULT_WIDTH;
              BASE    : in NUMBER_BASE := DEFAULT_BASE);
```

Outputs the value of the parameter ITEM as an integer literal, with no underlines, no exponent, and no leading zeros (but a single zero for the value zero), and a preceding minus sign for a negative value.

If the resulting sequence of characters to be output has fewer than WIDTH characters, then leading spaces are first output to make up the difference.

Uses the syntax for decimal literal if the parameter BASE has the value ten (either explicitly or through DEFAULT_BASE); otherwise, uses the syntax for based literal, with any letters in upper case.

```
procedure GET(FROM : in STRING; ITEM : out NUM; LAST : out POSITIVE);
```

Reads an integer value from the beginning of the given string, following the same rules as the GET procedure that reads an integer value from a file, but treating the

end of the string as a file terminator. Returns, in the parameter ITEM, the value of
type NUM that corresponds to the sequence input. Returns in LAST the index
value such that FROM (LAST) is the last character read.

The exception DATA_ERROR is raised if the sequence input does not have the   15
required syntax or if the value obtained is not of the subtype NUM.

```
procedure PUT(TO    : out STRING;                                              16
              ITEM  : in NUM;
              BASE  : in NUMBER_BASE := DEFAULT_BASE);
```

Outputs the value of the parameter ITEM to the given string, following the same   17
rule as for output to a file, using the length of the given string as the value for
WIDTH.

Examples: 18.

```
package INT_IO is new INTEGER_IO(SMALL_INT); use INT_IO;
-- default format used at instantiation, DEFAULT_WIDTH = 4, DEFAULT_BASE = 10

PUT(126);                            -- "b126"
PUT(-126, 7);                        -- "bbb-126"
PUT(126, WIDTH => 13, BASE => 2);    -- "bbb2#1111110#"
```

References: based literal 2.4.2, blank 14.3.5, data_error exception 14.4, decimal literal 2.4.1, field subtype 14.3.5,   19
file_type 14.1, get procedure 14.3.5, integer_io package 14.3.10, integer literal 2.4, layout_error exception 14.4, line
terminator 14.3, put procedure 14.3.5, skipping 14.3.5, width 14.3.5

14.3.8 Input-Output for Real Types

The following procedures are defined in the generic packages FLOAT_IO and FIXED_IO, which   1
must be instantiated for the appropriate floating point or fixed point type respectively (indicated by
NUM in the specifications).

Values are output as decimal literals without underline characters. The format of each value output   2
consists of a FORE field, a decimal point, an AFT field, and (if a nonzero EXP parameter is supplied)
the letter E and an EXP field. The two possible formats thus correspond to:

```
FORE . AFT
```

and to: 3

```
FORE . AFT E EXP
```

without any spaces between these fields. The FORE field may include leading spaces, and a minus   4
sign for negative values. The AFT field includes only decimal digits (possibly with trailing zeros).
The EXP field includes the sign (plus or minus) and the exponent (possibly with leading zeros).

For floating point types, the default lengths of these fields are defined by the following variables   5
that are declared in the generic package FLOAT_IO:

```
DEFAULT_FORE  : FIELD := 2;
DEFAULT_AFT   : FIELD := NUM'DIGITS-1;
DEFAULT_EXP   : FIELD := 3;
```

For fixed point types, the default lengths of these fields are defined by the following variables that are declared in the generic package FIXED_IO :

```
DEFAULT_FORE   : FIELD := NUM'FORE;
DEFAULT_AFT    : FIELD := NUM'AFT;
DEFAULT_EXP    : FIELD := 0;
```

The following procedures are provided:

```
procedure GET(FILE  : in FILE_TYPE; ITEM : out NUM; WIDTH : in FIELD := 0);
procedure GET(ITEM  : out NUM; WIDTH   : in FIELD := 0);
```

> If the value of the parameter WIDTH is zero, skips any leading blanks, line terminators, or page terminators, then reads a plus or a minus sign if present, then reads according to the syntax of a real literal (which may be a based literal). If a nonzero value of WIDTH is supplied, then exactly WIDTH characters are input, or the characters (possibly none) up to a line terminator, whichever comes first; any skipped leading blanks are included in the count.
>
> Returns, in the parameter ITEM , the value of type NUM that corresponds to the sequence input.
>
> The exception DATA_ERROR is raised if the sequence input does not have the required syntax or if the value obtained is not of the subtype NUM .

```
procedure PUT(FILE   : in FILE_TYPE;
              ITEM   : in NUM;
              FORE   : in FIELD := DEFAULT_FORE;
              AFT    : in FIELD := DEFAULT_AFT;
              EXP    : in FIELD := DEFAULT_EXP);

procedure PUT(ITEM   : in NUM;
              FORE   : in FIELD := DEFAULT_FORE;
              AFT    : in FIELD := DEFAULT_AFT;
              EXP    : in FIELD := DEFAULT_EXP);
```

> Outputs the value of the parameter ITEM as a decimal literal with the format defined by FORE , AFT and EXP . If the value is negative, a minus sign is included in the integer part. If EXP has the value zero, then the integer part to be output has as many digits as are needed to represent the integer part of the value of ITEM , overriding FORE if necessary, or consists of the digit zero if the value of ITEM has no integer part.
>
> If EXP has a value greater than zero, then the integer part to be output has a single digit, which is nonzero except for the value 0.0 of ITEM .
>
> In both cases, however, if the integer part to be output has fewer than FORE characters, including any minus sign, then leading spaces are first output to make up the difference. The number of digits of the fractional part is given by AFT , or is one if AFT equals zero. The value is rounded; a value of exactly one half in the last place may be rounded either up or down.
>
> If EXP has the value zero, there is no exponent part. If EXP has a value greater than zero, then the exponent part to be output has as many digits as are needed to represent the exponent part of the value of ITEM (for which a single digit integer part is used), and includes an initial sign (plus or minus). If the exponent part to be output has fewer than EXP characters, including the sign, then leading zeros precede the digits, to make up the difference. For the value 0.0 of ITEM , the exponent has the value zero.

procedure GET(FROM : **in** STRING; ITEM : **out** NUM; LAST : **out** POSITIVE);   17

Reads a real value from the beginning of the given string, following the same rule   18
as the GET procedure that reads a real value from a file, but treating the end of the
string as a file terminator. Returns, in the parameter ITEM, the value of type NUM
that corresponds to the sequence input. Returns in LAST the index value such that
FROM(LAST) is the last character read.

The exception DATA_ERROR is raised if the sequence input does not have the   19
required syntax, or if the value obtained is not of the subtype NUM.

procedure PUT(TO   : **out** STRING;   20
          ITEM : **in** NUM;
          AFT : **in** FIELD   := DEFAULT_AFT;
          EXP : **in** INTEGER := DEFAULT_EXP);

Outputs the value of the parameter ITEM to the given string, following the same   21
rule as for output to a file, using a value for FORE such that the sequence of
characters output exactly fills the string, including any leading spaces.

Examples: 22

```
package REAL_IO is new FLOAT_IO(REAL); use REAL_IO;
-- default format used at instantiation, DEFAULT_EXP = 3

X : REAL := -123.4567;  --  digits 8      (see 3.5.7)

PUT(X); -- default format                 "-1.2345670E+02"
PUT(X, FORE => 5, AFT => 3, EXP => 2);  --  "bbb-1.235E+2"
PUT(X, 5, 3, 0);                        --  "b-123.457"
```

Note:

For an item with a positive value, if output to a string exactly fills the string without leading spaces,   23
then output of the corresponding negative value will raise LAYOUT_ERROR.

References: aft attribute 3.5.10, based literal 2.4.2, blank 14.3.5, data_error exception 14.3.5, decimal literal 2.4.1,   24
field subtype 14.3.5, file_type 14.1, fixed_io package 14.3.10, floating_io package 14.3.10, fore attribute 3.5.10, get
procedure 14.3.5, layout_error 14.3.5, line terminator 14.3.5, put procedure 14.3.5, real literal 2.4, skipping 14.3.5,
width 14.3.5

14.3.9   Input-Output for Enumeration Types

The following procedures are defined in the generic package ENUMERATION_IO, which must be   1
instantiated for the appropriate enumeration type (indicated by ENUM in the specification).

Values are output using either upper or lower case letters for identifiers. This is specified by the   2
parameter SET, which is of the enumeration type TYPE_SET.

```
type TYPE_SET is (LOWER_CASE, UPPER_CASE);
```

The format (which includes any trailing spaces) can be specified by an optional field width   3
parameter. The default field width and letter case are defined by the following variables that are
declared in the generic package ENUMERATION_IO:

```
DEFAULT_WIDTH   : FIELD := 0;
DEFAULT_SETTING : TYPE_SET := UPPER_CASE;
```

The following procedures are provided:

procedure GET(FILE   : **in** FILE_TYPE; ITEM : **out** ENUM);
procedure GET(ITEM   : **out** ENUM);

After skipping any leading blanks, line terminators, or page terminators, reads an identifier according to the syntax of this lexical element (lower and upper case being considered equivalent), or a character literal according to the syntax of this lexical element (including the apostrophes). Returns, in the parameter ITEM, the value of type ENUM that corresponds to the sequence input.

The exception DATA_ERROR is raised if the sequence input does not have the required syntax, or if the identifier or character literal does not correspond to a value of the subtype ENUM.

procedure PUT(FILE   : **in** FILE_TYPE;
             ITEM   : **in** ENUM;
             WIDTH   : **in** FIELD := DEFAULT_WIDTH;
             SET   : **in** TYPE_SET := DEFAULT_SETTING);

procedure PUT(ITEM   : **in** ENUM;
             WIDTH   : **in** FIELD := DEFAULT_WIDTH;
             SET   : **in** TYPE_SET := DEFAULT_SETTING);

Outputs the value of the parameter ITEM as an enumeration literal (either an identifier or a character literal). The optional parameter SET indicates whether lower case or upper case is used for identifiers; it has no effect for character literals. If the sequence of characters produced has fewer than WIDTH characters, then trailing spaces are finally output to make up the difference.

procedure GET(FROM : **in** STRING; ITEM : **out** ENUM; LAST : **out** POSITIVE);

Reads an enumeration value from the beginning of the given string, following the same rule as the GET procedure that reads an enumeration value from a file, but treating the end of the string as a file terminator. Returns, in the parameter ITEM, the value of type ENUM that corresponds to the sequence input. Returns in LAST the index value such that FROM (LAST) is the last character read.

The exception DATA_ERROR is raised if the sequence input does not have the required syntax, or if the identifier or character literal does not correspond to a value of the subtype ENUM.

procedure PUT(TO   : **out** STRING;
             ITEM : **in** ENUM;
             SET   : **in** TYPE_SET := DEFAULT_SETTING);

Outputs the value of the parameter ITEM to the given string, following the same rule as for output to a file, using the length of the given string as the value for WIDTH.

Although the specification of the package ENUMERATION_IO would allow instantiation for an integer type, this is not the intended purpose of this generic package, and the effect of such instantiations is not defined by the language.

Notes:

There is a difference between PUT defined for characters, and for enumeration values. Thus

TEXT_IO.PUT('A');   --   outputs the character A

package CHAR_IO **is new** TEXT_IO.ENUMERATION_IO(CHARACTER);
CHAR_IO.PUT('A');   --   outputs the character 'A', between single quotes

The type BOOLEAN is an enumeration type, hence ENUMERATION_IO can be instantiated for this   17
type.

References: blank 14.3.5, data_error 14.3.5, enumeration_io package 14.3.10, field subtype 14.3.5, file_type 14.1,   18
get procedure 14.3.5, line terminator 14.3.5, put procedure 14.3.5, skipping 14.3.5, width 14.3.5

14.3.10 Specification of the Package Text_IO

```
with IO_EXCEPTIONS;
package TEXT_IO is

   type FILE_TYPE  is limited private;

   type FILE_MODE is (IN_FILE, OUT_FILE);

   type COUNT is range 0 .. implementation_defined;
   subtype POSITIVE_COUNT is COUNT range 1 .. COUNT'LAST;
   UNBOUNDED : constant COUNT := 0; -- line and page length

   subtype FIELD        is INTEGER range 0 .. implementation_defined;
   subtype NUMBER_BASE is INTEGER range 2 .. 16;

   type TYPE_SET is (LOWER_CASE, UPPER_CASE);

   -- File Management

   procedure CREATE  ( FILE  : in out FILE_TYPE;
                       MODE : in FILE_MODE := OUT_FILE;
                       NAME : in STRING    := "";
                       FORM : in STRING    := "");

   procedure OPEN    ( FILE  : in out FILE_TYPE;
                       MODE : in FILE_MODE;
                       NAME : in STRING;
                       FORM : in STRING := "");

   procedure  CLOSE   (FILE : in out FILE_TYPE);
   procedure  DELETE  (FILE : in out FILE_TYPE);
   procedure  RESET   (FILE : in out FILE_TYPE; MODE : in FILE_MODE);
   procedure  RESET   (FILE : in out FILE_TYPE);

   function   MODE    (FILE : in FILE_TYPE) return FILE_MODE ;
   function   NAME    (FILE : in FILE_TYPE) return STRING;
   function   FORM    (FILE : in FILE_TYPE) return STRING;

   function   IS_OPEN (FILE : in FILE_TYPE) return BOOLEAN;

   -- Control of default input and output files

   procedure  SET_INPUT  (FILE : in FILE_TYPE);
   procedure  SET_OUTPUT (FILE : in FILE_TYPE);


   function   STANDARD_INPUT   return FILE_TYPE;
   function   STANDARD_OUTPUT  return FILE_TYPE;

   function   CURRENT_INPUT    return FILE_TYPE;
   function   CURRENT_OUTPUT   return FILE_TYPE;
```

— Specification of line and page lengths

```
procedure  SET_LINE_LENGTH   (FILE : in FILE_TYPE; TO : in COUNT);
procedure  SET_LINE_LENGTH   (TO : in COUNT);

procedure  SET_PAGE_LENGTH   (FILE : in FILE_TYPE; TO : in COUNT);
procedure  SET_PAGE_LENGTH   (TO : in COUNT);

function   LINE_LENGTH (FILE : in FILE_TYPE) return COUNT;
function   LINE_LENGTH   return COUNT;

function   PAGE_LENGTH (FILE : in FILE_TYPE) return COUNT;
function   PAGE_LENGTH return COUNT;
```

— Column, Line, and Page Control

```
procedure  NEW_LINE    (FILE : in FILE_TYPE; SPACING : in POSITIVE_COUNT := 1);
procedure  NEW_LINE    (SPACING : in POSITIVE_COUNT := 1);

procedure  SKIP_LINE   (FILE : in FILE_TYPE; SPACING : in POSITIVE_COUNT := 1);
procedure  SKIP_LINE   (SPACING : in POSITIVE_COUNT := 1);

function   END_OF_LINE (FILE : in FILE_TYPE) return BOOLEAN;
function   END_OF_LINE   return BOOLEAN;

procedure  NEW_PAGE    (FILE : in FILE_TYPE);
procedure  NEW_PAGE;

procedure  SKIP_PAGE   (FILE : in FILE_TYPE);
procedure  SKIP_PAGE;

function   END_OF_PAGE (FILE : in FILE_TYPE) return BOOLEAN;
function   END_OF_PAGE return BOOLEAN;

function   END_OF_FILE (FILE : in FILE_TYPE) return BOOLEAN;
function   END_OF_FILE   return BOOLEAN;


procedure  SET_COL (FILE : in FILE_TYPE; TO : in POSITIVE_COUNT);
procedure  SET_COL (TO   : in POSITIVE_COUNT);

procedure  SET_LINE (FILE : in FILE_TYPE; TO : in POSITIVE_COUNT);
procedure  SET_LINE (TO   : in POSITIVE_COUNT);


function COL  (FILE : in FILE_TYPE) return POSITIVE_COUNT;
function COL    return POSITIVE_COUNT;

function LINE (FILE : in FILE_TYPE) return POSITIVE_COUNT;
function LINE return POSITIVE_COUNT;

function PAGE (FILE : in FILE_TYPE) return POSITIVE_COUNT;
function PAGE   return POSITIVE_COUNT;
```

```
-- Character Input-Output

procedure  GET(FILE   : in   FILE_TYPE; ITEM : out CHARACTER);
procedure  GET(ITEM   : out  CHARACTER);
procedure  PUT(FILE   : in   FILE_TYPE; ITEM : in CHARACTER);
procedure  PUT(ITEM   : in   CHARACTER);

-- String Input-Output

procedure  GET(FILE   : in   FILE_TYPE; ITEM : out STRING);
procedure  GET(ITEM   : out  STRING);
procedure  PUT(FILE   : in   FILE_TYPE; ITEM : in STRING);
procedure  PUT(ITEM   : in   STRING);

procedure  GET_LINE(FILE : in   FILE_TYPE; ITEM : out STRING; LAST : out NATURAL);
procedure  GET_LINE(ITEM : out  STRING; LAST : out NATURAL);
procedure  PUT_LINE(FILE : in   FILE_TYPE; ITEM : in STRING);
procedure  PUT_LINE(ITEM : in   STRING);

-- Generic package for Input-Output of Integer Types

generic
   type NUM is range <>;
package INTEGER_IO is

   DEFAULT_WIDTH  : FIELD := NUM'WIDTH;
   DEFAULT_BASE   : NUMBER_BASE := 10;

   procedure GET(FILE   : in   FILE_TYPE; ITEM : out NUM; WIDTH : in FIELD := 0);
   procedure GET(ITEM   : out NUM; WIDTH : in FIELD := 0);

   procedure PUT(FILE   : in FILE_TYPE;
                 ITEM   : in NUM;
                 WIDTH  : in FIELD := DEFAULT_WIDTH;
                 BASE   : in NUMBER_BASE := DEFAULT_BASE);
   procedure PUT(ITEM   : in NUM;
                 WIDTH  : in FIELD := DEFAULT_WIDTH;
                 BASE   : in NUMBER_BASE := DEFAULT_BASE);

   procedure GET(FROM   : in STRING; ITEM : out NUM; LAST : out POSITIVE);
   procedure PUT(TO     : out STRING;
                 ITEM   : in NUM;
                 BASE   : in NUMBER_BASE := DEFAULT_BASE);

end INTEGER_IO;
```

```
-- Generic packages for Input-Output of Real Types

generic
   type NUM is digits <>;
package FLOAT_IO is

   DEFAULT_FORE  : FIELD := 2;
   DEFAULT_AFT   : FIELD := NUM'DIGITS-1;
   DEFAULT_EXP   : FIELD := 3;

   procedure  GET(FILE : in FILE_TYPE; ITEM : out NUM; WIDTH : in FIELD := 0);
   procedure  GET(ITEM : out NUM; WIDTH : in FIELD := 0);

   procedure PUT(FILE    : in FILE_TYPE;
                 ITEM    : in NUM;
                 FORE    : in FIELD := DEFAULT_FORE;
                 AFT     : in FIELD := DEFAULT_AFT;
                 EXP     : in FIELD := DEFAULT_EXP);
   procedure PUT(ITEM    : in NUM;
                 FORE    : in FIELD := DEFAULT_FORE;
                 AFT     : in FIELD := DEFAULT_AFT;
                 EXP     : in FIELD := DEFAULT_EXP);

   procedure GET(FROM : in STRING; ITEM : out NUM; LAST : out POSITIVE);
   procedure PUT(TO      : out STRING;
                 ITEM    : in NUM;
                 AFT     : in FIELD := DEFAULT_AFT;
                 EXP     : in FIELD := DEFAULT_EXP);
end FLOAT_IO;

generic
   type NUM is delta <>;
package FIXED_IO is

   DEFAULT_FORE  : FIELD := NUM'FORE;
   DEFAULT_AFT   : FIELD := NUM'AFT;
   DEFAULT_EXP   : FIELD := 0;

   procedure GET(FILE   : in FILE_TYPE; ITEM : out NUM; WIDTH : in FIELD := 0);
   procedure GET(ITEM   : out NUM; WIDTH : in FIELD := 0);

   procedure PUT(FILE    : in FILE_TYPE;
                 ITEM    : in NUM;
                 FORE    : in FIELD := DEFAULT_FORE;
                 AFT     : in FIELD := DEFAULT_AFT;
                 EXP     : in FIELD := DEFAULT_EXP);
   procedure PUT(ITEM    : in NUM;
                 FORE    : in FIELD := DEFAULT_FORE;
                 AFT     : in FIELD := DEFAULT_AFT;
                 EXP     : in FIELD := DEFAULT_EXP);

   procedure GET(FROM : in  STRING; ITEM : out NUM; LAST : out POSITIVE);
   procedure PUT(TO      : out STRING;
                 ITEM    : in NUM;
                 AFT     : in FIELD := DEFAULT_AFT;
                 EXP     : in FIELD := DEFAULT_EXP);

end FIXED_IO;
```

-- Generic package for Input-Output of · Enumeration Types

```
generic
   type ENUM is (<>);
package ENUMERATION_IO is

   DEFAULT_WIDTH    : FIELD := 0;
   DEFAULT_SETTING  : TYPE_SET := UPPER_CASE;

   procedure GET(FILE    : in FILE_TYPE; ITEM : out ENUM);
   procedure GET(ITEM    : out ENUM);

   procedure PUT(FILE    : in FILE_TYPE;
                 ITEM    : in ENUM;
                 WIDTH   : in FIELD      := DEFAULT_WIDTH;
                 SET     : in TYPE_SET   := DEFAULT_SETTING);
   procedure PUT(ITEM    : in ENUM;
                 WIDTH   : in FIELD      := DEFAULT_WIDTH;
                 SET     : in TYPE_SET   := DEFAULT_SETTING);

   procedure GET(FROM : in    STRING; ITEM : out ENUM; LAST : out POSITIVE);
   procedure PUT(TO   : out   STRING;
                 ITEM : in     ENUM;
                 SET  : in     TYPE_SET := DEFAULT_SETTING);
end ENUMERATION_IO;

-- Exceptions

STATUS_ERROR   : exception renames IO_EXCEPTIONS.STATUS_ERROR;
MODE_ERROR     : exception renames IO_EXCEPTIONS.MODE_ERROR;
NAME_ERROR     : exception renames IO_EXCEPTIONS.NAME_ERROR;
USE_ERROR      : exception renames IO_EXCEPTIONS.USE_ERROR;
DEVICE_ERROR   : exception renames IO_EXCEPTIONS.DEVICE_ERROR;
END_ERROR      : exception renames IO_EXCEPTIONS.END_ERROR;
DATA_ERROR     : exception renames IO_EXCEPTIONS.DATA_ERROR;
LAYOUT_ERROR   : exception renames IO_EXCEPTIONS.LAYOUT_ERROR;

private
   -- implementation-dependent
end TEXT_IO;
```

14.4   Exceptions in Input-Output

The following exceptions can be raised by input-output operations. They are declared in the
package IO_EXCEPTIONS, defined in section 14.5; this package is named in the context clause for
each of the three input-output packages. Only outline descriptions are given of the conditions
under which NAME_ERROR, USE_ERROR, and DEVICE_ERROR are raised; for full details see
Appendix F. If more than one error condition exists, the corresponding exception that appears
earliest in the following list is the one that is raised.

The exception STATUS_ERROR is raised by an attempt to operate upon a file that is not open, and
by an attempt to open a file that is already open.

The exception MODE_ERROR is raised by an attempt to read from, or test for the end of, a file
whose current mode is OUT_FILE, and also by an attempt to write to a file whose current mode is
IN_FILE. In the case of TEXT_IO, the exception MODE_ERROR is also raised by specifying a file
whose current mode is OUT_FILE in a call of SET_INPUT, SKIP_LINE, END_OF_LINE, SKIP_PAGE,
or END_OF_PAGE; and by specifying a file whose current mode is IN_FILE in a call of
SET_OUTPUT, SET_LINE_LENGTH, SET_PAGE_LENGTH, LINE_LENGTH, PAGE_LENGTH,
NEW_LINE, or NEW_PAGE.

The exception NAME_ERROR is raised by a call of CREATE or OPEN if the string given for the parameter NAME does not allow the identification of an external file. For example, this exception is raised if the string is improper, or, alternatively, if either none or more than one external file corresponds to the string.

The exception USE_ERROR is raised if an operation is attempted that is not possible for reasons that depend on characteristics of the external file. For example, this exception is raised by the procedure CREATE, among other circumstances, if the given mode is OUT_FILE but the form specifies an input only device, if the parameter FORM specifies invalid access rights, or if an external file with the given name already exists and overwriting is not allowed.

The exception DEVICE_ERROR is raised if an input-output operation cannot be completed because of a malfunction of the underlying system.

The exception END_ERROR is raised by an attempt to skip (read past) the end of a file.

The exception DATA_ERROR may be raised by the procedure READ if the element read cannot be interpreted as a value of the required type. This exception is also raised by a procedure GET (defined in the package TEXT_IO) if the input character sequence fails to satisfy the required syntax, or if the value input does not belong to the range of the required type or subtype.

The exception LAYOUT_ERROR is raised (in text input-output) by COL, LINE, or PAGE if the value returned exceeds COUNT'LAST. The exception LAYOUT_ERROR is also raised on output by an attempt to set column or line numbers in excess of specified maximum line or page lengths, respectively (excluding the unbounded cases). It is also raised by an attempt to PUT too many characters to a string.

References: col function 14.3.4, create procedure 14.2.1, end_of_line function 14.3.4, end_of_page function 14.3.4, external file 14.1, file 14.1, form string 14.1, get procedure 14.3.5, in_file 14.1, io_exceptions package 14.5, line function 14.3.4, line_length function 14.3.4, name string 14.1, new_line procedure 14.3.4, new_page procedure 14.3.4, open procedure 14.2.1, out_file 14.1, page function 14.3.4, page_length function 14.3.4, put procedure 14.3.5, read procedure 14.2.2 14.2.3, set_input procedure 14.3.2, set_line_length 14.3.3, set_page_length 14.3.3, set_output 14.3.2, skip_line procedure 14.3.4, skip_page procedure 14.3.4, text_io package 14.3

14.5   Specification of the Package IO_Exceptions

This package defines the exceptions needed by the packages SEQUENTIAL_IO, DIRECT_IO, and TEXT_IO.

```
package IO_EXCEPTIONS is

    STATUS_ERROR   : exception;
    MODE_ERROR`    : exception;
    NAME_ERROR     : exception;
    USE_ERROR      : exception;
    DEVICE_ERROR   : exception;
    END_ERROR      : exception;
    DATA_ERROR     : exception;
    LAYOUT_ERROR   : exception;

end IO_EXCEPTIONS;
```

14.6   Low Level Input-Output

A low level input-output operation is an operation acting on a physical device. Such an operation is handled by using one of the (overloaded) predefined procedures SEND_CONTROL and RECEIVE_CONTROL

A procedure SEND_CONTROL may be used to send control information to a physical device. A procedure RECEIVE_CONTROL may be used to monitor the execution of an input-output operation by requesting information from the physical device.

Such procedures are declared in the standard package LOW_LEVEL_IO and have two parameters identifying the device and the data. However, the kinds and formats of the control information will depend on the physical characteristics of the machine and the device. Hence, the types of the parameters are implementation-defined. Overloaded definitions of these procedures should be provided for the supported devices.

The visible part of the package defining these procedures is outlined as follows:

```
package LOW_LEVEL_IO is
  -   declarations of the possible types for DEVICE and DATA;
  --  declarations of overloaded procedures for these types:
  procedure SEND_CONTROL      (DEVICE : device_type; DATA : in out data_type);
  procedure RECEIVE_CONTROL   (DEVICE : device_type; DATA : in out data_type);
end;
```

The bodies of the procedures SEND_CONTROL and RECEIVE_CONTROL for various devices can be supplied in the body of the package LOW_LEVEL_IO. These procedure bodies may be written with code statements.

14.7 Example of Input-Output

The following example shows the use of some of the text input-output facilities in a dialogue with a user at a terminal. The user is prompted to type a color, and the program responds by giving the number of items of that color available in stock, according to an inventory. The default input and output files are used. For simplicity, all the requisite instantiations are given within one sub-program; in practice, a package, separate from the procedure, would be used.

```
with TEXT_IO; use TEXT_IO;
procedure DIALOGUE is
   type COLOR is (WHITE, RED, ORANGE, YELLOW, GREEN, BLUE, BROWN);
   package COLOR_IO is new ENUMERATION_IO(ENUM => COLOR);
   package NUMBER_IO is new INTEGER_IO(INTEGER);
   use COLOR_IO, NUMBER_IO;

   INVENTORY : array (COLOR) of INTEGER := (20, 17, 43, 10, 28, 173, 87);
   CHOICE : COLOR;

   procedure ENTER_COLOR (SELECTION : out COLOR) is
   begin
      loop
         begin
            PUT ("Color selected: ");   --   prompts user
            GET (SELECTION);            --   accepts color typed, or raises exception
            return;
         exception
            when DATA_ERROR =>
               PUT("Invalid color, try again.   ");  --  user has typed new line
               NEW_LINE(2);
               --  completes execution of the block statement
         end;
      end loop;  --   repeats the block statement until color accepted
   end;
begin --   statements of DIALOGUE;

   NUMBER_IO.DEFAULT_WIDTH := 5;

   loop

      ENTER_COLOR(CHOICE);   --  user types color and new line

      SET_COL(5);    PUT(CHOICE); PUT(" items available:");
      SET_COL(40);   PUT(INVENTORY(CHOICE));   --   default width is 5
      NEW_LINE;
   end loop;
end DIALOGUE;
```

Example of an interaction (characters typed by the user are italicized):   3

```
Color selected: Black
Invalid color, try again.

Color selected: Blue
   BLUE items available:          173
Color selected: Yellow
   YELLOW items available:         10
```

appendix XI

Glossary

D. Glossary

[This glossary is not part of the standard definition of the Ada programming language.]

This appendix is informative and is not part of the standard definition of the Ada programming language. Italicized terms in the abbreviated descriptions below either have glossary entries themselves or are described in entries for related terms.

Accept statement. See *entry*.

Access type. A value of an access type (an *access value*) is either a null value, or a value that *designates* an *object* created by an *allocator*. The designated object can be read and updated via the access value. The definition of an access type specifies the type of the objects designated by values of the access type. See also *collection*.

Actual parameter. See *parameter*.

Aggregate. The evaluation of an aggregate yields a value of a *composite type*. The value is specified by giving the value of each of the *components*. Either *positional association* or *named association* may be used to indicate which value is associated with which component.

Allocator. The evaluation of an allocator creates an *object* and returns a new *access value* which *designates* the object.

Array type. A value of an array type consists of *components* which are all of the same *subtype* (and hence, of the same type). Each component is uniquely distinguished by an *index* (for a one-dimensional array) or by a sequence of indices (for a multidimensional array). Each index must be a value of a *discrete type* and must lie in the correct index *range*.

Assignment. Assignment is the *operation* that replaces the current value of a *variable* by a new value. An *assignment statement* specifies a variable on the left, and on the right, an *expression* whose value is to be the new value of the variable.

Attribute. The evaluation of an attribute yields a predefined characteristic of a named entity; some attributes are *functions*.

Block statement. A block statement is a single statement that may contain a sequence of statements. It may also include a *declarative part*, and *exception handlers*; their effects are local to the block statement.

Body. A body defines the execution of a *subprogram*, *package*, or *task*. A *body stub* is a form of body that indicates that this execution is defined in a separately compiled *subunit*.

Collection. A collection is the entire set of *objects* created by evaluation of *allocators* for an *access type*.

Compilation unit. A compilation unit is the *declaration* or the *body* of a *program unit*, presented for compilation as an independent text. It is optionally preceded by a *context clause*, naming other compilation units upon which it depends by means of one more *with clauses*.

Component. A component is a value that is a part of a larger value, or an *object* that is part of a larger object.

Composite type. A composite type is one whose values have *components*. There are two kinds of composite type: *array types* and *record types*.

Constant. See *object*.

Constraint. A constraint determines a subset of the values of a *type*. A value in that subset *satisfies* the constraint.

Context clause. See *compilation unit*.

Declaration. A declaration associates an identifier (or some other notation) with an entity. This association is in effect within a region of text called the *scope* of the declaration. Within the scope of a declaration, there are places where it is possible to use the identifier to refer to the associated declared entity. At such places the identifier is said to be a *simple name* of the entity; the *name* is said to *denote* the associated entity.

Declarative Part. A declarative part is a sequence of *declarations*. It may also contain related information such as *subprogram bodies* and *representation clauses*.

Denote. See *declaration*.

Derived Type. A derived type is a *type* whose operations and values are replicas of those of an existing type. The existing type is called the *parent type* of the derived type.

Designate. See *access type*, *task*.

Direct visibility. See *visibility*.

Discrete Type. A discrete type is a *type* which has an ordered set of distinct values. The discrete types are the *enumeration* and *integer types*. Discrete types are used for indexing and iteration, and for choices in case statements and record *variants*.

Discriminant. A discriminant is a distinguished *component* of an *object* or value of a *record type*. The *subtypes* of other components, or even their presence or absence, may depend on the value of the discriminant.

Discriminant constraint. A discriminant constraint on a *record type* or *private type* specifies a value for each *discriminant* of the *type*.

Elaboration. The elaboration of a *declaration* is the process by which the declaration achieves its effect (such as creating an *object*); this process occurs during program execution.

Entry. An entry is used for communication between *tasks*. Externally, an entry is called just as a *subprogram* is called; its internal behavior is specified by one or more *accept statements* specifying the actions to be performed when the entry is called.

Enumeration type. An enumeration type is a *discrete type* whose values are represented by enumeration literals which are given explicitly in the *type declaration*. These enumeration literals are either *identifiers* or *character literals*.

Evaluation. The evaluation of an *expression* is the process by which the value of the expression is computed. This process occurs during program execution.

Exception. An exception is an error situation which may arise during program execution. To *raise* an exception is to abandon normal program execution so as to signal that the error has taken place. An *exception handler* is a portion of program text specifying a response to the exception. Execution of such a program text is called *handling* the exception.

Expanded name. An expanded name *denotes* an entity which is *declared* immediately within some construct. An expanded name has the form of a *selected component*: the *prefix* denotes the construct (a *program unit*; or a *block*, loop, or *accept statement*); the *selector* is the *simple name* of the entity.

Expression. An expression defines the computation of a value.

Fixed point type. See *real type*.

Floating point type. See *real type*.

Formal parameter. See *parameter*.

Function. See *subprogram*.

Generic unit. A generic unit is a template either for a set of *subprograms* or for a set of *packages*. A subprogram or package created using the template is called an *instance* of the generic unit. A *generic instantiation* is the kind of *declaration* that creates an instance.

A generic unit is written as a subprogram or package but with the specification prefixed by a *generic formal part* which may declare *generic formal parameters*. A generic formal parameter is either a *type*, a *subprogram*, or an *object*. A generic unit is one of the kinds of *program unit*.

Handler. See *exception*.

Index. See *array type*.

Index constraint. An index constraint for an *array type* specifies the lower and upper bounds for each index *range* of the array type.

Indexed component. An indexed component *denotes* a *component* in an *array*. It is a form of *name* containing *expressions* which specify the values of the *indices* of the array component. An indexed component may also denote an *entry* in a family of entries.

Instance. See *generic unit*.

Integer type. An integer type is a *discrete type* whose values represent all integer numbers within a specific *range*.

Lexical element. A lexical element is an identifier, a *literal*, a delimiter, or a comment.

Limited type. A limited type is a *type* for which neither assignment nor the predefined comparison for equality is implicitly declared. All *task* types are limited. A *private type* can be defined to be limited. An equality operator can be explicitly declared for a limited type.

Literal. A literal represents a value literally, that is, by means of letters and other characters. A literal is either a numeric literal, an enumeration literal, a character literal, or a string literal.

Mode. See *parameter*.

Model number. A model number is an exactly representable value of a *real type*. Opera-

tions of a real type are defined in terms of operations on the model numbers of the type.

The properties of the model numbers and of their operations are the minimal properties preserved by all implementations of the real type.

Name. A name is a construct that stands for an entity: it is said that the name *denotes* the entity, and that the entity is the meaning of the name. See also *declaration*, *prefix*.

Named association. A named association specifies the association of an item with one or more positions in a list, by naming the positions.

Object. An object contains a value. A program creates an object either by *elaborating* an *object declaration* or by *evaluating* an *allocator*. The declaration or allocator specifies a *type* for the object: the object can only contain values of that type.

Operation. An operation is an elementary action associated with one or more *types*. It is either implicitly declared by the *declaration* of the type, or it is a *subprogram* that has a *parameter* or *result* of the type.

Operator. An operator is an operation which has one or two operands. A unary operator is written before an operand; a binary operator is written between two operands. This notation is a special kind of *function call*. An operator can be declared as a function. Many operators are implicitly declared by the *declaration* of a *type* (for example, most type declarations imply the declaration of the equality operator for values of the type).

Overloading. An identifier can have several alternative meanings at a given point in the program text: this property is called *overloading*. For example, an overloaded enumeration literal can be an identifier that appears in the definitions of two or more *enumeration types*. The effective meaning of an overloaded identifier is determined by the context. *Subprograms*, *aggregates*, *allocators*, and string *literals* can also be overloaded.

Package. A package specifies a group of logically related entities, such as *types*, *objects* of those types, and *subprograms* with *parameters* of those types. It is written as a *package declaration* and a *package body*.

The package declaration has a *visible part*, containing the *declarations* of all entities that can be explicitly used outside the package. It may also have a *private part* containing structural details that complete the specification of the visible entities, but which are irrelevant to the user of the package. The *package body* contains implementations of *subprograms* (and possibly *tasks* as other *packages*) that have been specified in the package declaration. A package is one of the kinds of *program unit*.

Parameter. A parameter is one of the named entities associated with a *subprogram, entry,* or *generic unit,* and used to communicate with the corresponding subprogram body, *accept statement* or generic body. A *formal parameter* is an identifier used to denote the named entity within the body. An *actual parameter* is the particular entity associated with the corresponding formal parameter by a *subprogram call, entry call,* or *generic instantiation.* The *mode* of a formal parameter specifies whether the associated actual parameter supplies a value for the formal parameter, or the formal supplies a value for the actual parameter, or both. The association of actual parameters with formal parameters can be specified by *named associations,* by *positional associations,* or by a combination of these.

Parent type. See *derived type.*

Positional association. A positional association specifies the association of an item with a position in a list, by using the same position in the text to specify the item.

Pragma. A pragma conveys information to the compiler.

Prefix. A prefix is used as the first part of certain kinds of name. A prefix is either a *function call* or a *name.*

Private part. See *package.*

Private type. A private type is a *type* whose structure and set of values are clearly defined, but not directly available to the user of the type. A private type is known only by its *discriminants* (if any) and by the set of *operations* defined for it. A private type and its applicable operations are defined in the *visible part* of a *package,* or in a *generic formal part.* Assignment, equality, and inequality are also defined for private types, unless the private type is *limited.*

Procedure. See *subprogram.*

Program. A program is composed of a number of *compilation units,* one of which is a *subprogram* called the *main program.* Execution of the program consists of execution of the main program, which may invoke subprograms declared in the other compilation units of the program.

Program unit. A program unit is any one of a *generic unit, package, subprogram,* or *task unit.*

Qualified expression. A qualified expression is an *expression* preceded by an indication of its *type* or *subtype.* Such qualification is used when, in its absence, the expression might be ambiguous (for example as a consequence of *overloading*).

Raising an exception. See *exception.*

Range. A range is a contiguous set of values of a *scalar type.* A range is specified by giving the lower and upper bounds for the values. A value in the range is said to *belong* to the range.

Range constraint. A range constraint of a *type* specifies a *range,* and thereby determines the subset of the values of the type that *belong* to the range.

Real type. A real type is a *type* whose values represent approximations to the real numbers. There are two kinds of real type: *fixed point types* are specified by absolute error bound; *floating point types* are specified by a relative error bound expressed as a number of significant decimal digits.

Record type. A value of a record type consists of *components* which are usually of different *types* or *subtypes.* For each component of a record value or record *object,* the definition of the record type specifies an identifier that uniquely determines the component within the record.

Renaming declaration. A renaming declaration declares another *name* for an entity.

Rendezvous. A rendezvous is the interaction that occurs between two parallel *tasks* when one task has called an *entry* of the other task, and a corresponding *accept statement* is being executed by the other task on behalf of the calling task.

Representation clause. A representation clause directs the compiler in the selection of the mapping of a *type*, an *object*, or a *task* onto features of the underlying machine that executes a program. In some cases, representation clauses completely specify the mapping; in other cases, they provide criteria for choosing a mapping.

Satisfy. See *constraint, subtype*.

Scalar type. An *object* or value of a scalar *type* does not have *components*. A scalar type is either a *discrete type* or a *real type*. The values of a scalar type are ordered.

Scope. See *declaration*.

Selected component. A selected component is a *name* consisting of a *prefix* and of an identifier called the *selector*. Selected components are used to denote record components, *entries*, and *objects* designated by access values; they are also used as *expanded names*.

Selector. See *selected component*.

Simple name. See *declaration, name*.

Statement. A statement specifies one or more actions to be performed during the execution of a *program*.

Subcomponent. A subcomponent is either a *component*, or a component of another subcomponent.

Subprogram. A subprogram is either a *procedure* or a *function*. A procedure specifies a sequence of actions and is invoked by a *procedure call* statement. A function specifies a sequence of actions and also returns a value called the *result*, and so a *function call* is an *expression*. A subprogram is written as a *subprogram declaration*, which specifies its *name, formal parameters*, and (for a function) its result; and a *subprogram body* which specifies the sequence of actions. The subprogram call specifies the *actual parameters* that are to be associated with the formal parameters. A subprogram is one of the kinds of *program unit*.

Subtype. A subtype of a *type* characterizes a subset of the values of the type. The subset is determined by a *constraint* on the type. Each value in the set of values of a subtype *belongs* to the subtype and *satisfies* the constraint determining the subtype.

Subunit. See *body*.

Task. A task operates in parallel with other parts of the program. It is written as a *task specification* (which specifies the *name* of the task and the names and *formal parameters* of its entries), and a *task body* which defines its execution. A *task unit* is one of the kinds of *program unit*. A *task type* is a *type* that permits the subsequent *declaration* of any number of similar tasks of the type. A value of a task type is said to *designate* a task.

Type. A type characterizes both a set of values, and a set of *operations* applicable to those values. A *type definition* is a language construct that defines a type. A particular type is either an *access type*, an *array type*, a *private type*, a *record type*, a *scalar type*, or a *task type*.

Use clause. A use clause achieves *direct visibility* of *declarations* that appear in the *visible parts* of named *packages*.

Variable. See *object*.

Variant part. A variant part of a *record* specifies alternative record *components*, depending on a *discriminant* of the record. Each value of the discriminant establishes a particular alternative of the variant part.

Visibility. At a given point in a program text, the *declaration* of an entity with a certain identifier is said to be *visible* if the entity is an acceptable meaning for an occurrence at that point of the identifier. The declaration is *visible by selection* at the place of the *selector* in a *selected component* or at the place of the name in a *named association*. Otherwise, the declaration is *directly visible*, that is, if the identifier alone has that meaning.

Visible part. See *package*.

With clause. See *compilation unit*.

Index